LIFE SCIENCE LIBRARY

THE PHYSICIAN

LIFE SCIENCE LIBRARY

CONSULTING EDITORS
René Dubos
Henry Margenau
C. P. Snow

THE PHYSICIAN

by Russel V. Lee, Sarel Eimerl
and the Editors of TIME-LIFE BOOKS

TIME-LIFE BOOKS   NEW YORK

ABOUT THIS BOOK

THE MODERN PHYSICIAN is the product of millennia of change. This book traces his emergence from the medicine man of primitive times to the highly trained specialist who practices in today's urban hospitals and clinics. It pays particular attention to the latest trends in medicine —the growth of specialization, and the increasing tendency of physicians to practice in groups rather than individually. Finally it examines some of the advanced techniques that are shaping the practice of medicine today and for the future.

The text chapters of the book are supplemented by picture essays. For example, Chapter 1, "The Progress of an Ancient Calling," describes the early history of medicine. Essay 1, "A Renaissance in Medicine," focuses on the medieval University of Bologna, where the first tentative groping toward scientific medicine took place.

THE AUTHORS

DR. RUSSEL V. LEE, founder of one of the country's largest and best-known group practices, the Palo Alto (California) Medical Clinic, has been teaching and practicing medicine since the early 1920s. During World War II he was the Chief of Preventive Medicine for the U.S. Army Air Forces. After that he served on the Magnuson Commission, which studied national health needs and recommended measures that were to form the basis for the Medicare law.

The father of four sons and a daughter, all distinguished physicians, Dr. Lee is consultant to the Palo Alto Medical Clinic, and clinical professor emeritus of the Stanford University School of Medicine.

SAREL EIMERL, a graduate of Oxford living in the U.S., is a novelist who has also written books on scientific subjects and on the history of art. He was coauthor of *The Primates* in the Life Nature Library.

THE CONSULTING EDITORS

RENÉ DUBOS, a member and professor of The Rockefeller University, is a distinguished microbiologist and experimental pathologist who was awarded the Arches of Science Award in 1966. His books include *Mirage of Health* and *Man Adapting*. He is also coauthor of *Health and Disease* in this series.

HENRY MARGENAU is Eugene Higgins Professor of Physics and Natural Philoso-

phy at Yale, and an authority in spectroscopy and nuclear physics. He wrote *Open Vistas, The Nature of Physical Reality*, and is coauthor of *The Scientist* in this series.

C. P. SNOW has won an international audience for his novels, including *The New Men, The Affair* and *Corridors of Power*, which explore the effects of science on today's society.

ON THE COVER

Two of the physician's basic tools are pictured on the cover: the chest X-ray, which he uses in diagnosing tuberculosis, cancer and other ailments, and the stethoscope, which helps him listen to the heart and lungs. On the back cover is the caduceus, the ancient symbol of Hermes, the messenger of the gods, and today a device that identifies the physician.

© 1967 Time Inc. All rights reserved. Reprinted 1969.
Published simultaneously in Canada. Library of Congress catalogue card number 67-20331.
School and library distribution by Silver Burdett Company, Morristown, New Jersey.

CONTENTS

TIME-LIFE BOOKS

EDITOR
Maitland A. Edey

EXECUTIVE EDITOR
Jerry Korn

TEXT DIRECTOR   ART DIRECTOR
Martin Mann   Sheldon Cotler

CHIEF OF RESEARCH
Beatrice T. Dobie

PICTURE EDITOR
Robert G. Mason

Assistant Text Directors:
Harold C. Field, Ogden Tanner
Assistant Art Director: Arnold C. Holeywell
Assistant Chief of Research: Martha T. Goolrick

PUBLISHER
Rhett Austell
Associate Publisher: Walter C. Rohrer
Assistant Publisher: Carter Smith
General Manager: Joseph C. Hazen Jr.
Business Manager: John D. McSweeney
Production Manager: Louis Bronzo

Sales Director: Joan D. Manley
Promotion Director: Beatrice K. Tolleris
Managing Director, International: John A. Millington

LIFE SCIENCE LIBRARY

SERIES EDITOR: Martin Mann
Editorial Staff for *The Physician:*
Associate Editor: Robert G. Mason
Text Editors: William K. Goolrick, Nancy Gross,
William Frankel, James A. Maxwell
Picture Editor: Simone Daro Gossner
Designer: Charles Mikolaycak
Assistant Designer: Raymond Ripper
Staff Writers: Peter Chaitin, Marianna Pinchot,
Frank Kendig, Bryce Walker
Chief Researcher: Marjorie Pickens
Researchers: Sarah Bennett, Suzanne Braun,
Leah Dunaief, Joan C. Gerard, Alice Kantor,
Irene Kleinsinger, James MaHood,
Brooke Newman, Carol Phillippe, Shirley Small

EDITORIAL PRODUCTION
Color Director: Robert L. Young
Assistant: James J. Cox
Copy Staff: Rosalind Stubenberg,
Madge Raymond, Florence Keith
Picture Department: Dolores A. Littles,
Joan T. Lynch
Traffic: Arthur A. Goldberger
Art Assistants: Gloria Cernosia, Joel Margulies

This book, from conception to final editing, was under the professional direction of Russel V. Lee. Text chapters were written by Sarel Eimerl, picture essays by the editorial staff. The following individuals and departments of Time Inc. were helpful in the production of the book: Medical Director, F. T. Kirkham Jr.; LIFE staff photographers Alfred Eisenstaedt, Fritz Goro, Leonard McCombe, Ralph Morse; Editorial Production, Robert W. Boyd Jr.; Editorial Reference, Peter Draz; Picture Collection, Doris O'Neil; Photographic Laboratory, George Karas; TIME-LIFE News Service, Murray J. Gart.

INTRODUCTION

One physician superbly qualified to describe his own profession to the average reader is Russel V. Lee, a salty man and a memorable raconteur. In this book Dr. Lee takes the reader on a delightful tour through medical history, from Hippocrates, Galen, Claude Bernard, and the development of modern medical education, into the complexities of specialized medical practice and social medicine.

Dr. Lee's father was a missionary who migrated to Utah in about 1880 —his purpose to convert the Mormons to Calvinism. Failing in this—Dr. Lee states—he tried to outnumber the Mormons by producing eight children in seven years. Russel and his twin brother, Paul (who later became a distinguished admiral in the U.S. Navy), were the last of three pairs of twins and two singles.

Dr. Lee's early life is the story of a driving, dedicated youngster who let no obstacles stop him on his road to an education. He worked at everything from raising bees to serving as a "bound boy" in Salt Lake City before he received his medical degree in 1920 from Stanford University in Palo Alto, California. Entering practice there, he formed a partnership that later developed into the Palo Alto Medical Clinic, one of the largest and most successful group practices in the country.

Experience in his own clinic persuaded Dr. Lee that group practice, described in detail in this book, was the only way that the rapidly advancing new knowledge of medical technology could be carried to the bedside of the patient at a cost the patient could afford. This led him into the broad, uncharted field of social medicine. He studied prepayment plans with the acuity of an actuary. He became convinced that better medical care could be delivered at a lower cost through group practice and prepaid insurance, and he preached this doctrine across the country.

Dr. Lee has also been a leader in efforts to improve the treatment of older people—socially as well as medically. His concern with efforts to modernize teaching methods in tradition-bound medical schools, particularly through the use of modern visual aids, is reflected in several sections of this book.

Perhaps most important of all, Dr. Lee is a "patient's doctor." The care of the patient and the sensitive relationship between patient and physician have always been his passion. His diagnostic ability and his intuitive sense of his patients' physical and emotional needs have made him a physician extraordinary. As doctor, raconteur, evangelist, educator, economist and world traveler, Dr. Lee offers the readers of this book an exciting and educational view of the modern physician.

—Howard A. Rusk, M.D.
Director, Institute of Rehabilitation Medicine
New York University Medical Center

1

The Progress of an Ancient Calling

A physician who became a god, Aesculapius was an ancient Greek said to be so proficient a healer that he could revive the dead. He was worshiped for centuries in both Greece and Rome, and his snake-coiled staff still symbolizes the physician.

SOON AFTER the end of World War II, when Britain was suffering an acute fuel shortage, an English anthropologist who had just received his Ph.D. moved to a new city. There he found he was being sent a generous extra ration of coal—a blessing, apparently providential, that was finally explained when the local coal dealer telephoned to ask if the "doctor" was satisfied.

This misunderstanding, though trivial in itself, indicates the unique and privileged status the physician enjoys in today's society. The respect he is accorded is not merely a tribute to his education and intelligence, although he is assumed to possess both. It reflects the depth of the need the physician is called upon to satisfy. A person in good health may speak scornfully of doctors. But when he is sick, it is to the doctor he must turn. Illness, as the Greek physician Herophilus observed some 2,000 years ago, "renders science null, art inglorious, strength effortless, wealth useless, and eloquence powerless." Most people value their health above all else, and it is the physician's ability to overcome illness that has given him his status and his privileges.

The doctor's prowess has won him honor in all times and in all societies. Primitive people esteem their medicine men at least as highly as modern nations do their men of medicine; indeed, they are regarded not merely as physicians, but as holy men as well. In these primitive societies, spirits are held responsible not only for the fall of the rain, the heat of the sun and the growth of the crops, but for many serious illnesses too, and the medicine man must deal with the spirits if he is to cure his patients of disease. To do this the Eskimo angakok goes into a trance, makes a "trip" to the supernatural world and returns to this one with a cure. The African witch doctor tries to frighten disease, chasing an evil spirit by biting, beating, punching, kicking or even stamping its host. If spirit and patient survive this drastic therapy, the witch doctor attempts to lure the spirit away to take up residence in an animal, or in one of the patient's enemies, or in some inanimate object. Or, if the spirit is considered too clever to be fooled, he may appease it with gifts and sacrifices.

Such treatments, of course, attack a nonexistent enemy. Yet the medicine men maintain their prestige because their patients often do respond, as many modern scientists have observed. And an understanding of the primitive ability to heal reveals much about the craft of physicians everywhere.

Three distinct factors seem to be involved. The first is psychological: the patient's belief that the doctor and his treatment will produce a cure. As anyone who has ever been sick will testify, just to see the doctor enter is a great comfort. The phrase "bedside manner" is often used disparagingly, to suggest artifice and insincerity. But the fact is that a good bedside manner—the ability to inspire confidence and trust—is not only a comfort to the patient, but one of the physician's most effective weapons. Many illnesses are generated or intensified by anxiety, depression or loneliness—by a sense that no one cares. Through the centuries, the men of medicine have cared. Their sympathy and the faith they instill in their patients can work wonders, and not only among the scientifically naïve. Every modern doctor has at least a few patients who insist on medication even for illnesses that do not require it, and who benefit from placebos—pills that have no physical value at all. The effect of placebos is psychological. In most cases where they are used the illness would have cured itself, without either pills or doctor.

This is the second constant on which physicians have always relied: at least three quarters of the diseases that affect people are in time overcome by the body's own action, whether or not it is assisted by the physician's remedies. The human body has great recuperative powers, and these natural defenses are among the physician's most important allies in the fight against disease.

The third reason for the doctor's success, of course, is his knowledge of effective remedies—and this is as true of the primitive medicine man as it is of the trained physician. The witch doctor knows how to use poultices, massages and such pain-reducing drugs as opium and coca. He knows how to reduce dislocations, set fractures, open abscesses and suture wounds. Indeed, the primitives had remedies for some diseases long before Europeans did. The Count of Chinchon, who is credited with the introduction of quinine to Spain in the first half of the 17th Century, learned about it from the Indians of Peru: it was their standard remedy for the treatment of fevers.

What makes the modern doctor succeed

Although the same three factors that help the primitive medicine man are also the basis of the scientific physician's success, there are crucial differences in the way they are used. The medicine man does not really know what he is doing, nor precisely why he achieves cures. He may not recognize the influence he has on his patients' minds, he does not understand the reparative mechanisms of their bodies, and he has no idea how his remedies accomplish their effects. The scientific physician, on the other hand, is very much aware of what he is doing. He knows that a large proportion of illnesses are psychosomatic—resulting from the mind's effect on the body—and he knows that his ability to inspire his patients with trust and confidence is one of his most powerful remedies. His understanding of the functioning of the body guides him when he must supplement the body's own defenses with drugs or surgery. Finally, he has at hand an armamentarium of specific medications.

In these differences between primitive and advanced medicine can be traced the progress of the physician's craft. So long as the doctor subscribed to a supernatural theory of disease, he could not determine why any given treatment worked, and his functions could not be distinguished from the priest's. Until he recognized that disease is a natural occurrence, he could not find rational remedies nor understand the actions of the patient's body and mind. The history of Western medicine—and of the physician—is largely the story of the shift from magic to science.

A PRIMITIVE MEDICINE MAN may have been the subject of this 15,000-year-old painting found at Les Trois Frères cave in southern France. Wearing the pelts of animals and adorned with stag antlers and a wolf tail, the figure is apparently performing a ritual dance, its purpose now unknown. Some anthropologists believe that the painting depicts a hunting god, but others feel that the figure represents a prehistoric healer—a point of view strengthened by the figure's resemblance to the 19th Century American Indian medicine man shown on the opposite page.

It is impossible to tell precisely what prehistoric medicine was like. But it was probably very similar to the medicine now practiced by primitive tribes. In certain respects it was remarkably sophisticated. For example, archeologists have found bones and instruments indicating that prehistoric people knew how to perform the delicate surgical procedure called trephining—the removal of a circular section of bone from the skull. Trephining reduced pressure on the brain, and the operation may have been performed for this purpose. But it seems to have had magical connotations as well. The disks of excised bone served as amulets—good-luck charms to ward off evil spirits. In the prehistoric world, magic and medicine were undoubtedly thoroughly intermixed.

By the time written records appear, the two were beginning to separate. The ancient Egyptians divided diseases into two distinct categories—those that could be cured only by invoking the supernatural and those that were susceptible to physical remedies. Supernatural treatment—the only therapy available for hopeless conditions, such as snakebite—was the sole province of the temple priests. Professional physicians were called in for ailments that were known to benefit from natural remedies. The physicians, like the priests, undoubtedly depended heavily on their patients' own bodies and minds to work the cures. But they also knew a great many practical treatments, as is clear from the Ebers papyrus, a 3,500-year-old medical record uncovered in 1873 in Thebes by Georg Ebers, a German Egyptologist. The papyrus lists more than 700 potions, among them such useful specifics as senna and castor-oil laxatives, and gentian and coriander tonics. Egyptian physicians properly used colchicum for gout, and even applied a salve made from moldy wheat to skin infections—an accidental (and ineffective) use of mold extracts which antedated the discovery of penicillin by some 3,500 years.

Hippocrates: the first physician-scientist

But it was not until nearly a thousand years later, in the Greece of the Fifth Century B.C., that medicine turned decisively away from magic. At that time, the most illustrious of all physicians, Hippocrates of Cos, declared that epilepsy—which the Greeks, like the Egyptians, had always considered a "sacred disease," curable only by the gods—was no more supernatural in its origins than any common illness. "The disease called sacred," Hippocrates wrote, "is not, in my opinion, any more divine or more sacred than other diseases, but has a natural cause, and its supposed divine origin is due to men's inexperience, and to their wonder at its peculiar character." With this pronouncement, with its implication that all diseases are susceptible to physical treatment, Hippocrates turned the physician firmly in the direction of science.

Very little is known about Hippocrates as a person; the only mention of him by his contemporaries is one brief reference in Plato's *Dialogues*. Apart from this, all knowledge of the man and his work is based on medical writings produced by him and his followers, but they made clear that Hippocrates must have been a brilliant physician. He repeatedly

AN INDIAN MEDICINE MAN belonging to the Blackfoot tribe is depicted in this painting by the 19th Century American artist George Catlin. The American Indian shaman, like his prehistoric colleague *(opposite page)*, dressed in animal skins to perform cures. Ritual dances and incantations were the major part of the treatment, but the medicine men also prescribed herb remedies and performed simple surgery, sometimes with considerable skill. In many cases, this combination of psychological influence and practical care was surprisingly effective in restoring the patient to health.

stressed the importance of the one skill that is basic to all science—careful observation. "To know is one thing," he wrote, "but merely to believe one knows is another. To know is science but merely to believe one knows is ignorance." And, he mourned, "Life is short and the art [of medicine] long; the occasion fleeting; experience fallacious and judgment difficult." His descriptions of diseases and his recommendations for treatment indicate that he followed his own prescriptions. He described empyema—a collection of pus in the chest—in terms that any modern physician would easily recognize. His suggested treatment—a thrust of a knife between the ribs to permit the liquid to emerge—later became a standard surgical procedure. And his description of the signs of approaching death still guides physicians.

For several centuries after Hippocrates, his successors in Greece, in Alexandria and later in the Roman Empire followed where he had led. They believed that all human ills were their concern, and they identified a number of previously mysterious diseases, including meningitis and dozens of skin afflictions. They recognized the symptoms of heart disease, learned how to stop hemorrhages and used a crude method of electrotherapy, applying electric eels to the victims of facial neuralgia. They dissected corpses to determine the structure of the body, investigating the brain, the liver, the prostate gland and the duodenum.

The Roman "wonder-worker"

This long period of enlightened medicine flowered in another great physician, Galen, who was born in the Second Century A.D., in the Roman province of Pergamum. His father was an engineer; his mother seems to have been, at the least, eccentric: according to her son, she used to bite her serving maids in fits of anger. Galen attended the famous medical school in Alexandria, served as surgeon to a troupe of gladiators and then went on to Rome. There he was a provincial, young and unknown. But shortly after his arrival, fever struck a fellow native of Pergamum, Eudemus, who had already become prominent in the capital. Under the care of Rome's most distinguished physician, Eudemus grew steadily worse until, in desperation, he sent for Galen. After the young physician took over, Eudemus recovered, and Galen's reputation was made.

Galen, like Hippocrates, must have been a fine doctor. He became known as the "wonder-worker," and served as physician to two emperors. But his ambition soared beyond the practice of medicine. He conceived the idea of writing an encyclopedia of all medical knowledge—to include anatomy, physiology, pathology and therapeutics—and he did so in a vast work compiled over many years. It was a stupendous achievement, but it was riddled with errors. Because the Romans frowned upon the dissection of human bodies, Galen used pigs and monkeys instead, and then attributed to man some of the anatomical characteristics he had found in the animals. Still more misleading were his physiological descriptions of bodily processes: he maintained, for example, that the blood does not circulate, but moves back and forth inside the blood ves-

THE PHYSICIAN GALEN, a Second Century Greek who practiced in Rome, was one of the most influential of ancient physicians. He preserved the medical knowledge of his time in a series of more than 300 treatises that became the bible of physicians for the next 1,400 years. As late as the 16th Century, when the woodcut above was made, Galen's words were still sacrosanct. Although many of his conclusions were inaccurate, he correctly described some aspects of human anatomy, such as the gross structure of the brain, the valves of the heart and the muscles of the diaphragm.

sels rather like the tides. And his pharmacology was untrustworthy: he recommended a vast number of traditional herbal remedies that were of no value, along with others that were definitely harmful.

Worst of all, Galen was convinced of his own infallibility. "Never as yet," he wrote, "have I gone far astray, whether in treatment or in prognosis, as have so many other physicians of great reputation. If anyone wishes to gain fame . . . all that he needs is to accept what I have been able to establish." This counsel, unfortunately, was followed for many years. The authority established by his monumental work was later strengthened by a religious element. Medieval theologians were attracted to Galen's medical philosophy—a God-ordained balance between disease and remedy—and his supremacy was fixed by the approval of the Church, which dominated intellectual life in Western Europe for a thousand years after the sack of Rome.

The dark age of medicine

During this period, the scientific approach fell completely out of favor. As dogma was enshrined, observation was abandoned. Dissection, the indispensable tool for acquiring knowledge of the human body, was forbidden on the grounds that it was impious to cut up a corpse that had been made in "the image of God." Besides, medieval people simply did not think in terms of establishing facts by observation. They put their trust in authority. Since the Bible had described Eve as made from a rib taken from Adam, nobody doubted that women had one more rib than men. No one, apparently, ever bothered to count. Indeed, to do so would have implied disbelief in the Bible and might have led, like other heresies, to the stake.

The decline of the spirit of inquiry during the Middle Ages disastrously hampered the physician in his efforts to save human lives. Cities were growing, sanitation was inadequate, and contagious diseases spread unchecked through crowded, filthy streets. Influenza, tuberculosis, diphtheria, smallpox and cholera swept over Europe in periodic waves. In the six years between 1347 and 1353, in the worst pandemic ever recorded, the plague killed 25 million people.

Rational treatment was half forgotten; more and more people turned to magic. Astrology was so widely accepted that it was taught in medical schools as a method of diagnosis. Palmistry and superstition flourished. Sick people hung cards around their necks on which the word *abracadabra* was elaborated in fantastic designs. To cure a sword wound, a physician often treated not the wound but the sword, rubbing it with the so-called weapon salve, a mixture of blood and fat.

Probably the most highly regarded of these outlandish remedies was the bezoar stone, a deposit found in the intestines of ruminant animals and offered as a cure for every human misfortune. In the 16th Century one of these rare cure-alls was the talisman of King Charles IX of France until his independent-minded surgeon, Ambroise Paré, suggested that the King test the stone by giving it to a criminal who had been condemned

A STAG'S STONE TEARS, which legend says were formed when the animal was bitten by a snake, were believed by early Persian and Arabian physicians to be snake-venom antidotes called bezoar stones. Actually they were concretions, similar to gallstones, from the digestive systems of deer and other ruminant animals, and their curative powers were imaginary. But the legend, depicted in the 15th Century woodcut above, persisted and spread to Europe, where some physicians counterfeited bezoar stones from ordinary rocks and sold them to the credulous as cure-alls.

to death. The King agreed, and the criminal was given the stone to hold and a vial of poison to swallow. Seven hours later, he was dead. Shortly thereafter, legend has it, King Charles threw his bezoar stone into the fire.

This story suggests the new and more questioning attitude that, by the 16th Century, had begun to spread across Western Europe. The Renaissance had revived the classic respect for reason, observation and experiment, and many long-sacred beliefs were re-examined. But physicians were slow to take advantage of their opportunity. They continued to cling, more rigidly than any other group except perhaps the clergy, to the assumptions of the past.

Physicians have always tended to be conservative—and with good reason. Dealing, as they do, with life and death, they must be cautious about accepting novel theories and unproved remedies. But caution and rigidity are very different things. And it was rigidity—the dead weight of medical conservatism—that blocked the early advance of the physician, as a young and brilliant Flemish doctor was to discover. Andreas Vesalius was 17 years old when he arrived in Paris in 1531 to enroll in the Paris University medical school. The school itself was a bastion of tradition, and Vesalius' teacher, Sylvius, was as firmly attached to Galen's doctrines as a leech to blood. He taught by reading aloud from Galen's work on anatomy while pointing, with a long cane, to the appropriate portion of a corpse. The students did not have a chance to touch the body, and were thus saved both from contact with a cadaver and from learning anatomy at firsthand.

Vesalius: the first to learn by doing

Vesalius decided to study cadavers by himself. Dissection was still discouraged in France, so he had to dig for bones in the graveyards. Legend has it that he even went so far as to cut down the body of a criminal left hanging in chains outside the walls of the city of Louvain.

When he was only 23, Vesalius was appointed professor of surgery and anatomy at the University of Padua, in Italy. There a more liberal attitude toward dissection permitted Vesalius to broaden his studies. He soon discovered that the human body was not constructed exactly as Galen had specified. One day, when he was dissecting an ape, he observed in the animal several of the characteristics which Galen had attributed to humans. He realized that Galen had been attributing the anatomical peculiarities of the monkey to humans, and this experience persuaded him to trust his own observations above the assertions of unproved authority.

In 1543, when he was 28, Vesalius published the elaborate and superbly illustrated textbook which was to lay the foundations for modern anatomy. It was violently attacked, and his old teacher, Sylvius, was among his most outraged critics. Galen had said that the human thighbone is curved. Vesalius showed that it is straight. That only proved, Sylvius retorted, that it had been straightened by the tight breeches in which man encased it. "Sensuality and luxury," said Sylvius, accounted for other discrepancies, such as the "intermaxillary" bone which Galen had listed and which Vesalius could not find; if the human body was not as described by Galen, then it must have altered since his time—and, Sylvius sourly remarked, "not for the better."

When Vesalius died in 1564, his findings were still disputed by his fellow professionals, but his imaginative and questioning approach to medicine was becoming established as the mark of a new breed of physicians. Only 64 years later, his clarification of anatomy was complemented by the investigations of an English physician, William Harvey. Although Harvey is best known for his discovery of the way the heart keeps the blood circulating continuously throughout the body, the significance of his work goes much deeper. For his studies made clear that the way bodily structures work (i.e., their physiology) depends on the way they are constructed (i.e., their anatomy). After Harvey, it became an axiom of medicine that a physiological explanation must be compatible with the facts of anatomy. Once Harvey's work had demonstrated how the blood circulates, physicians could begin to understand the way this fluid vehicle carries oxygen, food and waste products through the body, and thus interacts with such organs as the liver, the kidneys and the lungs. Only then did it become possible to discover the functions these organs actually perform.

Thus the stage was being set for the appearance of the modern physician, no longer the healer who relied mainly on his power to evoke faith, but the man of science who understood why his remedies did—or did not—work. Scientists such as the Dutch microscopist Anton van Leeuwenhoek, who first described red blood cells, and Thomas Willis, the English anatomist who gave the first complete account of the nervous system, began to discover the facts that later led to rational therapy. Great physicians such as Thomas Sydenham of 17th Century England learned to combine new knowledge with their own careful, sympathetic observations to provide superior treatment.

Jenner and vaccination: the birth of modern medicine

One development, occurring in England in the very last decade of the 18th Century, can be singled out as heralding the revolution in medical practice that was to erupt in the 19th Century. In 1796 a daring Gloucestershire surgeon, Edward Jenner, inoculated a country boy with liquid from the arm of a milkmaid who was then recovering from the relatively mild disease of cowpox. Jenner thus immunized the youngster against smallpox, the dread disease which killed 60 million people during the 18th Century. But he did more than show how to prevent a terrible infection. His pioneering trial demonstrated vividly the great benefits to mankind of informed experimentation. The time was ripe. During the next 100 years, experimentation was to be exploited so fruitfully that the art of medicine was transformed and the physician established as a practitioner of science.

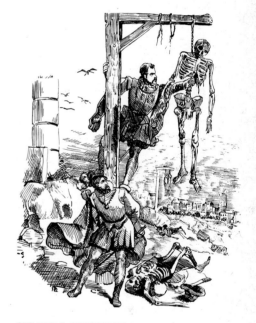

STEALING SKELETONS from the public gallows was one way in which the 16th Century Flemish physician Andreas Vesalius (above) is said to have obtained subjects for his pioneering study of the human body. Dissecting human cadavers despite the disapproval of both church and state, Vesalius collected the first comprehensive and accurate data on human anatomy, which he described in his definitive, superbly illustrated treatise, *The Fabric of the Human Body*.

A Renaissance in Medicine

Europe in the mid-14th Century was a continent in despair. The Black Death plague held Europe in a murderous grip. Between 1347 and 1353 one fourth of its 100 million people died, and from Scandinavia to Italy penitents wandered the dismal landscape scourging their bodies with spiked whips, hoping that the lash's sting would purge them of sin and spare them from God's wrath. Certainly physicians offered scant help, for medicine, after lying dormant since Rome's decline 10 centuries earlier, had just begun to stir.

The renaissance of medicine can be traced to one country, Italy, and in particular to one city, Bologna, where a remarkable medical school was founded in the 13th Century. Here, in an atmosphere of free inquiry unusual for the times, physicians and students welcomed new ideas and challenged old superstitions, such as the legendary transplantation of a leg by Sts. Cosmas and Damian (opposite). The faculty introduced the dissection of cadavers, furtively at first, but then as an open and important part of the study of the human body, making Bologna a training center for great physicians. It was from Bologna that this progressive approach spread, providing the foundation for the scientific medicine of today.

A MEDICINE OF MIRACLES
The patron saints of medicine and of the medical school at Bologna, Sts. Cosmas and Damian, are shown, in this painting of a famous legend of the Middle Ages, grafting a dead Moor's leg onto a cancer victim's stump. According to the legend, the patient dreamed that he had been the beneficiary of a miracle —and awoke to find his diseased leg replaced.

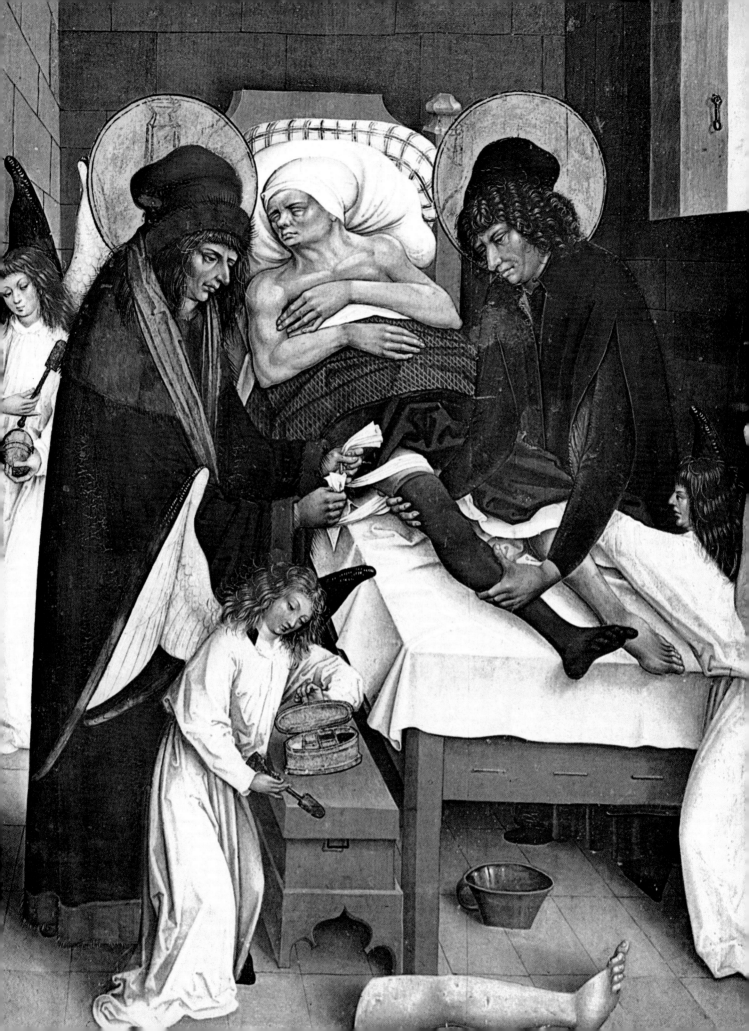

THE CITY AND THE UNIVERSITY
The skyline of Bologna in 1505 was marked by fortresslike structures surmounted by high towers—private homes in which families could defend themselves against all attackers. Most of the students and professors lived near the center of town, but there was no real campus as classes usually met in the professors' quarters.

A City Famed for Its Physicians

The city of Bologna began its existence as a Stone Age settlement and flourished as a Roman colony. Its position as a center of medical learning can be traced to its medieval status as a self-governing, free city. Here scholars could teach and learn relatively free of interference from either the Church or a distant emperor.

By the early 12th Century, the skeleton of the university was forming. First there was the law school, a direct forerunner of the medical school: the first dissections were performed not to teach anatomy but to determine if murder had been committed. By the 13th Century classes in medicine had been officially organized and the medical school became a separate institution within the university.

Unlike other universities, which were controlled by their faculties, Bologna was firmly ruled by its student guilds; the students were bound only by their own laws. Professors were less lucky. They were totally at the mercy of their pupils, who fixed salaries, scheduled classes, hired and fired. One professor was actually sentenced to death for leaving the university without permission (there is no record that the sentence was carried out). The unprecedented power of the students was a major element in maintaining Bologna's intellectual greatness; so long as their influence persisted, Bologna held its position as Europe's greatest school of medicine.

PLACE OF HONOR
Flanking the Virgin and Child, the patron saints of the medical school—St. Cosmas, holding a surgical knife, and St. Damian, wearing the red robe of a student—figure prominently in this 15th Century fresco. It adorns a wall in the Bologna church dedicated to St. Petronio, who is shown at left holding a model of the city. (The figure shown kneeling is the painting's donor.)

Learning Medicine from the Ancients

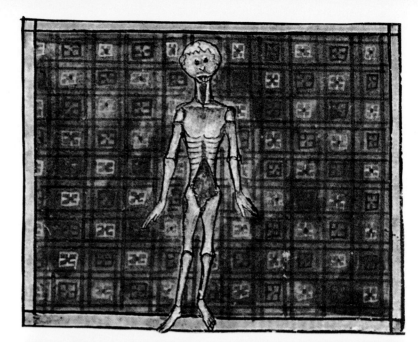

The medieval physician was a man imprisoned by the past. For the most part he merely accepted what earlier practitioners had written about the cause and cure of disease.

Even at Bologna in the mid-14th Century the basic text was the *Canon* by the 11th Century Arab physician Avicenna. This manuscript coordinated most of Western man's medical information—and misinformation—dating back to Hippocrates. It gave great weight to the Second Century Greco-Roman Galen—the discoverer of the sympathetic nervous system and of the lungs' blood-aerating function—who unfortunately based his descriptions of human anatomy on the dissection of pigs and monkeys.

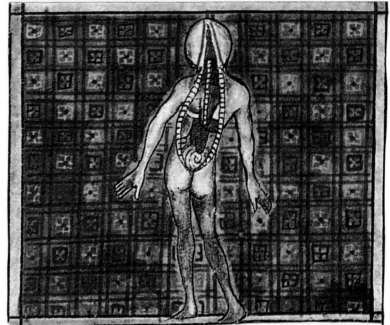

Yet the medieval physician was not totally mired in ignorance. His readings of the ancients had taught him that the most effective remedy for disease was the body's own recuperative powers. He also knew hundreds of herbal palliatives for common ailments, and these were distributed by pharmacies such as the one at left.

Not all these remedies were helpful: Tuberculosis was not likely to respond to the application of radish root to the throat nor was a sore likely to be cured by a treatment of pig dung mixed with herb. Persistent ailments were often treated by bleeding the patient, a dangerous practice that was thought to be effective for every affliction from headaches to cancer.

A GUIDE TO TREATMENT
A page from a translation of Avicenna's *Canon (left)* shows an open-air pharmacy and several treatments. At upper left a patient is exposed to the sun's rays; the three panels below show therapeutic baths. Hot cups are used at lower left to draw out disease, and the last two panels depict bloodletting. Many books were in Hebrew because Jews were prominent physicians.

PICTORIAL ANATOMY
Based on Galen's descriptions, these 14th Century drawings *(right)* were teaching aids for Henri de Mondeville, a physician who studied at Bologna. From top to bottom they show a skeleton, the internal organs as seen from the back, and the organs as seen from the front.

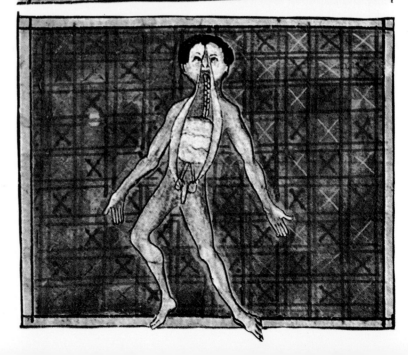

Discovering the Human Body

Medieval Bologna's greatest contribution to medicine was in the field of anatomy. At a time when other medical colleges forbade dissection as a desecration of the human body, Bologna was scheduling dissections for students in the final three years of their five-year course.

For centuries, however, the corpse was viewed not as a source of anatomical knowledge but merely as a teaching aid: The lecturer, seated upon a high platform, read Galen's anatomical works while assistants dissected, exposing organs as confirmation of Galen's hallowed word.

Bologna's most noted pioneer in the study of anatomy was Mondino de Luzzi (c. 1270-1326), whose text on dissection became the bible of anatomy students for 250 years. Like other medieval physicians, he disregarded the evidence of his own eyes when it conflicted with Galen's statements, and if necessary performed feats of mental gymnastics to make the facts of anatomy conform with ancient writ. Whenever this proved impossible, the corpse was said to be defective or the error was blamed on a faulty translation of Galen's work.

But for all this hedging, dissection was a great step forward; eventually the student and lecturer alike would learn from the corpse what human anatomy really was—and how mistaken Galen had been for all those years.

DIVISION OF LABOR
A woodcut from a 1493 edition of Mondino's manuscript *Anathomia* shows the great physician upon his thronelike chair. While he lectures from an ancient text, an assistant illustrates the discourse by revealing appropriate organs of the cadaver. Mondino often had two assistants: one to make incisions in the corpse and another to point out the organs under discussion.

A COOPERATIVE CORPSE
A cadaver helps in its own dissection by peeling back its skin to reveal abdominal muscles, in this illustration from a 1521 commentary on Mondino's work. Mondino taught dissection by separating layers of the body rather than by systematically exposing entire physiological systems; the illustration shows that this method was still in use two centuries after his death.

An Apostle of Surgery

One of Bologna's most brilliant students during Mondino's tenure was the Frenchman Guy de Chauliac (c. 1300-1367). After graduating in 1325, de Chauliac returned to his homeland, where he used his knowledge of anatomy—gained through dissection—to establish himself as a surgeon of wide renown. So great was his fame that during the period of the Black Death he was appointed physician to Pope Clement VI, then reigning from Avignon in the south of France.

De Chauliac was perhaps the first medieval physician who also practiced serious surgery, and in his own work he extended the role of the surgeon; instead of being a mere healer of wounds he became an expert on a wide range of ailments. De Chauliac also pioneered in the surgical removal of cancerous growths, performed operations on hernias and cataracts, and reintroduced slings and weights in the treatment of fractures.

But it was for his treatise *Chirurgia* that de Chauliac gained his most lasting fame. This textbook on surgical training, procedures and implements was eventually accepted by medical schools throughout the Continent as a work fully as important as Mondino's text on anatomy. De Chauliac himself paid tribute to anatomy with this stern advice to generations of students: "It is necessary that [the surgeon] especially know anatomy" for without it he "can do nothing."

De Chauliac's career was a tribute to the quality of the medical education which Bologna offered in the early 14th Century. Nowhere else did a curriculum include so many dissections; in no other medical school was surgery taught as an important adjunct to the training of a physician.

PORTRAIT OF THE SURGEON
This 17th Century portrait of Guy de Chauliac now hangs in a medical museum in Paris. De Chauliac was not only an innovator in surgery but also a moralist who told students to be "pious and merciful, not greedy of gain."

SEEKING TREATMENT
Clad in a physician's robe and surgeon's cap, Guy de Chauliac is shown *(opposite)* at a lectern while patients file by. The man closest to the surgeon holds out a badly ulcerated arm while the patient at the left points to the bloody bandage covering his injured eye. As Guy examines the patients he consults his own manuscript to determine the proper course of treatment. This illustration appears in a 15th Century manuscript of de Chauliac's treatise on surgery, which served as a definitive text for hundreds of years.

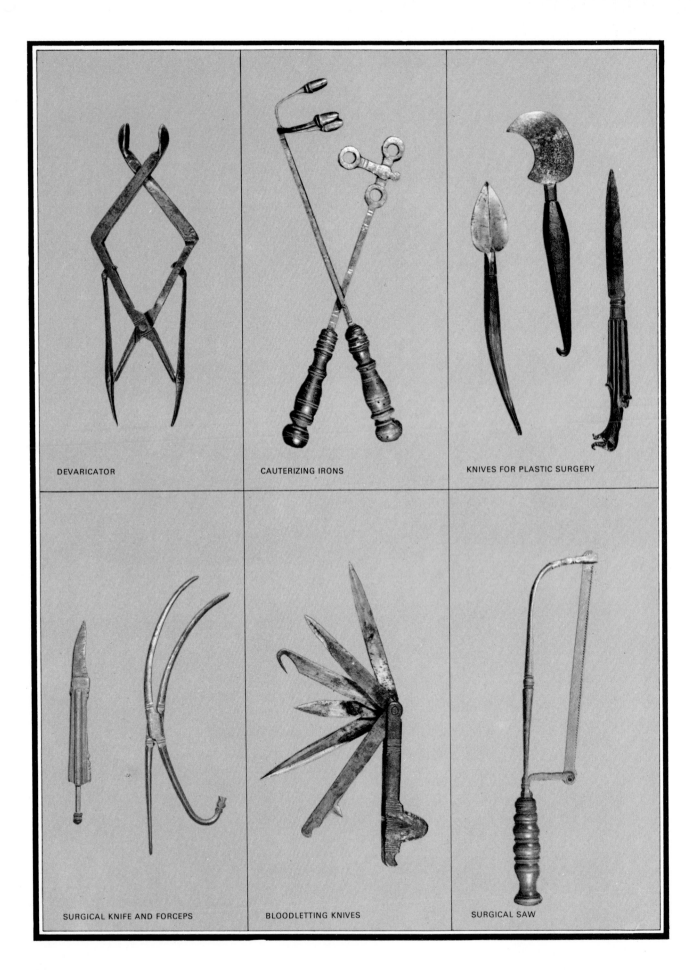

DEVARICATOR

CAUTERIZING IRONS

KNIVES FOR PLASTIC SURGERY

SURGICAL KNIFE AND FORCEPS

BLOODLETTING KNIVES

SURGICAL SAW

The Slow Progress of the Surgeon

Although the medical school in Bologna emphasized anatomy and surgery—all students learned surgical techniques and the use of tools such as those shown opposite—the surgeon himself remained a man of only slight prestige. In many areas surgery was the province of poorly educated itinerant barbers who traveled the country treating wounds or injuries.

Even at Bologna, surgical teaching was based on the theory that disease was caused by an imbalance of body fluids. This was the doctrine of humors, first stated by Hippocrates and restated by Galen. It held that the mixture of four fluids, or humors—black bile, yellow bile, phlegm and blood—determined health or illness. Since a sick man was often considered to have too much of one fluid, it seemed that his health could be restored by draining off the excess.

To draw out the offending humor, medieval surgeons employed several techniques, almost all harmful rather than curative. One of the most frequently used was the application of heat with scorching irons like those pictured opposite at top center. Even more popular was bloodletting—the deliberate cutting of a vein with a knife *(bottom center)*. To determine when and where to make an incision for bloodletting, surgeons referred to elaborate charts. Liver trouble, for example, was treated by the letting of blood from between the middle and fourth fingers. Often such operations ended with the collapse—or death—of the patient.

Surgery did make gains, however slowly. Bologna's stress on anatomy and Guy de Chauliac's innovations pointed the way. But it would be many centuries before surgery would assume its place among the most important of medicine's many branches.

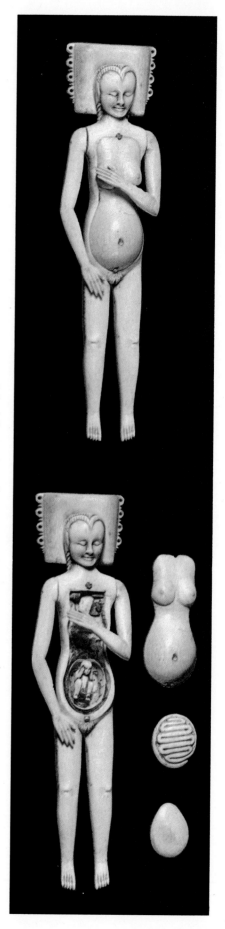

TOOLS OF THE TRADE
Typical of the medieval surgeon's instruments are the tools at left, 15th Century versions of ancient prototypes. The devaricator *(upper left)* was used to pry open wounds. The tri-pronged iron and ringed guard device *(top center)* are cauterizing tools. The rings were placed over the areas to be cauterized and the scorching-hot prongs were then inserted into the rings.

ANATOMY SIMPLIFIED
This 15th Century doll is believed to have been an anatomical teaching aid, used to instruct surgeons and midwives in northern Europe at a time when Bologna's students were studying human cadavers. The front of the doll was detached, as at lower right, to reveal chest and abdominal organs. When the uterus wall was taken off, the viewer saw a fully formed fetus.

Bologna's Last Great Physician

At the start of the 16th Century the medical school at Bologna began a long decline. The administration of the university was taken over by the Church, which was then struggling against the Reformation and was intent on stamping out heresy everywhere. Oppressive restrictions were placed on physicians; all, for example, now took an oath not to treat nonbelievers for longer than three days. But despite this atmosphere, Bologna knew a final flowering in the work of Gaspare Tagliacozzi.

While teaching anatomy, Tagliacozzi developed an advanced technique of plastic surgery; in 1597 he wrote a famous text on the subject. To Bologna trooped hundreds whose ears had been mutilated in duels, whose noses had been cut off as punishment for crimes, whose lips had been decayed by disease.

But genius had little place in Bologna by Tagliacozzi's time, and even he was called a heretic. The spirit of freedom now found expression elsewhere, particularly at Padua's medical school, 77 miles away. Padua became a magnet for Europe's most celebrated physicians, the greatest of whom was Vesalius. An occasional lecturer at Bologna, Vesalius completed the work timidly begun by Mondino two centuries earlier. At Padua he came down from the professor's throne to perform dissections himself and to base lectures not on Galen's misinformation but on observation. Through him medicine entered the era of scientific inquiry.

BUILDING A NOSE
Panels from Tagliacozzi's text show four stages in the reconstruction of a nose. At upper left a noseless patient has had a flap of skin partly cut loose from his arm. The loose end of the flap is then grafted onto his face *(upper right)* while he is held rigid by a harness so that blood from the arm can nourish skin for the new nose. After 14 days the flap is cut away from the arm *(lower left)* and bandaged *(lower right)*. In another fortnight the surgeon will begin the painful and delicate three-week process of shaping the formless skin into a nose.

THE MASTER SURGEON
A portrait of Tagliacozzi shows him pointing to a page from his text. Though he was reputed to have tugged on one patient's reconstructed nose to demonstrate its durability, many wearers fitted metal caps to these noses to help protect them against injury and cold weather.

2

The New Science
of Healing

One of the most respected surgeons of the 19th
Century, Dr. D. H. Agnew directs an operation
for the removal of a cancer. The picture was
painted by Thomas Eakins in 1889, when the
modern age of surgery was still in its infancy.

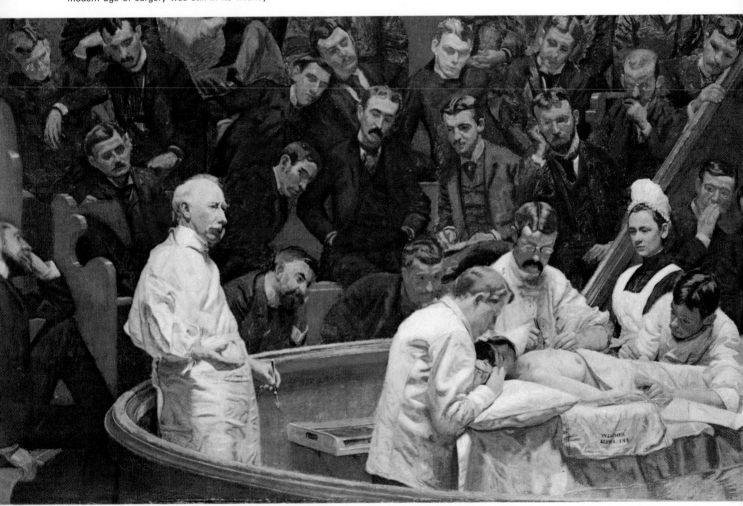

OBSTETRICIAN IGNAZ PHILIPP SEMMELWEIS was the laughing stock of the Viennese medical fraternity during the mid-19th Century. Physicians were amused—when not outraged—by his constant insistence that they themselves were spreading childbed fever among the patients in the maternity wards of Vienna. True, the death rate from the disease was appallingly and mysteriously high in the hospitals, far higher than among women whose babies were born at home. But Semmelweis was obviously a fool, the doctors agreed, to believe that they were guilty of carrying the fever from one patient to another simply because they did not waste valuable time washing their hands after each examination or treatment. The ridicule and frustration drove Semmelweis insane.

The unfortunate Semmelweis was only one of a number of men who challenged the methods and concepts of orthodox physicians in the 19th Century. Like Semmelweis they questioned established ideas, advanced startling new theories, made daring experiments and announced results that shattered tradition. These radicals ultimately brought about a revolution in medical science without precedent in history. But at first—like Semmelweis—they met doubt and derision. What was the conventional 19th Century physician to think of the French physiologist who stated that a balance of certain substances inside the body was essential to good health? Or of the German pathologist who said that disease is basically a conflict between cells, brought about by an external force?

Hardest of all to believe was the new germ theory, postulated most explicitly by a French scientist—and he not even a physician but a chemist! Could he possibly be correct in saying that microscopic organisms on a physician's hands, on a surgeon's instruments or in the air itself were the cause of infection? Had Semmelweis, who died before the germ theory was accepted, been on the right track?

Fortunately for mankind, the skepticism and sarcasm these suggestions aroused did not deter the men who introduced them. Their contributions to physiology, pathology, bacteriology, antisepsis and anesthesia have made medicine the life-saving science we know today and have become basic to the work of every modern physician.

Of all the medical practitioners who benefited from the advances of the 19th Century, the one who probably gained the most was the surgeon. With antiseptic techniques, he was at last able to avoid the danger of postoperative infection, once almost inevitable. Anesthetics permitted him to perform operations that had been impossible for his predecessors. The new insights into physiology and pathology gave him surer knowledge than ever before of what could and could not be done surgically, and of the probable results of a given operation.

Progress in science also played a major role in another 19th Century development of crucial importance to the modern surgeon: the complete reunification of his calling with that of medicine. Until the Middle Ages, surgery had functioned as a branch of medicine. Then, largely because of religious strictures, medicine and surgery were completely separated in many parts of the world, and for hundreds of years the physician and surgeon had no more professional relationship than an airline pilot and a locomotive engineer do today.

In retrospect, it seems almost inconceivable that this division of medicine ever took place. Early writings, some of them believed to date back at least 2,500 years before the Christian era, give ample evidence that the surgeon was first of all a physician. He was a well-trained, skillful and sophisticated practitioner, capable of delicate operations. A cataract operation, which restored sight by delicately moving an opaque lens within the eye, was routine in 1000 B.C. in India. Early Hindus also repaired hernias, delivered babies by Caesarian section and performed such complex skin-grafting operations as rhinoplasty—the reconstruction of the nose by taking skin from the cheek.

A forgotten body of knowledge

The Greeks and Romans were also skilled in surgery. But with the disintegration of the Roman Empire during the Fourth and Fifth Centuries, the Dark Ages encompassed Europe, and both surgery and medicine went into sharp decline there. Almost everything that had been learned was discarded or forgotten. Fortunately for Europeans, some of the medical and surgical knowledge of India and the classical world was kept alive by the Arabs during this period, and it eventually found its way back to Europe by way of Arab writings.

Most Arab treatises were useful, but one document, written in the 11th Century, had a profound and disastrous effect. This medical work was the *Canon* by Avicenna, a well known Arab physician. He considered surgery inferior to medicine and recommended that the two be separated. He further urged that the surgeon's vital tool, the knife, be abandoned and that injuries be treated by cauterization with a hot iron.

The Church had long discouraged surgery on the human body. Now Avicenna had provided a technical justification for the stand. Because most medical schools were operated by the Church, it was able to enforce this misguided approach. Cauterization became a cure-all, and medicine and surgery split into completely different fields. In some countries surgery became a sideline for barbers.

Throughout the next five centuries faltering attempts to raise the level of medicine and surgery were made in parts of Europe; progressive schools arose and then declined in Italy, France and Sweden. But not until the 16th Century were the baleful doctrines of Avicenna successfully attacked. Ironically, the innovator was a member of the lowly barber-surgeon caste. Ambrose Paré, who was born in the small French village of Bourg Hersent in 1510, went to Paris as a young man and apprenticed himself to a barber-surgeon. By the time he was 26, Paré was serving as a surgeon in the French army. During his first campaign, in a war between France and Spain, he made a discovery that raised serious questions about one of the most common—and harmful—of the procedures inherited from Avicenna: the cauterization of battle wounds.

One evening while treating wounded men on the battlefield, Paré's supply of cauterizing oil gave out. Unwilling to leave the soldiers without any aid, he applied a cold dressing of turpentine and oil of roses. His unorthodox treatment made him uneasy. He later wrote: "I expected to find them all dead the next morning. . . . Greatly to my surprise, I found that those whom I had treated with the salve had very little pain in their wounds, no inflammation, no swelling, and they had passed a comfortable night. The others, whose wounds had been treated with boiling elder oil, were in a high fever, while their wounds were inflamed, swollen and acutely painful. I determined, therefore, that I would no longer cauterize the unfortunate wounded in so cruel a manner."

Soon Paré was introducing other bold measures. He tied off cut blood vessels instead of cauterizing them with red-hot irons, and he popularized the use of a truss for a hernia. Because of his remarkable skill and knowledge, royalty demanded his services, and during his lifetime he was court surgeon to four French kings.

While Paré's success improved the position of the surgeon in France, the beginning of modern science was slowly freeing both medicine and surgery from the ignorance that had stifled them. During the following years, human anatomy was explored by Vesalius and his followers, the elementary facts about bodily functions were discovered, and such basic instruments as the microscope and thermometer were invented. Progress was small until the latter half of the 18th Century, when the great revolution in medicine that was soon to come was foreshadowed in the work of several pioneers. Among them was a quick-tempered Scot, a medical scientist by inclination, a surgeon by profession. His name was John Hunter and he was the precursor of the modern physician-surgeon.

Born in 1728, John Hunter was the youngest, and apparently the most difficult, of 10 children. He was a dismal failure in school and by the time he was 20 he had tried and abandoned several careers. Finally he was apprenticed to his oldest brother William, a London surgeon.

The "surgeon extraordinary"

When John took scalpel in hand, he found his calling. He became Britain's most famous surgeon, and in 1776 was named "surgeon extraordinary" to King George III of England. His lectures and writings influenced generations of students. Success, however, did nothing to soften Hunter's character. He remained irascible, blunt in his dealings with colleagues, and a kicker of sacred cows.

One of the cows that felt his boot was the enforced separation of surgery and medicine insisted upon by physicians. Passionately interested in medical research, Hunter observed and experimented until he became an outstanding authority in fields that were then considered no concern of a surgeon: physiology and pathology. He maintained his own private zoo and used his animals for experiments, just as modern scientists do.

One animal experiment led to a surgical discovery of great importance. Hunter operated on a young male deer and tied off a large artery that supplied blood to a half-grown antler. The antler, deprived of its blood

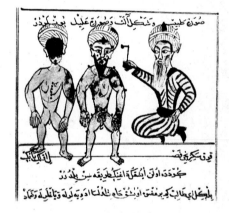

TO HEAL WITH FIRE, a Persian doctor is about to apply a hot iron to a leper's sores in the painful treatment called cauterization, seen in an illustration *(above)* from a 14th Century manuscript. Although originally advocated as a replacement for surgery by Albucasis, an 11th Century Arab physician, this generally harmful remedy became standard for all kinds of ailments from epilepsy to dislocated shoulders. So great was the Arab's influence on European medicine that cauterization remained the regular treatment for open wounds for five centuries.

supply, soon became cold to the touch, as Hunter had expected. However, when he returned a couple of weeks later, he was astonished to discover that the antler was once more warm and growing. When he dissected the buck, he found that smaller blood vessels near the sealed-off artery had grown larger and had taken over the job of nourishing the antler.

This was a phenomenon, never before observed, that Hunter was to recall months later when he examined a patient with an aneurysm of an artery behind the knee. Because the seriously distended and weakened artery might easily rupture, causing a fatal hemorrhage, such a case was usually treated by amputating the leg. Hunter, however, decided that his experience with the deer showed a way to save the leg. He tied off the artery above the aneurysm, on the theory that collateral vessels would assume the task of circulating blood to the lower limb and thus relieve the pressure on the weakened artery. In six weeks the patient walked out of the hospital on his own two legs. This procedure continued in use for more than a century.

Hunter's willingness to try out his ideas—to develop a theory and then test it by actual experiment—was one of his most remarkable characteristics because it was so rare in his time. His example helped establish the experimental method as the most valuable tool for advancing medicine.

"But why think? Why not try the experiment?" he wrote his protégé Edward Jenner, the discoverer of smallpox vaccination. Experiment Jenner did. So, too, did the sophisticated scientists who followed in the 19th Century. Many of them made important contributions, but the modern physician and surgeon probably owe their greatest debt to the research of four men: Rudolf Virchow in pathology, Louis Pasteur in bacteriology, Joseph Lister in antisepsis and Claude Bernard in physiology.

From theater to medicine

Bernard was born in 1813 in the small French village of Saint-Julien. He began his career as an apothecary's apprentice, but he was also a part-time playwright—until a perceptive critic advised him to take up medicine. After receiving his degree in 1843, he set up a laboratory in the gloomy, damp cellar of the Collège de France. There, with equipment that he himself had made, he began his momentous experiments.

He first investigated the effect of poisons on animals—and proved that, contrary to accepted belief, most of them do not act on the entire body but on a localized region. For instance, one will disturb the central nervous system, another impair the ability of the blood to absorb oxygen. If poisons acted so selectively, Bernard reasoned, remedies probably did too. This meant, he said, that drugs should not be administered blindly as general therapy; rather each should be tested for its specific effect. Pharmacology has proceeded on that basis ever since.

While testing the effects of drugs, Bernard was pursuing his major concern, physiology, the study of the functioning of the body's organs. He discovered the relationship between juices from the pancreas and the stomach, and how under- and over-secretion adversely affect digestion.

SCARLESS STITCHES are one of the techniques developed by Ambroise Paré. In the 16th Century, this French surgeon played a key role in raising surgical standards from the low levels of medieval times. This 1594 woodcut shows his method for minimizing the scars left by cuts: he stuck adhesive material to each side of the wound and pulled the flesh together with stitches through the cloth, rather than through the patient's skin.

He also made the important finding that the liver stored energy-giving sugar and released it to the blood stream when needed.

Until Bernard showed what some basic body organs did, physicians and surgeons had been severely hampered in diagnosis and treatment. Now, however, the doctors could distinguish among several of many possible causes for digestive ailments, for example, and in some cases give specific relief. They began to see why certain organs could safely be removed and why others could not because they were essential to life.

The cell as a citizen

Bernard's contemporary, the German pathologist and anthropologist Rudolf Virchow, was less concerned with the functions of the organs than with their cellular structure. His research led him to the conclusion that every living organism is "a cell state in which every cell is a citizen." And a disease, he said, was "a conflict of citizens in this state, brought about by the action of external forces."

Virchow's careful study of cells enabled him to describe the physical appearance of diseased organs. Now a physician was able to recognize an ailment by looking at an organ and examining its cells under a microscope. With this development, autopsy became an invaluable tool for training and research, for often the examination of the cells of organs could positively identify the cause of a patient's death and suggest ways of diagnosing and treating the affliction in other persons. Today, refined techniques make it possible to detect diseases of the liver, heart, kidney and other organs in their earliest stages by microscopic examination of the living patient's cells. Study of a few cells sliced, scraped or swabbed from the body can now identify cancer; blood disorders, such as anemia, also reveal themselves in the number and type of cells in the blood.

The direct value of Virchow's study of cells was matched by the influence of his view of disease, which he saw as a conflict between cells and some "external force." This was the idea that had bedeviled Semmelweis. And finally it was to be supported by experimental evidence—from a French chemist.

In 1877 Louis Pasteur established beyond any doubt that germs can cause infectious disease. This discovery, effected almost simultaneously in Germany by Robert Koch, was the most important contribution ever made to the practice of medicine and surgery. Pasteur was led to his proof through his efforts to find the cause of the spoilage of beet-sugar mash used to make alcohol in the north of France. After repeated experiments, he was able to prove that the souring of the beet sugar was effected by minute organisms in the air. Later he showed that air-borne organisms were also responsible for the spoilage of wine, beer and milk. He found that heat killed the organisms and prevented the spoilage. He went on to develop a process of controlled heat sterilization that protected the liquid without changing its taste. The process—now known as pasteurization—today guards against infections transmitted in milk.

Once Pasteur had discovered the effect of germs and had learned how to kill them in food, he sought a way to combat them inside the human body. From this search came the entire theory of immunization. Vaccination was not new. Jenner had made a successful smallpox vaccine a century earlier. However, he had had no idea of how the inoculation worked. Pasteur thought he knew. He theorized that a minor infection of a disease would cause the body to create its own forces of resistance—now called antibodies—which would thereafter remain in reserve, ready to fight off a major infection when it came.

An epidemic of anthrax that was decimating the cattle and sheep of France gave Pasteur an opportunity to test his theory under actual conditions. He first went to an area where the animals were afflicted with the disease and took blood from some of the sick animals. From these samples he was able to isolate the anthrax germ. His next step was to develop an attenuated, or weakened, strain of the organism. He found that he could achieve this result either by heating the germs or letting them stand in containers until they lost much of their virulence. Now he was ready to try his vaccine on animals that had not yet been affected by the epidemic.

He conducted his experiments on healthy herds of sheep and cattle. In each herd, some animals were inoculated with the attenuated strain of the anthrax germ but others were not. When the experimental groups were struck by the anthrax epidemic, Pasteur's theory was proved beyond doubt. His experiments were brilliantly successful. The sheep and cattle that had been inoculated with Pasteur's vaccine were completely immune to anthrax; those that had not been vaccinated died.

Every preventive vaccine developed afterward—from typhoid shots to Dr. Albert Sabin's oral vaccine for polio—is a direct outgrowth of Pasteur's work. It brought him fame and honor during his lifetime, although his concepts, especially his germ theory, met formidable opposition from many of his contemporaries.

Killing germs, saving patients

One who did recognize the importance of the germ theory and saw its relevance to surgery was the British surgeon Joseph Lister. Early in his career he had noted that a fracture that did not break through the skin never became infected. On the other hand, a fracture that had pierced the skin usually developed serious infection. The germ theory solved the riddle. Bacteria in the air could reach the open injury, but were kept away by unbroken skin.

From this deduction, Lister jumped to a momentous conclusion: bacteria in the air and on instruments must also be responsible for the infections that were killing as many as 50 per cent of surgical patients. This toll could be prevented, Lister realized, by killing the germs with a chemical. He washed his instruments with a carbolic acid solution and sprayed the same solution around the operating room. After surgery, a heavy dressing that had been soaked in the solution was applied to the wound. The results were immediate and dramatic—mortality from ampu-

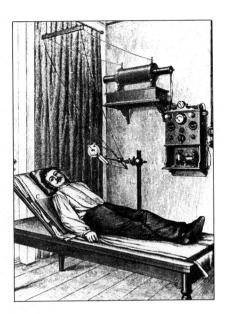

X-RAYING THE CHEST to diagnose lung ailments was a common procedure as early as 1900, when this drawing was made. Although X-rays had been discovered only five years before, doctors immediately realized the new tool's value. Unfortunately they were not so quick to appreciate the rays' harmful effects. To get a clear picture of a fracture, for example, they would turn on the rays for so long that some patients received burns far worse than their original injuries.

tations dropped from nearly 50 per cent, to about 15 per cent, and more modern techniques have since reduced surgical infections even further.

At almost the same time that Lister was applying Pasteur's germ theory to make surgery safe, another development was extending the scope of surgery. This was the discovery of anesthesia. Without anesthesia, the pain of surgery made speed all important. A three-minute amputation was not uncommon. Obviously, careful surgery was impossible under the circumstances; the screaming victim, tied to the operating table, might die of shock if the surgeon took time to do his job well. But pain was not the only problem. The surgeon's incision caused the patient's muscles to contract uncontrollably, moving intestinal structures so much that operations on the abdomen were almost impossibly difficult and hazardous.

"Gentlemen, this is no humbug"

Neither of these obstacles could be overcome by ancient pain relievers like alcohol and opium; if such a drug were administered in a dose large enough to induce total insensibility, the result all too often was death. New drugs were needed, and chemical experimenters found them early in the 19th Century. Who first used them for surgical anesthesia is still a matter of dispute, but their acceptance in medicine can be traced to one thrilling confrontation on October 16, 1846, in the operating theater of Massachusetts General Hospital in Boston. There, before a skeptical —even hostile—audience of students and distinguished physicians, William Morton, a dentist from Charlton, Massachusetts, administered ether to George Abbott, a painter who was about to have a tumor removed from his neck. Dr. John Collins Warren, head of surgery in the hospital and one of the country's foremost surgeons, performed the operation. When the painless, relaxed procedure was completed, Dr. Warren announced, "Gentlemen, this is no humbug."

The modern era of surgery had begun. Basic medical knowledge became as essential to surgeons as to other physicians, so that surgeons were necessarily physicians first and operating specialists second. Scientific discovery thus forced the complete reunification of surgery and medicine, just as it revolutionized the practice of all kinds of physicians.

The progress of the 19th Century may best be reckoned by measuring the gap between the physician of 1800—who did not even have a stethoscope to aid him in diagnosis—and his counterpart in 1900, who used the X-ray to reveal the inside of the body. Of equal, or perhaps of even greater, importance was the change of attitude toward medical science that occurred during those 100 years. Earlier medical men had been satisfied if they could answer, from experience, one practical question: "Does this treatment work?" In the 19th Century men of medicine wanted other answers as well: they sought to learn how and why a treatment worked. And this shift of emphasis was probably the 1800s' greatest gift to the modern physician and surgeon. It marked the difference of viewpoint between the rule-of-thumb empiricist and the inquiring scientist.

AN AUTO-POWERED X-RAY was used by one turn-of-the-century physician, who took the newly invented diagnostic tool to his patient's bedside. The early X-ray machine was small enough to be portable, and its tube could be operated on a car battery's low-voltage electricity, fed over wires leading through a bedroom window.

Doctor in the Backwoods

Hand in hand with the remarkable advances made by medicine in this century went the gradual decline in prestige of the general practitioner, the physician who had been the mainstay of the healing art. As science moved into the sickroom, specialists took over more and more areas of medical practice. By the middle of the 20th Century, the old-fashioned G.P. had lost his preeminence, but those who still practiced were of greatest importance in isolated rural areas.

At first glance, this seems to be the explanation of the backwoods practice to which Dr. Gaine Cannon (right) devoted his last years. The physical conditions of his life in the Blue Ridge Mountain country around Balsam Grove, North Carolina, almost exactly resembled those of the early-20th Century G.P. Yet Dr. Cannon was a paradox, for he possessed skills nurtured in leading medical schools and an up-to-date knowledge of medicine gained in modern hospitals. His patients idolized him; when he died in August 1966 they discovered that he was a hard man to replace. The medical profession is making the same discovery: authorities are urging medical schools to train a new kind of doctor—a specialist in family practice—to fill the shoes of the Gaine Cannons.

ROUTINE OF DAILY VISITS
At 11 in the morning Cannon trudges through mud to a two-room cabin housing the nine members of the Owen family. He examined not only Mrs. Owen, who had just borne a baby, but the rest of the children while he was at it. On this day, Cannon had risen at sunup to treat patients at his clinic before setting out to make 15 to 20 house calls around the countryside.

House Call in a Mountain Cabin

Most modern physicians see their patients during office hours or in a hospital. By contrast, Gaine Cannon's practice often took him some 50 miles daily to see families like the one shown here. He used a two-way radio to keep in touch with the nurse at his clinic. In bad weather, or when calls for help sent him to isolated cabins on washboard roads, he drove a four-wheel-drive vehicle.

On just such a rough lane is situated the home of Cecil Owen, where Dr. Cannon made this morning call. Owen is an illiterate television repairman, using batteries to supply testing current in a cabin without electricity. The opportunity to practice preventive medicine, afforded by this visit, is as important as the treatment of illness. Stopping in to check Mrs. Owen and her new baby, Cannon found that the other children had runny noses and fevers. He examined them to make sure that they had nothing more serious than a cold.

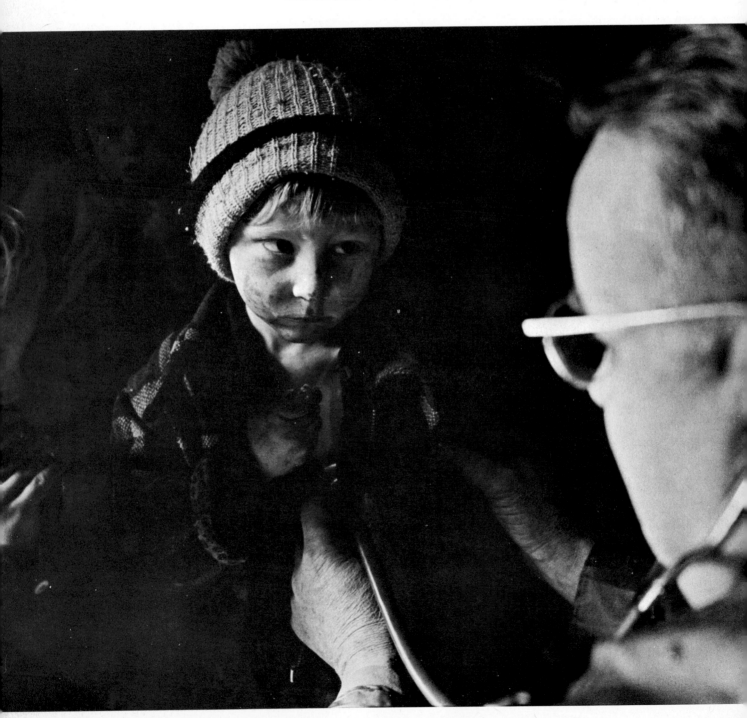

CANDY FOR CONFIDENCE

Like many a busy pediatrician Dr. Cannon found that candy was a specific antidote for the fear and suspicion of his youthful patients. Here he applies liberal doses of the time-honored therapy to the Owen children before getting down to the more serious business of examining them.

A TWO-WAY EXAMINATION

Under the scrutiny of a wary sharpshooter *(opposite),* the doctor listens for sounds that might indicate pneumonia, a potentially dangerous complication that can result from common respiratory ailments. Colds usually get short shrift in the mountains but the doctor takes no chances.

CHECKING FOR DANGER SIGNS

A contented youngster *(above)* sucks on a piece of candy while Cannon checks his ear for signs of infection. When he first came to Balsam Grove, the doctor found many children suffering from diseases spawned by malnutrition and poor sanitation. Cannon waged war against such causes by educating parents in hygiene and occasionally by giving families much-needed food.

Message Centers for Shut-ins

Since most of Cannon's patients had no telephones, he worked out other ways for them to communicate with him when they were ill. On Mondays and Fridays, for example, he would make a 25-mile drive to a general store in Jackson County *(left)*, across the mountain from his clinic. The store was a message center where requests for house calls could be left by patients in the vicinity.

As the doctor traveled from Balsam Grove to Jackson County and back again, he also called on elderly patients, many of whom suffered from high blood pressure. During these visits, Cannon was able to spot danger signs and take preventive measures.

INFORMAL EXAMINATION ROOMS
After picking up messages from all the patients who needed house calls, Cannon takes blood pressure readings on the proprietress of a general store in Jackson County *(left)* and the postmistress in Balsam Grove *(above)*. It was no trouble for him to check on the postmistress— he visited the tiny post office nearly every day, for the majority of its mail was addressed to him.

A One-Man Ambulance Service

Transporting seriously ill patients to the nearest hospital—some 60 miles away—was a real chore. Cannon fitted his Jeep station wagon with a mattress. In nearly any weather, this makeshift ambulance, with its four-wheel drive, was able to bring his patients from out-of-the-way cabins to a paved road and a conventional ambulance. But when the snow lay so deep that even this rugged vehicle could not get through, Cannon radioed the state police for a bulldozer to dig a path to his patient.

This carefully planned rescue service was called into action to save the life of 75-year-old Charlie McCall, shown at right being taken out of Cannon's Jeep. During one bad blizzard, Dr. Cannon bulldozed his way into McCall's cabin for a routine call and found him struggling for breath at a dying fire, the door of his cabin open to the freezing cold outside. Cannon treated him on the spot and saw to his care, but a few months later McCall became acutely ill again. This time Cannon took him out in the Jeep. As the doctor worked his way along the road leading from the cabin, he radioed for an ambulance to pick up McCall at the nearest paved road, 15 miles away. Though nearly dead of heart disease and kidney disease, McCall pulled through again. He later reported to Dr. Cannon that he felt "pert as a cricket."

A ROADSIDE TRANSFER
After bringing Charlie McCall down a slippery mountain road in a Jeep, Cannon meets an ambulance which he had summoned and helps its driver move the patient to a stretcher. Several of McCall's friends and relatives, seeking to be of help, have followed the doctor's Jeep down to the meeting place, at the junction of a paved road and the track leading to McCall's cabin.

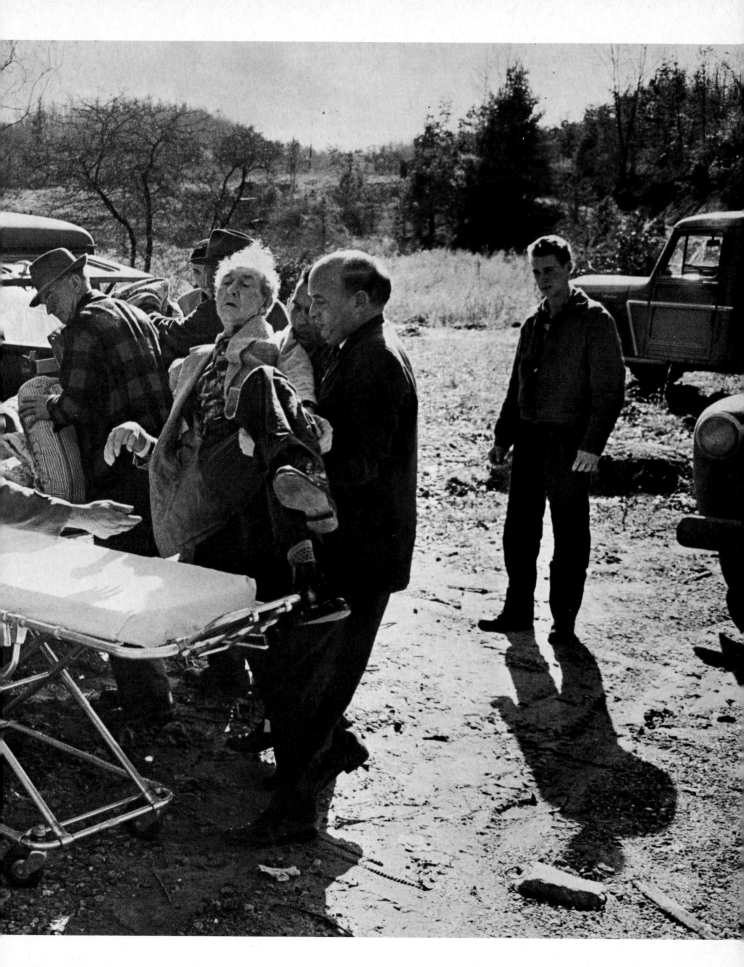

Lifesaving Care for the Old

An extraordinarily high proportion of Cannon's patients were old people. A survey conducted in nearby Canada township showed that people over 70 made up 13 per cent of the residents, although this age group constitutes only 4 per cent of the total population of the state. The apparent longevity of these mountain people is difficult to explain. Cannon himself ascribed it to the slow, easy tempo of their lives, while other people point out that many of the young people move away from the mountains, leaving behind mostly the old and the children. Whatever the rea-

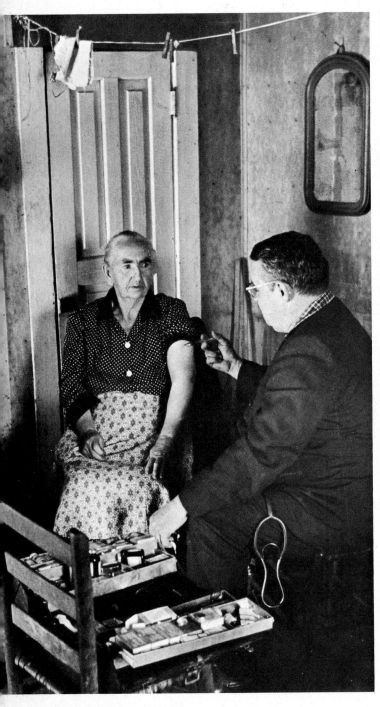

RELIEF FOR ARTHRITIS
On one of his many routine house calls to his elderly patients, Cannon gives an injection to Mrs. Parlee Smith to alleviate the stiffness of her chronic arthritis.

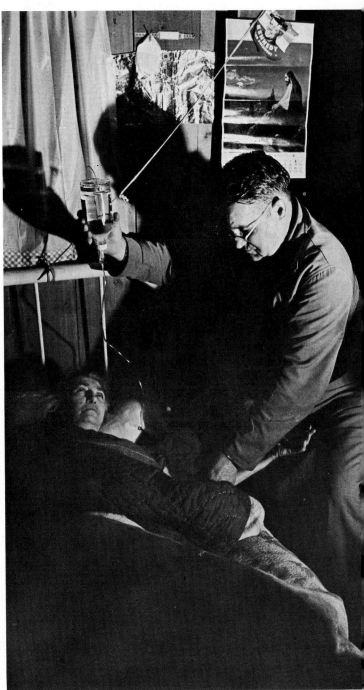

HOSPITAL TREATMENT AT HOME
The doctor administers blood plasma to Carrie McCall to relieve dehydration caused by influenza, to which Cannon's elderly patients were so susceptible.

son, Cannon often had to act as a geriatrician—a specialist in the diseases of the aged.

In this role his ability to relieve illness and prolong lives would have seemed like magic to a 19th Century G.P. Dr. Cannon had the most modern drugs and techniques available for alleviating arthritis, high blood pressure and the respiratory ailments common among the elderly. Occasionally, he was able to carry out emergency treatments, usually administered only in hospitals, to those patients who were too ill—or simply unwilling—to leave their homes.

THERAPY FOR HYPERTENSION
Prescribing for Henry Owen's chronic high blood pressure, Cannon had available a choice of several different drugs that reduce blood pressure to a safe level.

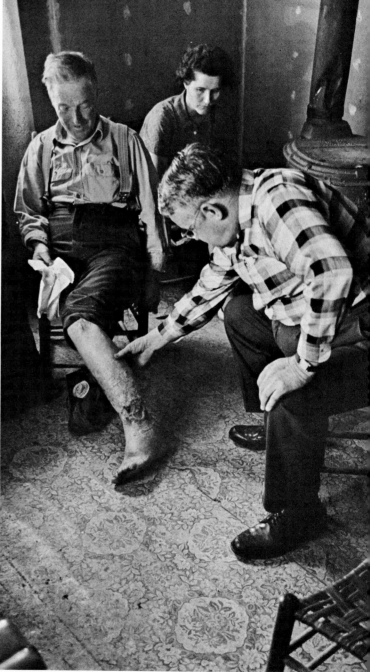

HELP FOR A RELUCTANT PATIENT
The doctor inspects a healing ulcer on the leg of Cannon McCall, who at the age of 80 still cut down laurel trees for a living but was reluctant to seek treatment.

A Clinic in an Old Farmhouse

After his daily rounds, Cannon usually returned to his clinic at about 5:30. Then he saw patients on their way home from work, for no matter how sick they were, few of his patients took time off from work to come to the clinic during the day. Dr. Cannon often found a roomful of patients waiting for treatment.

Cannon himself was keenly aware of the inadequacies of the clinic, and when he died he was building a hospital to replace it. For a one-man establishment, however, the clinic was well equipped and fairly self-sufficient. In an old farmhouse he had set up his office, a large reception room, a treatment room and a dispensary, where he filled his own

prescriptions—there was no drugstore closer than an hour and a half drive. In a nearby building, he maintained a four-bed maternity ward.

The maternity ward was perhaps the most important part of the clinic for, like every rural G.P., Cannon spent much of his time delivering babies. He estimated that in 13 years he had delivered about 5,000, a case load many specialists in obstetrics would never match. Though Cannon begged prospective mothers to come to the clinic well before delivery, many arrived at the last possible minute. Sometimes they did not get there at all: a number of Cannon's patients were born in his station wagon or even at the side of a road.

A PROGRAM OF CONSTANT CARE
In the treatment room of his small clinic, Dr. Cannon makes a routine check on Charlie McCall, one of his most difficult patients *(page 44)*. Because McCall suffered from a variety of serious ailments, Cannon had to maintain a constant watch over him both at home and in the clinic.

WARM GREETING FOR A NEW BABY
Still in his delivery room smock and gloves, Cannon beds down a new arrival in the maternity ward. He tried to get new mothers to stay on at the ward for two or three days of postnatal care, but despite his pleas they often packed up their babies and went home in a few hours.

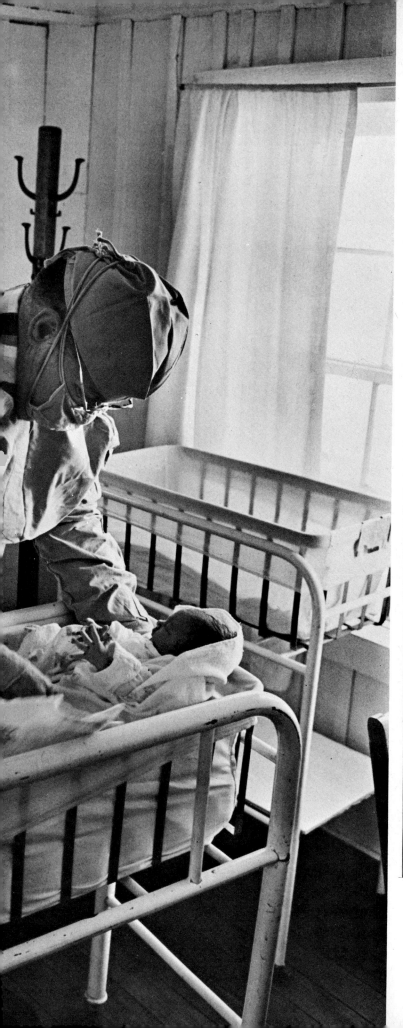

FILLING A PRESCRIPTION
Cannon not only wrote his patients' prescriptions but filled nearly all of them. Here, seen in his dispensary, he is being assisted by his cousin Helen McCall, a medical technician whom he trained to act as his nurse and assistant, and to run the clinic while he was out on house calls.

The Day Ends, the Night Begins

At 8:30 or so, after treating the patients in his waiting room, Cannon was finally ready for dinner. It was his first real meal of the day; he rarely stopped for lunch, but snatched a soft drink or a bowl of soup between his visits to his patients. But he was often interrupted in the middle of his meal, and even after dinner his work did not end, for his nights were sometimes as busy as his days. He was frequently roused to deliver a baby in the clinic or to go out to tend one of his old people. Hardly ever was he able to get an entire night's sleep.

The strain of this kind of life finally overcame Gaine Cannon. He had heart disease when he came to Balsam Grove in 1953 and died of it in 1966; he was 68. His death has left the mountain people stranded. Though they get part-time medical attention from an old colleague of Cannon's, located in Rosman, several miles away, they have been unable to find a G.P. willing to take on the job full time.

LAST PATIENT OF THE DAY
On his way home from work a patient reports to the treatment room of the clinic for an injection. Though patients like this one and other emergencies kept Cannon up late at night and almost every night, he never thought of refusing to see them. As he himself once said in a Christmas card greeting to his patients and friends, his real office hours were "twenty-four hours daily."

A FINAL SPELL OF PAPER WORK
It is 11 p.m. For the moment, Cannon has seen his last patient, given his last shot, written and filled the last prescriptions. Now he can settle down in his office to straighten out his patients' records before going to bed. He is finally reaching the end of another exhausting 18-hour day.

3
The Making
of an M.D.

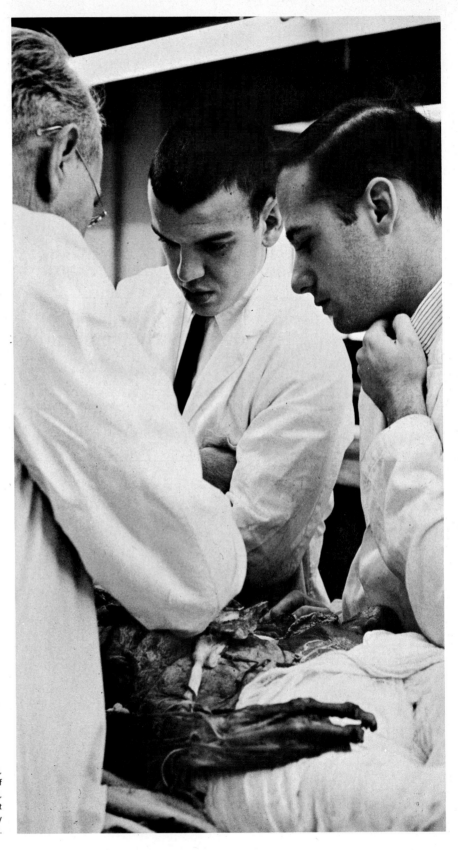

While their anatomy professor supervises, two first-year students at the University of Illinois medical school dissect a cadaver, beginning four years of laborious study that will prepare them to diagnose and remedy the ailments that afflict the human body.

"YOU JUST DON'T REALLY KNOW what it's like until evening. Last night we got our books and got all ready to study, and then it came to us how much there was to do, and we were so scared we couldn't do anything." Those despairing words from a first-year medical student at the University of Kansas convey the frustrations every American physician feels during the ordeal of learning his profession. His training is longer and more arduous than that required for almost any other calling. After high school and college he must devote four years to intensive, 70-hour-week study in medical school and a year to internship. Then, if he is among the more than 85 per cent who plan to specialize, he usually spends two to five years as a hospital resident physician. Most doctors cannot complete their training and begin to support families of their own until they are about 30 years old.

The young men (and a few young women) who are willing to subject themselves to this demanding preparation are an elite group. They have to be good students, achieving grades that usually average at least a B. Only about 80 per cent of them have to wait until they are graduated from college to be accepted as medical students; 20 per cent enter medical school before they have their bachelor's degree because they have attained such outstanding records in undergraduate study. Most come from middle-class, well-educated families; 1 in 10 is the child of a doctor. They expect to live comfortably as physicians, and they know that they will be treated with respect. They also know that physicians are among the most independent of men and give orders far more often than they have to take them. The would-be doctor is therefore likely to be self-confident, with a taste for independence and the exercise of authority. And, if he is to do his job well, he must have a strong streak of idealism as well.

To these qualities of intellect and character, training must add the knowledge and skills that will make him an efficient physician. Today, most American medical schools offer a program of education which, while criticized by some authorities, is still of such high quality that it attracts students from all over the world. But this was not always the case. In the 19th Century, the low standards of American medical education were a national scandal. A few universities—among them Harvard, Pennsylvania, Western Reserve and Dartmouth—had good medical schools, but most of the institutions were tragically inadequate. Many of them were nothing more than diploma mills, operated primarily to make a profit for their owners.

These proprietary schools were generally run by groups of doctors who pooled resources, rented a building, bought a minimum of equipment and went into business. There were no real standards of admission; virtually anyone could enter and would be graduated if he paid the fees. Laboratory facilities were primitive or nonexistent. The teaching consisted mainly of lectures drawn from antiquated textbooks. And there was little or no clinical training: most of the graduates went into practice without having had any experience in treating the sick. They learned on their patients—at what cost in human suffering no one now can even guess.

The hopeless inadequacy of the schools was widely recognized. They were assailed by the officials of the good medical schools, by the American Medical Association, which had been founded in 1847 to raise medical standards, and by a number of state governments which had set up licensing boards to ensure that only properly trained doctors could practice. But for years the proprietary schools managed to defy all attempts to reform them, and they continued to flourish until they were put out of business by a one-man crusade.

The man was Abraham Flexner. Flexner was not a physician, but a scholar and educator who had written a critical survey of higher education, *The American College*. In 1908 he was commissioned by the Carnegie Foundation for the Advancement of Teaching to study American medical schools. He went at the job with the sophisticated perception of a learned man and with the zeal of a muckraking reformer. In less than a year he visited all of the 155 medical schools in the U.S. and Canada, investigating laboratories and classrooms, courses and requirements. If officials were uncooperative, he did not hesitate to spy. In Iowa one dean showed Flexner doors marked "Anatomy," "Physiology" and "Pathology" and assured him that they led to laboratories. But the doors were locked and the janitor, who had the keys, could not be found. Flexner pretended to be satisfied and permitted the dean to take him to the railway station. He waited until his host had gone, then returned to the school, found the janitor and gave the man five dollars to open the doors. Inside the rooms he found desks, blackboards and chairs, but no laboratory equipment at all.

Bombshell for medical education

Flexner's report, *Medical Education in the United States and Canada*, appeared in 1910 and it was damning. One after another he listed the schools and their shortcomings, naming names and giving details. "The medical profession," as he wrote later, "and the faculties of the medical schools . . . were absolutely flabbergasted by the pitiless exposure. We were threatened with lawsuits, and in one instance actually sued for libel for $150,000." Flexner even received anonymous letters warning him that he would be shot if he returned to Chicago, a city in which he had uncovered several particularly unsavory institutions. But the shock of his disclosures stimulated action. The enrollments—and profits —of the schools he condemned dropped sharply, and within five years 60 of them closed. Almost all of those that continued to operate or that were built after his report appeared followed Flexner's recommendations for improvements in curricula, faculties, and clinical and laboratory facilities.

The standard of medical education that the Flexner Report gave America was based on the courses of study already in use at the better medical schools. It most closely reflected the program at a then rela-

A GREAT MEDICAL EDUCATOR, Dr. William Henry Welch, and his most distinguished protégés are affectionately caricatured in this 1910 cartoon—"Some Welch Rabbits"— drawn to honor his 60th birthday. A founder of the influential Johns Hopkins School of Medicine in 1893, he later helped organize the Rockefeller Institute of Medical Research (now The Rockefeller University) and the Johns Hopkins School of Hygiene and Public Health.

tively new institution, the medical school of the Johns Hopkins University of Baltimore. That single institution, started in 1893, had quickly attracted two of the nation's most influential medical educators and had established a pattern of scientifically oriented medical training that has endured to the present day.

The model medical school

The school was founded by Johns Hopkins, a Baltimore whiskey merchant whose will divided seven million dollars into two bequests—half to establish a hospital and half to establish a university with a medical school. Hopkins endowed more wisely than he could have known. Rarely before had an American medical school and hospital been so closely associated, and the importance of this juxtaposition cannot be overestimated. Now medical students could be given thorough clinical training at the bedside of the sick. The innovation was made even more effective by the man who was appointed chief of the hospital medical staff. He was William Osler, the great physician whose skill, perseverance and compassion inspired not only his own students but his students' students, and whose methods and goals still continue to guide the physician today.

The second great contribution made by the new school was its emphasis on basic training in the principles of science. Students were no longer given rule-of-thumb procedures to follow blindly. Instead they were taught the fundamental structure and operation of the human body, whether healthy or diseased, so that they would understand the causes of illnesses and the effects that could be expected of treatments. For this scientific approach to medical education, the greatest credit must go to William Welch, professor of pathology and later dean of the school.

Welch was nicknamed "Popsy" for his fatherly attitude toward his colleagues, and he was truly the father of scientific medical education in the United States. He had studied in Germany, where medical science was blossoming, and he understood the importance of a firm grounding in scientific knowledge. Under his guidance, Johns Hopkins set up departments in the basic medical sciences—anatomy, pharmacology, physiology and pathology—and staffed them with superb teachers, all of whom worked full time, on salary. This, too, was an innovation; previously, medical school professors had been private physicians who taught a few hours a week as a sideline. The change was enormously important: it enabled the instructors to devote all their time to teaching and research, and it made the school a center for the discovery and dissemination of new medical knowledge.

The educational approach that Johns Hopkins developed and that the Flexner Report established as a standard remains in force in virtually every American medical school today. In all but about a half dozen of the almost 90 schools now accredited, the first two years are devoted primarily to academic study and laboratory instruction, and the last two to clinical study in a teaching hospital. In his first year, the student concentrates on anatomy, biochemistry and physiology—learning how the human body is constructed and how it functions. He learns from books, lectures and long hours in the laboratory, where he dissects cadavers. The students work together in the laboratory. While one reads out directions from a lab manual, another dissects and attempts to identify muscles, nerves and blood vessels from paintings and diagrams in a textbook. The work is physically exhausting and the learning gleaned from it frustrating, for the organs dissected rarely look like the pictures in the book.

The strain of this first year is ably described in *Boys in White*, a 1961 sociological study of medical students at the University of Kansas. This report quotes the faculty of the university as advising its students: "Start work immediately because there will be no time to catch up. . . . There are 5,000 names and parts of the body you will have to learn." To master all the material and pass his exams, the student has to work 12-hour days. He works under supervision from 8 or 9 in the morning until 5 in the afternoon. He works on his own in the evening and on weekends, and he often works far into the night, flogging himself to study despite insufficient sleep. One first-year student told the authors of *Boys in White*, "I'm now getting a little behind in everything, and I can't see any prospect of catching up." His experience was far from unusual; more students drop out during the first year than at any other time. The second year continues a routine that has become familiar—more of the textbook and laboratory grind. Now the student learns about the abnormalities created by disease, the action of infectious agents, drug therapy and physical diagnosis.

From classroom to clinic

After these two years of study, most students are thoroughly fed up with academic work. They want to watch doctors in action, and they want to work with patients themselves. Extensive experience begins in the third year, which is spent in the teaching hospital affiliated with the medical school. The student continues to read textbooks and attend lectures, but these are now oriented more toward work with patients. This change in training is symbolized by a change in clothing—the student replaces his laboratory coat with the physician's white jacket. And as he moves around the wards, he begins to feel that he will indeed one day become a doctor. He accompanies senior physicians on their rounds; standing at bedsides, he watches his teachers handle patients and listens as they explain their diagnoses and the treatments that are necessary.

He also looks after patients of his own. If a patient has just been admitted to the hospital, the student conducts the routine physical examination and takes down the medical history. He performs laboratory tests, such as a urinalysis and blood-cell count, evaluates other laboratory tests that have been made and examines the patient's X-rays. Then

FIRST YEAR
BIOCHEMISTRY, ANATOMY, HUMAN PHYSIOLOGY, GENETICS, BIOMATHEMATICS, BEHAVIOR, HISTORY AND PHILOSOPHY OF MEDICINE.

SECOND YEAR
PATHOLOGY AND MICROBIOLOGY, PHARMACOLOGY, TECHNIQUES OF PHYSICAL DIAGNOSIS, CLINICAL MEDICINE, PRINCIPLES OF EPIDEMIOLOGY, RESEARCH.

THIRD YEAR
PUBLIC HEALTH; CLINICAL TRAINING IN MEDICINE, SURGERY, PEDIATRICS, PSYCHIATRY, GYNECOLOGY AND OBSTETRICS, RADIOLOGY, OPHTHALMOLOGY.

FOURTH YEAR
APPRENTICESHIP IN MEDICINE, SURGERY, PEDIATRICS, PSYCHIATRY, NEUROLOGY, RADIOLOGY.

MEDICAL SCHOOL COURSES, listed above in the traditional curriculum of the Johns Hopkins University, make rigorous demands on the student. During his first year, he studies basic sciences. While continuing this work in his second year, the student also begins to observe patients, preparing for the third year when he will work in the hospital, assisting interns and residents. In his fourth year, the student becomes an apprentice doctor, caring for patients assigned to him and, under the supervision of his instructor, recommending treatment and medication.

he makes his diagnosis. When he next accompanies his seniors on ward rounds, the student "presents" his patient, describing the test results, offering a diagnosis and suggesting treatment. He is expected to have read up on the disease he has diagnosed and to be able to answer questions about it. Then the senior physician will take over and give his opinion, often using the student's patient as a starting point for a lecture on the disease.

Bedside and corridor lectures are often couched in very practical terms. A teacher may describe an imaginary patient who, forgetting that his swimming pool had been drained, dived in, landed on his head and was brought unconscious to the hospital emergency room. "The man is lying there," the teacher says, "bleeding to death. But he doesn't have to die. You can save his life if you know how to. Now what would you do?" The teacher then leads the discussion, correcting any mistakes the students make.

Occasionally a student will experience the excitement of recognizing a rare disease, or of identifying unusual symptoms, or even of saving a patient's life in an emergency. But so dramatic an event comes rarely; for most students clinical experience is a routine but essential initiation into the emotionally charged society of the hospital. Here they see at first hand how great and yet how limited is the power of the physician, and they gain a profound insight into human nature.

"In those three years," wrote physician-novelist Somerset Maugham of his days as a student in St. Thomas' Hospital in London, "I must have witnessed pretty well every emotion of which man is capable. . . . I saw how men died. I saw how they bore pain. I saw what hope looked like, fear and relief: I saw the dark lines that despair drew on a face: I saw courage and steadfastness."

Such intimate observations mold the student to his future role. He sees that in the hospital the physician is in command. Outside the hospital, a patient may be the doctor's equal, or even his superior. Inside it, he is at the doctor's mercy. Sometimes he is not even consulted about what is done to him. And when he is consulted, he generally lets the physician do what he thinks best, even if the proposed treatment is painful or dangerous.

Training for uncertainty

While awakening to the scope of this power to command, the student also begins to recognize the limitations on the physician's power to heal. During the first two years in medical school, he may think that medicine is an exact science. But clinical experience persuades him differently. He sees that disagreement about a diagnosis is common even among experienced physicians, especially when they are of different specialties.

In the midst of these disagreements, the student acquires what sociologist Renée Fox has described as "training for uncertainty." He sees, to quote from Dr. Fox, that "doctors aren't always sure what caused the patient's death" and that "they come to the autopsy to find out what was really wrong." On many occasions, the student observes that when the physician is most certain of his diagnosis the autopsy fails to bear it out.

The sobering experiences in the hospital often corrode the student's confidence in his own capacity and his chances for success in his chosen career. He never encounters some of the diseases he has read about, and he sees others—such as cases of ulcers—repeated so often that he comes to think he is wasting his time if he looks at any more. He may not recognize any of the signs and symptoms of a disease his professors have described. He may not be able to feel that a liver or a spleen is enlarged, or to notice the characteristic sounds of heart disease. There are few students who have not concluded at some time, with a sense close to hopelessness, that they would never learn the basic facts that seem to come so easily to their seniors.

The student's greatest frustrations arise when he attempts to practice the techniques he is learning. Throughout medical school, he is continually reminded of the immense burden of responsibility he will bear, and naturally he wants to start exercising this responsibility as soon as possible. But his inexperience makes it unwise to permit him to perform any but routine tasks. He is allowed to perform examinations and to write up diagnoses of even the most complex conditions; his diagnoses cannot hurt anybody so long as they are not acted upon until a senior physician has verified them. But actually treating a patient is another matter. He is permitted—and even required—to deliver babies, but only when the birth is uncomplicated. The obstetrician is always present in the delivery room, and he takes over if the birth presents any difficulties. The student may feel perfectly competent to remove tonsils or even an appendix, but it is the surgeon who performs the operation. The student's frustrations are vividly expressed in a time-honored medical school joke: Teacher: "What would you do if . . ." Student: "Call a doctor."

These restrictions on the student's authority do not end even after he passes his final examinations and, in solemn academic ceremony, puts on the green-hooded medieval robe of a doctor of medicine. He can now write M.D. after his name, but in most states he cannot yet practice medicine. He still has more to learn.

First chance to practice: internship

First the newly graduated doctor must put in a year on a hospital staff as an intern. It may be a rotating internship; in this case, he will work with specialists in a number of fields, one after another. Or if he has decided on his own field of specialization—pathology perhaps, or pediatrics, or obstetrics and gynecology—the entire year will be spent in that department of the hospital.

To many physicians, the year of internship stands out as the most exciting in their lives. For now at last, after all the years of training, the intern is allowed to exercise some of the authority of a full-fledged physician. It is often the intern who first sees patients when they enter the hospital. It is he who examines them, makes diagnoses and recommends a course of treatment. He may be forced to make life-or-death decisions, for he is usually the first to see emergency cases. If a patient is brought in bleeding from a knife wound in the chest, it is the intern who may have to decide whether the patient requires surgery. If so, he will send the victim on to an operating room; if not, he will sew the wound up himself. A distraught husband may drive up with his wife already giving birth; there is no time to call the obstetrician and the intern must deliver the baby.

The right to practice medicine

When this ruggedly practical apprenticeship is completed, the young physician must still pass a licensing examination before the government will permit him to practice. Once he has been granted a license he is legally qualified to perform any kind of medical activity. As a general practitioner, or G.P., he is permitted to deliver babies, engage in diagnosis and surgery, accept patients of all ages, prescribe medicines and treat ailments of the eye, ear, heart, lung or any other part of the body. But this all-encompassing license conveys only a legal right; in reality the young G.P.'s opportunities to practice advanced modern medicine are severely limited. He knows that to provide many of the more difficult types of medical care his patients may require—to perform complex operations or to manage serious diseases of the eye, for example—he needs to acquire special skills and knowledge through additional years of study.

The physician's own desire for further education is strengthened by his relationship with the hospitals, many of which have adopted rules that, in effect, make advanced postgraduate training almost mandatory. The hospitals can exert this degree of control over the physician because their facilities have become so important to modern medical treatment; today nearly all seriously ill patients now receive at least part of their care inside hospitals. Doctors usually limit practice within their offices to routine examinations or treatment of minor ailments, and they make fewer and fewer house calls. The appendicitis operation on the kitchen table is now just a scene in a movie or a television show, and in the United States, only seven babies in every thousand are delivered at home. Today when a doctor is called for anything out of the ordinary, he most often commands his patient, "Go straight to the hospital. I'll meet you there."

But to be able to say that—to have the right to treat his patient in the hospital—the physician must be a member of the hospital staff. In many cities such an appointment is offered only to certified specialists, physicians who have completed advanced education in one of the 19 principal medical specialties—such as surgery, pediatrics or internal medicine. Lacking this training, the nonspecialist G.P. may be severely limited in his use of hospital facilities; when his patients require hospital care, he must often refer them to specialists who are members of a hospital staff. He may then retain a consultant status, but he cannot manage their hospital care, and he generally has to defer to the specialist's judgment of what needs to be done.

The demand for high-quality medicine, enforced by the restriction of hospital privileges to specialists, has dramatically influenced the training of physicians. In 1931, some 71 per cent of all physicians in the U.S. were general practitioners. Today the percentage is less than 25, and seven out of every eight newly licensed physicians elect to become hospital residents. The resident, although legally qualified to practice medicine, is still only in training. Working in the hospital, he treats patients under the close supervision of the senior hospital staff while he acquires the additional knowledge and skills that will qualify him as a specialist in his field. In most specialties, the residency period lasts for three or four years. In some branches of surgery, however, it lasts five years or more.

A careful grounding

The resident's training is thorough. His position in the hospital—usually a large one—gives him an opportunity to observe and treat a wide variety of cases in his field. If he is to be a surgeon, he performs operations—simple ones at first, more difficult ones later—but always under the watchful eye of a qualified surgeon who can intervene if necessary. If he is to be an internist, he conducts examinations, orders laboratory tests and interprets the results, then prescribes the drugs or recommends the surgery that may be indicated.

After his training period, the resident takes a set of examinations made up by boards of medical specialists. The first such agency, The American Board for Ophthalmic Examinations, was incorporated in 1917; today there are boards for every major specialty from pediatrics to psychiatry. The boards are not government agencies. They are private organizations established by distinguished specialists to improve medical standards. Although the specialty boards do not have any legal authority, as the state licensing boards do, they wield tremendous power because they are so highly respected both by hospitals and by practicing doctors.

The influence of the specialty boards has helped make U.S. postgraduate medical training the envy of the world. The basic technical education provided by medical schools is also excellent. But the undergraduate curricula are still locked within the pattern designed by Osler and Welch around the turn of the century, and this pattern is now being subjected to pointed criticism on two counts. First, it produces too few physicians. Simply to maintain the present ratio of physicians to population the nation will need at least 11,000 per year by 1975; at present only slightly more than 7,000 new doctors are being graduated per year and only a slight increase is proposed. The deficit is made up by a kind of wrong-way foreign aid—the United States imports over 1,000 physicians a year trained in other countries, which need their physicians more than we do. A more serious failing of the medical schools, according to many medical leaders, is an overemphasis on factual knowledge that encourages technical skill in treating diseases at the expense of human skill in treating people.

It is a measure of the severity of these problems that they have already prompted innovations in medical education, despite the medical profession's traditional conservatism. ("It is easier to move a cemetery," remarked one weary reformer, "than to change the curriculum of a medical school.")

The medical school of the future

To improve instruction, modern teaching techniques have been introduced. More than a third of U.S. medical schools now employ closed-circuit television systems as teaching aids. In surgery, television offers every student of a large class a close-up view of the operation as it is being performed, and in psychiatry, unobtrusive cameras permit students to observe the course of a patient's treatment. Even wider use of television—and other teaching tools, such as motion pictures—has been urged. Instead of forcing a student to go through the laborious process of dissecting cadavers himself, he might learn much of anatomy by watching films of dissections performed by distinguished anatomists. Instead of studying hundreds of slides under the microscope, the student could learn histology by looking at cells on a film.

More radical changes, altering the curriculum itself, have been tried at the medical school of Western Reserve University. This school has completely rearranged the traditional scheme for presenting the scientific foundations of medicine (pages 62-77). Instead of teaching the student all of anatomy in one year, all of pathology in another year, and so on, Western Reserve combines the academic disciplines into integrated units so that the student learns related facts from several fields. In one of these study units, for example, he may study the anatomy, physiology and biochemistry of the stomach, at the same time beginning to observe the treatment of patients suffering from ulcers, cancer and gastritis.

These new programs place much more emphasis on bedside medicine, and the student is involved in the management of individual patients from the very beginning of his medical education. During his very first week at school, the Western Reserve medical student is assigned to a patient whom he will serve as apprentice family physician. He learns at firsthand how social problems such as poverty or disrupted family relationships affect people's health. He sees that a sick woman may need more than drugs or a change of diet; perhaps the most useful treatment for her illness would be to find a job for her husband or a trustworthy babysitter while she works. He quickly discovers what every doctor must eventually learn: that there is far more to being a physician than can ever be taught in the classroom.

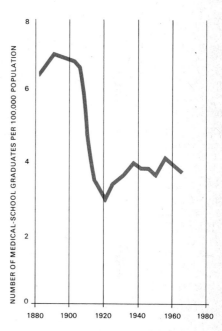

THE PHYSICIAN SHORTAGE in the United States and how it has grown are reflected by this graph, showing the ratio of medical-school graduates to the population. Late in the 19th Century, some seven newly graduated doctors entered practice each year for every 100,000 Americans. Sweeping reforms in medical education at the turn of the century forced many schools to close and lowered the ratio to 2.9 by 1920. Although the ratio improved slightly thereafter, it has been dropping steadily over the last decade as the number of graduates fails to keep pace with the swelling population.

A Revolution
in the Schools

"Divide your attention equally between books and men," advised Sir William Osler, the Canadian born physician-teacher who helped to set the pattern of American medical education in the 1890s. Many modern critics of medical teaching believe that the delicate balance urged by Osler has been lost, and that present-day medical schools overemphasize textbook facts and underemphasize patient care. Such dissatisfaction has plunged U.S. medical schools into a ferment of reorganization. Since 1961 modified curricula have been inaugurated at Northwestern, Duke and several other universities, but the most radical departure—involving a wholly new approach to medical teaching—is the program adopted at the School of Medicine of Western Reserve University in Cleveland, Ohio.

Western Reserve has restored emphasis to the human side of medicine by compressing textbook studies to provide more time for the student to work with patients. Each student is assigned a patient during his first week at school—not in his third year, as at most schools. From the start, he learns to care for, and to care about, the individual human being. He becomes, as shown in these photographs by Cornell Capa, a doctor trained to treat patients and not just their illnesses.

CLOSE-UP OF A SICK CELL

Eye fixed to the viewing lens of his microscope, a Western Reserve student focuses on the blood cells of a leukemia patient during a laboratory session on blood ailments. Students begin their study of diseased cells in the second year, after the first-year curriculum has made them familiar with healthy cells, the basic building blocks of the body.

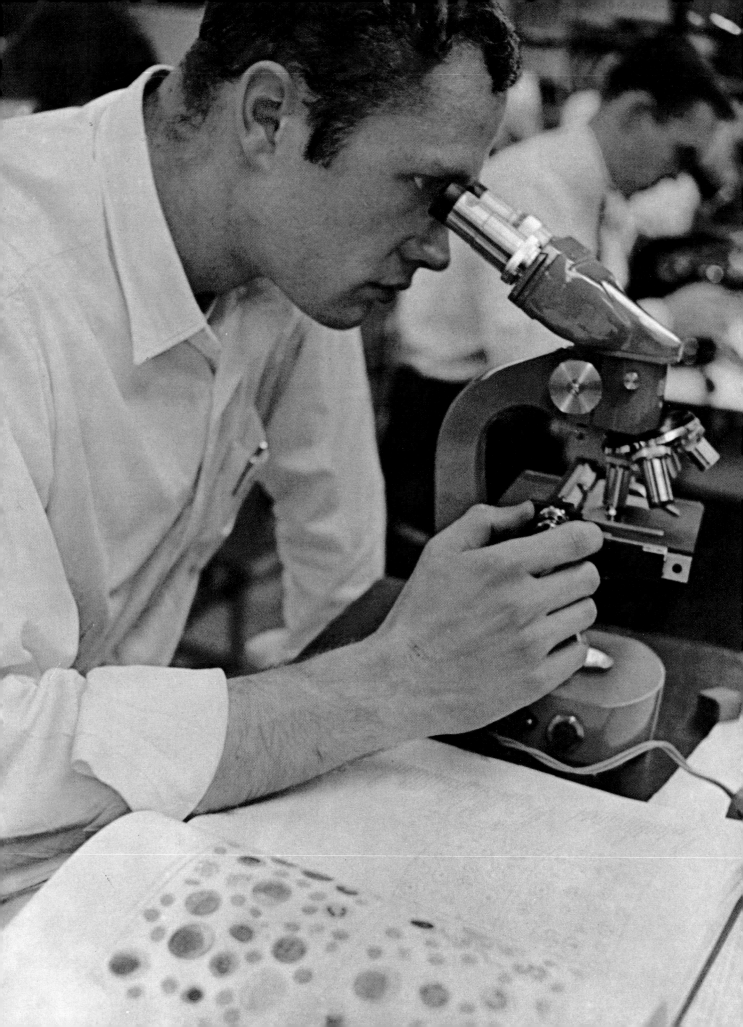

A First-Year Omnibus Course

Before Western Reserve reorganized its curriculum, repetition and duplication often plagued lecture and laboratory sessions. First-year students, for example, had to listen to five unrelated lectures on the thyroid gland given by five different departments. In the laboratory, the same experiments in anatomy were duplicated in physiology and in biochemistry.

At Western Reserve today, "multi-discipline" lectures and labs have ended such duplication. Professors from five departments now pool their talents for a coordinated nine-week course on the cell. Instructors from several departments teach one course on the endocrine glands, as shown here. The time saved enables students to work with patients. More important, the new approach shows that knowledge needed for treating patients is a coherent whole, not a patchwork of unrelated disciplines.

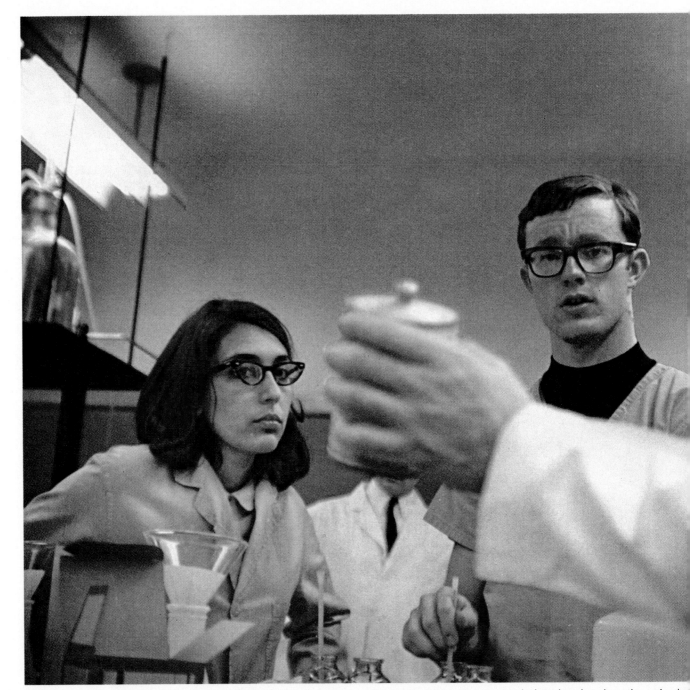

The ether in the hand of Dr. Howard Sachs will anesthetize an experimental animal in a laboratory course designed to show how the endocrin

WATCHING FOR A HORMONE

Under the instructor's supervision, student Lee Hyde has opened a vein of the anesthetized animal. Now he tests the effect of bleeding on the animal's pituitary gland. He studies a manometer—an instrument clamped above the bleeding animal that records its blood pressure. When the pressure falls to a predetermined point, he will test a sample of the blood for vasopressin, a hormone which the pituitary gland releases to constrict blood vessels and check bleeding.

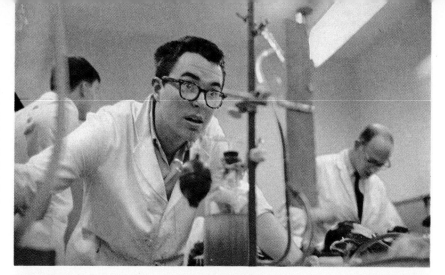

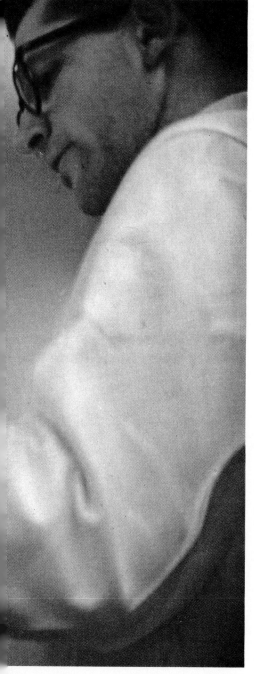

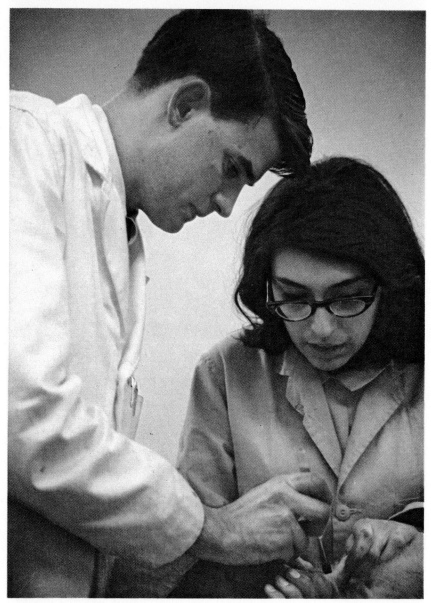

glands respond to and affect bodily processes.

TAPPING THE ADRENAL GLAND

Student Jim Holcroft exposes the adrenal gland in the endocrine system of the anesthetized animal. Blood from the gland will be collected by Holcroft and his lab partner, Lynne Zegiob; they will then analyze the blood to measure how much of an adrenal hormone called 17-ketosteroid is required to influence kidney functioning. This, too, is affected by blood pressure: as the pressure drops, the adrenal gland will excrete more 17-ketosteroid; under the effect of the hormone, the kidney will divert water to the bloodstream to counter the pressure drop.

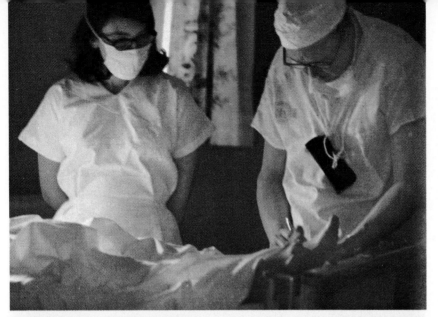

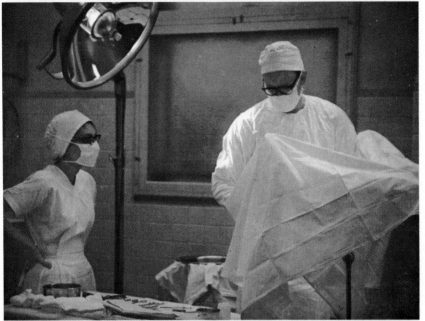

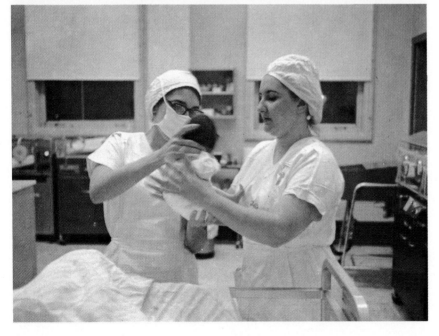

A Student's First Patient

Like a rookie ballplayer who sits out every game, the first-year student at a conventional medical school is restricted to the sidelines. He signs up to learn about keeping people well, but never works with a patient. He memorizes thousands of facts about anatomy, but seldom applies them to living people.

Western Reserve's new curriculum reverses this approach. Each first-year student becomes an apprentice family doctor to an expectant mother. Supervised by a "preceptor"—an experienced physician who acts as tutor and guide—the student helps give the mother physical checkups, writes a complete medical history of her family, attends the delivery of her baby and follows the child's development for two years or more.

During this long period of close involvement with one family's health problems, the student learns to treat patients as human beings. His very ignorance of medical detail is an asset, for it makes him concentrate on understanding the patient's personality. He begins to acquire the psychological horse sense that he will need later when, as a practicing physician, he must decipher the real meaning of his patients' vague descriptions of aches and twinges.

A CHILD IS BORN
Practical experience begins early for first-year student Lynne Zegiob when, summoned from home by telephone, she attends the delivery of her first "patient"—a healthy baby. In the top photograph, Lynne stands by while the anesthesiologist, who has just injected a limited anesthetic into the mother's spinal column to ease the pains of labor, begins to fill out his medical record of the case. In the delivery room *(center)*, Lynne and the obstetrician are ready to assist as the mother, her knees raised and draped in sterile linen, gives birth. Minutes later *(bottom)*, Lynne and the obstetrical nurse prepare the new baby, a robust 7-pound-12-ounce girl, for her crib in the hospital nursery.

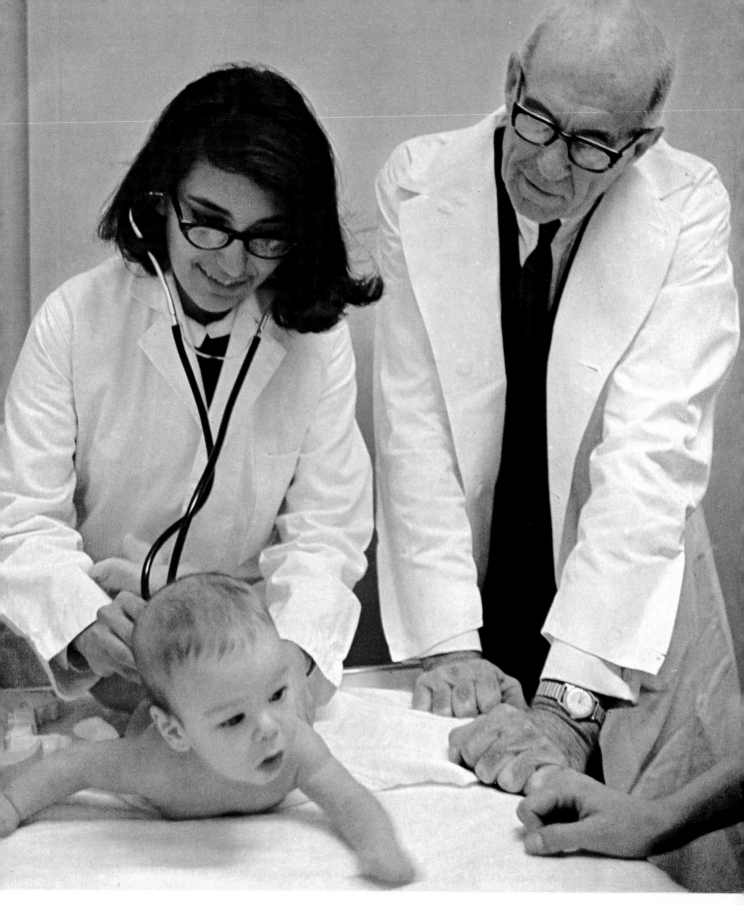

A STUDY IN GOOD HEALTH

Dr. Benjamin Spock, America's best-known authority on infant care, is also Professor of Child Development at Western Reserve, where he acts as a preceptor for eight students during their stint as apprentice doctors. Here he observes Lynne Zegiob's technique as she listens through a stethoscope to the respiration and heartbeat of a healthy four-month-old infant. Under the day-to-day guidance of her preceptor, Lynne will learn to take pulse rates, temperatures and blood pressures, and to treat the minor sniffles and aches of a growing baby.

Anatomy— Learning by Doing

These second-year students hunched over a metal-topped table at Western Reserve already know more about Percival's body than they do about their own. "Percival" is their cadaver; for a year and a half they will continue to dissect him, bone by bone, muscle by muscle, nerve by nerve.

Nothing less than this painstaking work with scalpel and probe can teach these students the actual complexities of the human body and prepare them to deal with its ailments.

For centuries, dissection has been the classic initiation to the medical profession, so essential to training

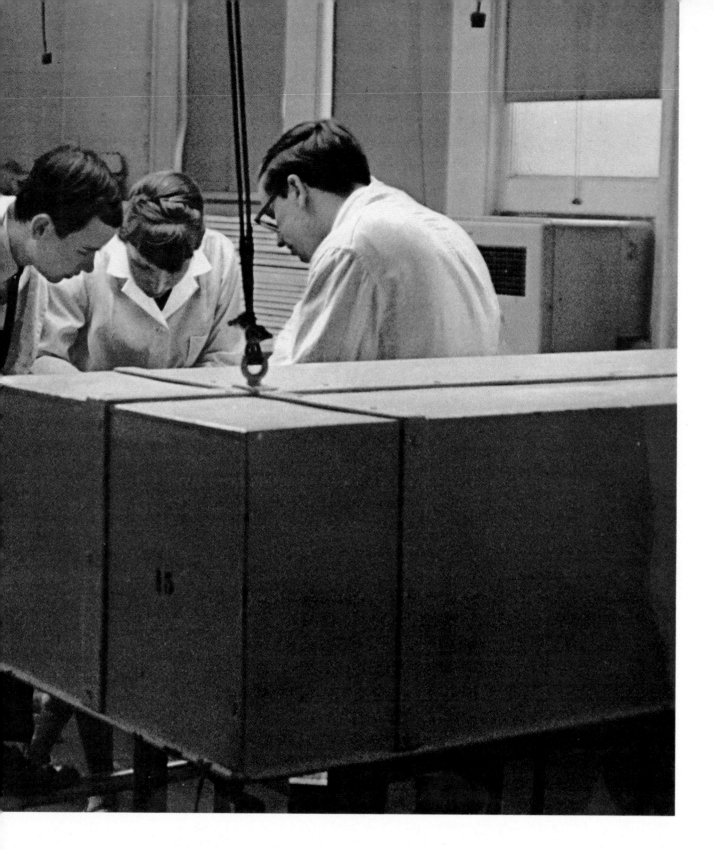

that the need for cadavers has always outstripped the supply. In 16th Century Padua, students haunted public executions to claim the corpses of the condemned. During one period in England, underworld "resurrectionists" robbed graves and sometimes even committed murder to supply medical schools with fresh bodies. In 18th Century Manhattan, dissections at New York Hospital once caused such outrage that the populace rioted, and doctors fled to the city jail for protection.

Today, most medical-school cadavers are unclaimed bodies from public morgues. In conventional schools they are used from the start of the first year to teach anatomy. But because Western Reserve emphasizes living processes during the first year, the dissection of cadavers is postponed until the second year, when students begin their study of disease.

The Second Year: Tracking Disease

Disease almost invariably has a visible effect upon the microscopic cells of the human body. To detect such changes, a doctor uses his microscope in much the same way that Sherlock Holmes used a magnifying glass: as a tool for uncovering the clues left by a possible killer. Learning to recognize these clues, second-year students in Western Reserve's laboratories spend hundreds of hours peering through the eyepieces of their microscopes, studying warped and crippled cells.

Microscopic examination is only one disease-locating method taught students. During all of the second year and part of the third, they study the many different effects of disease on the body's anatomy, microbiology and biochemistry. But the students do not take separate courses in these subjects. Instead, they study disease in terms of its total impact on each of the body's biological systems—the respiratory system, nervous system, cardiovascular system, and so on.

For example, lectures on respiratory diseases describe their pathology, the way in which emphysema collapses the lungs and tuberculosis dissolves its tissues. At the same time, students examine slides of lung tissue under their microscopes for evidence of structural changes and also dissect the chest cavities of cadavers in anatomical studies. Having learned to identify a wide range of respiratory diseases, the students move on to master the physician's crucial skills of treatment and cure.

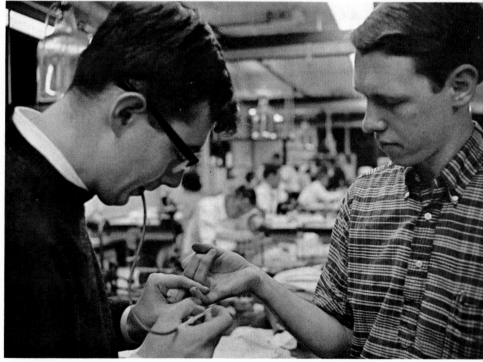

ON THE HUNT FOR DISEASE
In a lab session on blood-system illness, second-year students bend over their microscopes to estimate the number of white corpuscles in samples of blood. Normally, a cubic millimeter of human blood contains 5,000 to 7,000 white corpuscles; massive increases in the number of white cells may indicate disorders ranging from simple infection to incurable blood cancer.

A DROP FOR A BLOOD COUNT
A student draws blood from his lab partner into a glass tube in preparation for taking a blood count. He will release a diluted drop into a counting chamber, then view it under the microscope against a prepared scale. The scale enables him to count the white cells in a known area; from this figure the approximate number of cells per cubic millimeter can be determined.

71

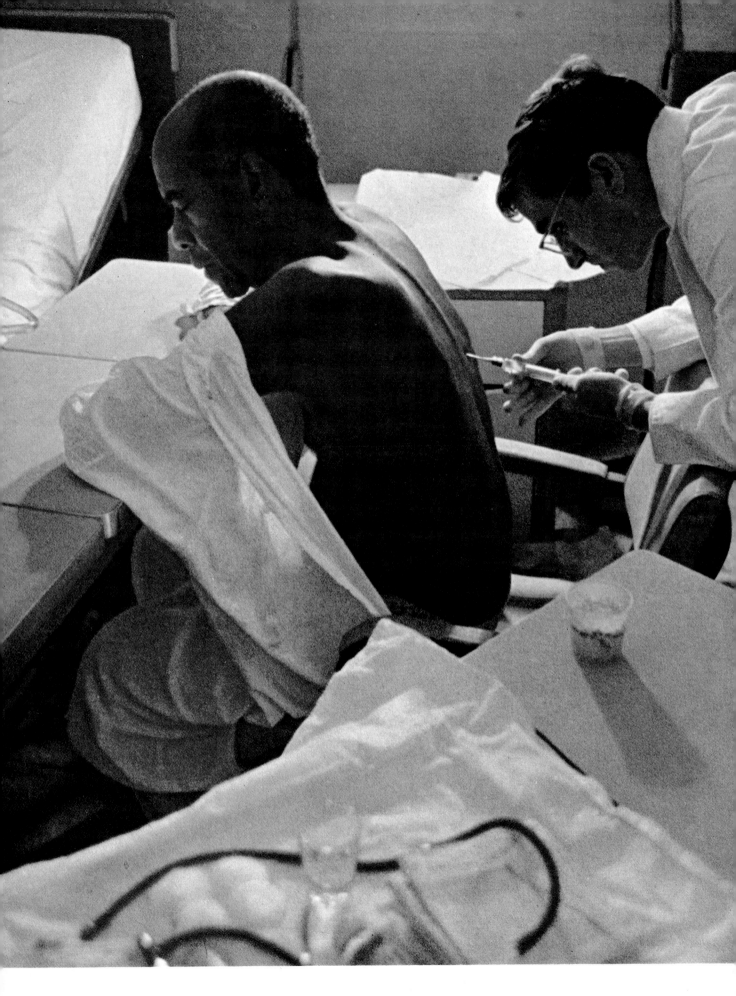

Apprenticeship in the Third Year

By the middle of their third year, medical students at Western Reserve have finished most routine lab training and lectures. Now they will concentrate on the care of patients. For the next year and a half, they will spend almost all their time in a series of "clerkships," or apprenticeships, in different wards of the 1,000-bed university hospital complex adjoining the school of medicine.

The arrangement is mutually advantageous to students and patients: the students get an opportunity to administer to real patients; the sick people, drawn from the low-income, largely Negro neighborhood around the school, get more individual attention than they otherwise would.

The first clerkship usually consists of a four-month period devoted to basic medicine; later clerkships cover such subjects as pediatrics, obstetrics and surgery. During his basic-medicine period, the student makes ward rounds with the resident physician, prepares and interprets temperature charts and case histories, and learns the practical techniques for battling disease. Sometimes, as in the pictures on these pages, he aids the resident in making diagnoses.

The students find working with sick people both a sobering and a profoundly satisfying experience, as they participate in the art of healing.

A LAB ANALYSIS
In a hospital laboratory David Joseph runs chemical tests on the fluid he has drawn from the chest cavity of the patient on the opposite page.

COLLECTING DATA IN A NEEDLE
Carefully inserting a hypodermic needle into the back of a heart patient, David Joseph prepares to draw out fluid which has accumulated in the chest cavity and hampered breathing. Laboratory tests of the fluid will indicate whether the patient has also contracted an infection.

A GROUP DIAGNOSIS
The findings submitted by David Joseph *(second from right)* are discussed by a committee of doctors and students headed by Assistant Professor of Medicine Dr. Thomas W. Moir *(center).*

The group decided that there was no infection, and that the fluid in the patient's chest cavity was the result of an alteration in body chemistry of a kind that often follows heart attacks.

Challenge of the Emergency Ward

Throughout one long night, Anne Colston, a fourth-year student at Western Reserve, kept a hectic, harried vigil in the university hospital's emergency ward. Her two-week clerkship required her to be on constant duty at the ward every other day from 9 in the morning until 9 the next morning, seeing patients with complaints ranging from a cut finger to a heart attack.

Anne shared in the task of diagnosing and treating every ailment she met. She had to draw upon all that she had learned in more than three years of study, for a half-forgotten line in an obscure textbook could hold the clue to the cause of a rasping cough or a soaring temperature.

Although the ultimate responsibility for diagnosis and treatment lay with the ward's resident doctor, Anne often saw the patients first, recorded their symptoms and proposed a course of treatment. If the complaint was minor and the treatment sound, she might be allowed to apply it while the resident supervised.

Many diagnoses and treatments

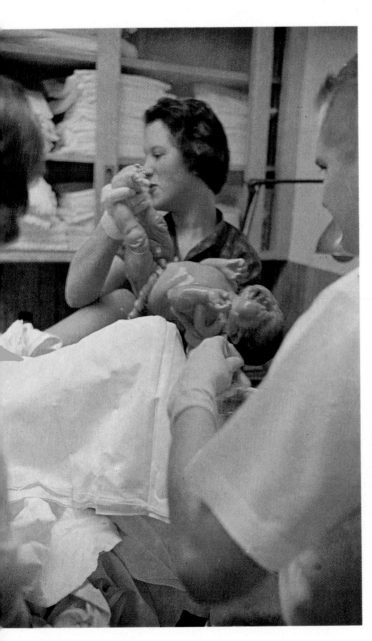

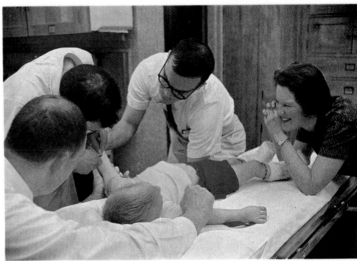

SETTING A BROKEN ARM
While an orthopedic specialist and the resident apply a cast to the broken arm of a four-year-old child, Anne helps by distracting him with funny faces. The casts on the boy's legs were put on at an earlier date to straighten his shin bones.

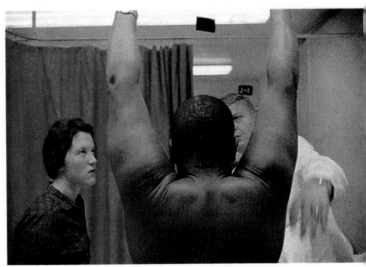

DELIVERING A CHILD
The evening's first case was an expectant mother, who arrived at the hospital in labor. Anne, prepared for this emergency by a previous clerkship in obstetrics, successfully delivered the baby, the 40th of her career.

TESTING FOR NERVE DAMAGE
This patient complained that he had lost all sensation in his right arm. Anne was unable to find any physical damage, but, suspecting an ailment of the man's nervous system, she asked the resident physician to diagnose the case.

were, of course, beyond Anne's skills, and her task was complicated by patients whose symptoms were purely imaginary. Some doctors estimate that as many as 50 per cent of all emergency patients are so-called "turkeys" who have no actual physical ailment. During the 24-hour emergency-ward duty shown here, Anne referred 10 possible "turkeys" to another clinic for diagnosis. She also turned to specialists for help in setting a fractured forearm and in diagnosing a possible heart attack.

But she herself—unaided, though supervised—delivered a baby, relieved an inflamed eye and patched up minor cuts and bruises. In one evening she acquired more medical experience than she might in a month of classroom or laboratory study.

For hundreds of upperclassmen like Anne Colston, the emergency ward is the crucible which helps to transform students into doctors. Said one, "This is what we have been waiting for. And this is where we really learn —when we have to do it ourselves."

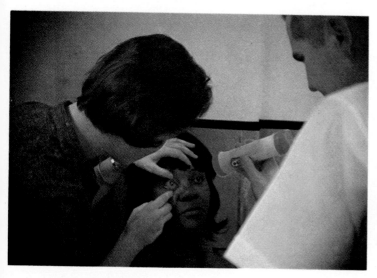

EXAMINING AN EYE WOUND
Peering into this woman's injured eye, Anne estimates the damage caused by a scratch on the cornea. A drop of local anesthetic has already eased the pain in the woman's eyeball, inflamed a fiery red as a result of her injury.

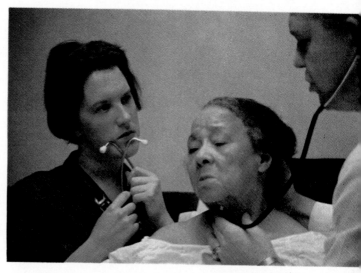

CHECKING A BLOCKED WINDPIPE
A resident, called in when Anne detected symptoms that suggested acute asthma, listens to the strangled breathing of this elderly woman. He decided that her symptoms were caused by hysteria, which had blocked her windpipe.

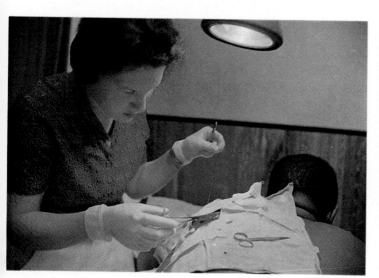

SEWING A WOUNDED BACK
Wielding her surgeon's needle like an expert, Anne sews 18 stitches into this man's back, which had been severely lacerated a few moments before in a truck accident. She later applied a surgical dressing and sent the man home.

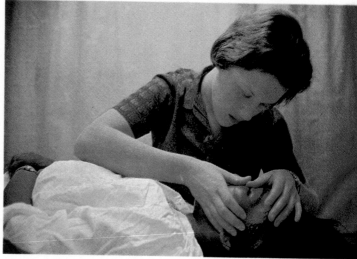

TREATING A BRUISED HEAD
Late in the evening, Anne examines a housewife's oozing head wounds, which had been inflicted by her husband in a family quarrel. Anne calmed the patient, then watched while an intern sewed up a cut over the woman's eye.

Tense Climax
to the Final Year

PLAN OF ATTACK
A senior resident surgeon, Dr. Roger Foster *(seated)*, studies X-rays and medical charts as he outlines the operation for the removal of a spleen to fourth-year student Robert Smink.

Under the glare of the operating-room lights, a human life hangs in a delicate balance; even when the surgery itself is relatively danger-free, the patient's future may be in question. The operation shown here is for the removal of a spleen. The patient, a woman, suffers from a disorder that causes hemorrhages in thousands of tiny blood vessels throughout her body. The doctors believe her spleen may be responsible, and estimate that there is at least a 50-50 chance that its removal will stop the hemorrhaging and save the patient's life.

For fourth-year student Robert D. Smink Jr., assisting at the splenectomy as part of a clerkship in surgery, the operation brings into focus some of the responsibility he will assume as a doctor, whether he becomes a surgeon, elects some other specialty or goes into general practice.

Before this responsibility can be his, Smink must spend a grueling year as a hospital intern and pass a licensing examination. Then he will probably spend from two to five years as a resident doctor in a hospital.

Later, he will add to his medical knowledge throughout his career—by reading the literature of his profession, by attending lectures, and by analyzing the results of his own and his colleagues' work. For Robert Smink, the four years of medical school are no more than first steps toward a never-ending course of study.

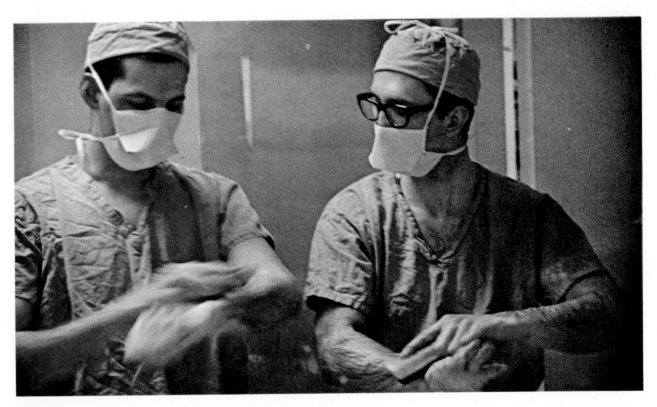

SCRUBBING UP
Eying Dr. Foster's technique, Smink learns the pre-operation ritual of "scrubbing up" with disinfectant to protect the patient from germs. Their gowns, masks and rubber gloves are further insurance against infection. Special cotton shoe coverings guard against a different hazard —sparks of static electricity, which might detonate the explosive gases used in anesthesia.

DEEP INCISION
Surgical clamp in hand, Smink *(center)* holds back the outer layers of flesh as Dr. Foster *(right)* cuts deeper into the patient's abdomen to reach the spleen. After the spleen was taken out, Smink was given the task of sewing together the outer layers of the patient's skin.

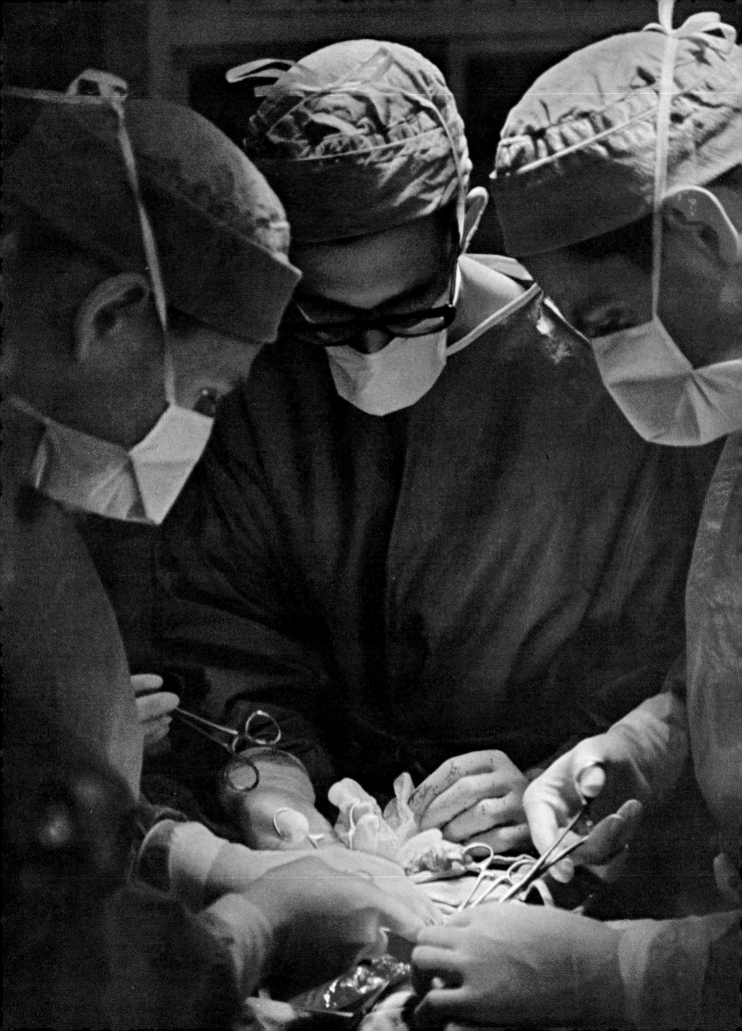

4
Physician to the Whole Man

Sir William Osler was a brilliant physician and educator. At the turn of the century he paved the way for the establishment of the internist—the combination generalist-specialist at the hub of medical practice today—as a new kind of personal doctor.

"THERE ARE NO DISEASES," runs one of the most hallowed of medical maxims, "there are only sick people." This guide for the physician is one with which everyone who has ever been a patient can agree. No one likes to be treated simply as a collection of symptoms, or as the dull but unavoidable appendage to a heart, an ear or a streptococcus germ. Everyone wants—and should have—a doctor who is concerned with him as a human being, a personal physician who understands him and not merely the diseases he may suffer from.

In the 19th Century, when the age of scientific medicine was just beginning, the typical doctor was a personal physician in this sense. He treated patients of all ages, seeing them through all their afflictions. He delivered babies, set broken bones, dealt with mumps and heart disease, and performed such major surgery as the removal of an appendix. In addition, he was a friend and counselor, providing patients with what we would now call psychiatric help.

The old-fashioned doctor owed much of his success to his personal qualities. Physically, he was an impressive figure, often bearded and formally dressed in high hat and frock coat. His manner was authoritative, and his reputation as a man of learning added weight to his words. He was dedicated and energetic—ready to sacrifice himself for his patients as few doctors will today. The city doctor was available at virtually any hour, and the country doctor took it for granted that he would have to get up in the middle of the night and ride for miles in his buggy across bad roads, frequently in appalling weather, to sit for hours with a sick child or a woman in labor.

The confidence the physician radiated must have cheered his patients, and the authority he commanded produced many cures. This authority may even have made him more effective than his modern successor in treating patients whose real trouble was anxiety or loneliness. With elaborate care, the doctor would bring out a pill and announce that he had prepared it himself especially for the patient. The pill may have been totally innocuous, but delivered with ceremony and the full force of the doctor's authority, it often produced a cure.

When he had to diagnose or treat organic disease, however, the powers of the 19th Century physician were pitifully limited. Skillful as he might have been, his diagnostic methods were primitive and so were his medications. Moreover, his approach to treatment was still empirical rather than scientific. He ordered treatments not because he knew how they worked but because other physicians had used them successfully in similar circumstances.

The scientific advances of the 19th Century offered the promise of considerable improvement. Pathologists had shown how to recognize diseases by their effects on body structures. Pharmacologists had created new drugs. Bacteriologists had discovered the causes of many illnesses and suggested methods of prevention. But the work had been done in the laboratory or at the autopsy table, and the findings still had to be applied in day-to-day practice at the patient's bedside.

Putting this knowledge into practice was more than the old-fashioned physician could manage. He lacked the training for the task. A new kind of doctor was needed—one who concerned himself with all aspects of physical well-being, as did the general practitioner, but who was better educated in the technical intricacies of his profession. This need was met around the turn of the century with the emergence of the physician who is now becoming the central figure of medicine: the internist.

The name "internist" is in a sense unfortunate; it is often confused with "intern." The intern is a young doctor in training, while the internist is a specialist in internal medicine, who has completed at least three years of postgraduate training as a resident and has passed a stiff examination prepared by the American Board of Internal Medicine. This formal training sets him apart from general practitioners—many of whom have acquired equivalent skills and knowledge through experience and study but lack the recognition of certification from a board. The U.S. has more board-certified internists—17,107 in 1965—than general surgeons, ophthalmologists or practitioners of any other medical specialty.

The internist is a specialist, but paradoxically he may also be a generalist. As a specialist he limits his practice to adults, and does not attend children or deliver babies (as most general practitioners do). He may specialize narrowly, treating only diseases of particular parts of the body, such as the heart or lungs. But usually he diagnoses all bodily ailments and sees to their treatment, either by himself or aided by another specialist. He is not satisfied simply to treat, say, high blood pressure or kidney disease as isolated disorders; instead he considers these conditions in relation to his patient's entire body. It is this all-inclusive approach that makes him a personal physician.

A model for internists

The American internist's prototype—the man who most clearly defined his role and best exemplified his methods—was a Canadian by birth. Sir William Osler, who played such an important part in the establishment of the Johns Hopkins medical school, was 35 years old when he left Montreal in 1884 to teach clinical medicine at the University of Pennsylvania. There Osler quickly became an object of admiration and love for everyone he dealt with—students, colleagues and patients alike. He had all the hallmarks of the great physician—compassion, intelligence, acute perceptiveness and dedication to science. These qualities are exemplified in many illuminating incidents related by his biographer and friend, the great neurosurgeon Harvey Cushing.

Osler's tremendous compassion is illustrated by the story Cushing tells of an occasion when Osler, still practicing in Montreal, struck up a casual acquaintanceship with a young Englishman who was visiting the city on business. The two men dined together several times. One evening, Osler noticed that his companion appeared ill and insisted that he go to bed immediately at Osler's club. It soon became clear that the young man had smallpox. During the three days in which the disease

THE BELOVED PHYSICIAN of the 19th Century, whose forceful personality often counted more than his scientific knowledge in treating illness, is epitomized in this 1870 magazine illustration. Its caption reads: "The good old doctor, indeed, is the oracle of the moment, and as he sits, watch in hand, counting the pulse of the household pet, the mother and nurse tremblingly await the next words that will fall from his lips. . . . 'A little bit under the weather.'"

ran its fatal course, Osler spent long hours with this man whom he hardly knew—even reading a prayer for him when he died—and later he wrote a warm letter to his father in England.

Osler never lost this old-fashioned, human touch. But to it he added a most modern application of the facts and methods of science. He was quick to follow up new discoveries. Just one month after *Ross's Journal*, a contemporary medical publication, announced the identification of the bacterium that causes tuberculosis, the same publication reported Osler's isolation of the guilty germ in a victim of the disease.

Once the malaria parasite was isolated, Osler carried out microscopic studies of blood from 70 malaria patients so that he could learn to recognize the organism himself. Then he ordered that future diagnoses of malaria be established by his staff only after the parasite had been identified in the patient's blood.

But while Osler was always receptive to new ideas, he never accepted them uncritically. In 1879, when Professor Moritz Benedikt of Vienna proclaimed that the brains of criminals are structurally different from those of law-abiding citizens, Osler quickly disproved the fanciful theory by examining the brains of two recently executed murderers.

Direct examination on the autopsy table was Osler's favorite technique for testing and training. He performed close to 1,000 autopsies, every one with scrupulous care. "He would hunt for hours," Cushing writes, "to find the small artery concerned in pulmonary hemorrhage or the still smaller one whose rupture produced [paralysis]." One of the greatest values of autopsies, Osler believed, was their brutal revelation of physicians' mistakes—his own included. "Once in the ward class," a student told Cushing, "there was a . . . man whom [Osler] demonstrated as showing all the classical symptoms of croupous pneumonia. The man came to autopsy later. He had no pneumonia but a chest full of fluid. Dr. Osler . . . sent especially for all those in his ward classes, showed them what a mistake he had made, how it might have been avoided, and how careful they should be not to repeat it."

A medical detective

Combining his talents for observation and deduction, Osler developed legendary prowess in diagnosis. He could, like a detective, draw correct conclusions from only one or two clues. Once he entered a ward where a young man was lying—paralyzed, and also widely and visibly tattooed. Quickly taking in these facts, Osler exclaimed: "Hello, where did you get this luetic encephalitis?"

The patient's condition had been an enigma to the house physician, and he was astounded by Osler's rapid diagnosis of the disease now known as syphilis. "Why" he asked, "do you call it that?" Osler's explanation, paraphrased, ran as follows:

The tattoos indicated that the young man was a sailor. Syphilis was at that time extremely common among sailors. In those days young people very rarely suffered from paralysis, except as a consequence of syphilis. Therefore Osler made a shrewd and—as it developed—correct guess.

Osler was also aware that discoveries in bacteriology and pathology showed how to keep people well, and his emphasis on preventive medicine may have been his greatest contribution to human welfare. He preached prevention to his students. He coaxed and bullied public officials to adopt and enforce health regulations. And the measures he fostered—immunization of children, isolation of infectious patients, rigid control of water and food supplies, sanitary disposal of wastes—have done more to prolong life and sustain well-being than any improvements in the diagnosis and treatment of disease.

It is virtually impossible to overestimate Osler's impact on his profession. His students revered him and copied his walk, his gestures—even his speech mannerisms. Most important, they copied his methods, passing them on to new generations of medical students, to establish the model that internists still follow today.

The modern internist, faithful to that model, sees himself as the commanding general in a battle against disease. He is first of all a strategist who perceives what must be accomplished, decides on a plan of action and supervises its execution. Since the success of his strategy depends on his diagnosis, quick, accurate recognition of illness is the most important part of his work. Once he knows what is wrong with a patient, deciding on treatment is relatively routine.

The four stages of diagnosis

Diagnosis itself is both a science and an art, requiring sensitive observation as well as medical knowledge. The diagnostic examination proceeds through four stages: the physician's first observation of the patient; the patient's recital of his symptoms and of his own and his family's medical history; the physical examination; and the laboratory tests. At each stage, the internist calls on everything he has learned about people and illness to give him clues.

If he knows his patient intimately, a single sign may be enough. One internist tells of a colleague who was hit by a truck, taken to the hospital and discharged soon thereafter as well. "But when I spoke to him," the internist reported, "I noticed that his personality had changed. Before, he was sweet-tempered and precise in his speech. Now he was irritable, critical and repetitious—symptoms that might indicate a blood clot on the brain. Which was what I suspected—correctly, it developed. Fortunately, a surgeon was able to remove the clot and my friend returned to his familiar and incisive self."

Such simple observations, even of patients the internist has never seen before, are often revealing. If the patient continually moistens his lips with his tongue, he may be nervous, suggesting troublesome anxieties —but if his skin is dry as well, he may have diabetes. While the doctor observes, he also asks his patient for information. The patient's statements may in some instances be enough to tell the internist what is wrong. A complaint of a peculiar disturbance of vision followed by in-

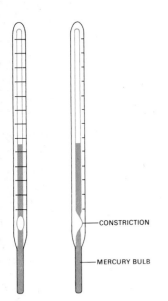

CONSTRICTION

MERCURY BULB

THE CLINICAL THERMOMETER, used by physicians to determine body temperature, differs from household thermometers in its ability to "freeze" its highest reading. A pinch in the lower bore of the hollow tube allows the mercury in the bulb to expand and rise to register internal body heat, but prevents it from falling until the thermometer is vigorously shaken. This permits the physician to obtain a reading that remains accurate to one tenth of a degree, unaffected by the cooler temperature of the atmosphere.

tense pain in one side of the head points to the agonizing headache called migraine. A middle-aged patient's report of swollen feet and shortness of breath suggests heart disease.

By the time the physician has recorded complaints and previous illnesses, he may have heard and seen enough to be quite sure of his diagnosis. But even so, he will insist on a close physical examination, using his own senses aided by instruments to learn what is going on inside the patient's body. With an ophthalmoscope he focuses light inside the eyeball so that he can see the red net of small blood vessels in the back—the only ones in the entire body that are easily visible. If they look thickened, the patient could have arteriosclerosis—hardening of the arteries.

Before the examination is over, most parts of the patient's body will have been peered at, probed into or pounded on. By pressing gently over internal structures—the lymph nodes, the liver, the bladder, the spleen— the internist feels for tumors. By tapping his finger over body organs, he drums sounds that signal disease; for example, a dull bump from the lungs instead of the normal loud, long and deep note could indicate tuberculosis or pneumonia.

When the internist has finished his examination, he sends the patient on for laboratory tests. If he suspects heart disease, he will order an electrocardiogram. This visual record of the heart's electrical signals may show damage to heart muscle. If the patient has mysterious headaches, X-rays may be taken of the head to show if a tumor is present. Such laboratory tests are often the final proof of disease when they confirm a pattern of symptoms. But taken alone they can be misleading. Syphilis is commonly detected through the Wassermann blood test. But a positive Wassermann test does not necessarily prove the presence of syphilis. It may indicate hepatitis or mononucleosis infections; or it may indicate a chronic disease of skin and connective tissue called lupus erythematosus.

Adding up the evidence

With this grab bag of information before him—his own observations, the patient's complaints, a medical history, laboratory findings—the internist must now select the significant items that add up to a disease. He then makes what is called a differential diagnosis, listing all the possibilities and the arguments for and against each, and finally eliminating the possibilities one by one, until he singles out the trouble.

To treat it, the internist may call on another specialist—a surgeon, a cardiologist or a urologist. With his colleague, he will integrate all information on the patient, and together they will plan treatment. But the internist, in his role as general in command of the campaign, should always retain control of the case. If a patient suffers from cancer of the stomach, a consulting surgeon might advise removal of the stomach. The surgeon may be convinced that the operation has a good chance of success and offers the only hope of saving the patient. The internist, basing his judgment on his greater familiarity with the patient, may be equally convinced that if the operation is performed, the patient will die. Such a conflict of views leaves the internist with a very difficult decision to make. But because he is the patient's personal physician, it is his opinion that will prevail.

The internist's ability to make the final decision on treatment rests on his intimate knowledge of his patient. During diagnosis, the internist who is serving as a personal physician usually asks whether members of the patient's family have suffered mental illness. But he also looks for less direct signs of psychological trouble—unusual physical tension, clammy hands or fidgeting. He knows that one third to one half of his patients suffer from illnesses inextricably intertwined with emotional disturbances. Such chronic diseases as stomach ulcers and high blood pressure are often associated with prolonged and continuing emotional stress. Many patients describe complaints, ranging in severity from fatigue, insomnia and headaches to paralysis, for which no organic basis can be found. To deal with such problems, the internist needs a sophisticated understanding of the human mind. The importance that doctors attach to this knowledge is evidenced in the fact that of all the part-time courses in medical specialties offered to practicing physicians in the mid-1960s, the greatest number—250—were in psychiatry.

Even a working knowledge of psychology may not be enough, however, to guide the internist to specific treatment. The complexity of his task is illustrated by the case of the middle-aged housewife who complained of insomnia. Physical examination uncovered no basis for the symptoms. When the doctor encouraged her to talk about her home life, she launched into a bitter diatribe. Her husband, she reported, was selfish and inconsiderate; he retired into his newspaper every evening and never took her out. His income was large, but he would not permit her to employ a maid and she had to do all the housework herself. Moreover, her adolescent daughter was sloppy and refused to keep her room clean.

To treat such a problem the internist needs further information—obtainable only from direct observation of the patient and her family in their home—before he can be certain of providing constructive advice. The lack of this knowledge often handicaps the internist; unlike the general practitioner, he seldom cares for all members of the family, he is unlikely to have treated his patient from youth onward, and he rarely visits the patient's home.

A study of family health

The extent to which home environment affects physical and emotional health was dramatically illustrated by an eight-year investigation of more than 200 families, all members of the same group medical plan, in New York City between 1950 and 1958. Half the families served as a control group, receiving no special care. The others were studied in detail by a health team directed by an internist and including a social worker, a public health nurse, a pediatrician and a psychiatrist. Under the internist's guidance, the nurse and the social worker visited the families' homes periodically and reported their observations to the health team.

Many shocking conditions were uncovered and described in the book-length report, *Family Medical Care*, written by Dr. George M. Silver, who directed the research. Although few of the families were poor, some were improperly fed. Even when the food was nutritious, emotional difficulties often led to loss of appetite or overweight. Homes were overcrowded, and space was not used to the best advantage. In several cases, there was obvious hatred between husband and wife. One family conference report runs as follows:

"Right from the beginning of the conference, some tension between Mr. and Mrs. X was apparent. At the same time they were calling each other "dear" in what seemed to be a rather guarded uncomfortable way. [Mr. X] hesitated somewhat when Dr. A asked him when [he suffered pains], but then said they occur mainly after he drinks beer. Mrs. X got obvious satisfaction out of his having to say this . . . There was discussion of her being overweight, and here Mr. X was the one who seemed glad that this was brought up. . . .

"There was a good deal of conversation concerning Mrs. X's being very tense, and while she agreed that she had a problem, she felt that it would get better as the children would get older and as her husband too would 'grow up.' After having said this, she turned to him and asked him 'Shall we talk?' and she then made him talk about his need to drink. They began to blame each other. . . ."

Patients as people

Such intimate knowledge of the test families' lives was put to practical medical use. During the home visits, the nurses and social workers suggested solutions to emotional problems. The nurses were able to guide some families toward better eating patterns or a more healthful arrangement of living quarters. Equally important, the information on home conditions enabled the health-team physicians to treat their patients much more effectively than would otherwise have been possible. Indeed, the control families, who did not receive this special care, showed less improvement in their physical health over the eight years of the study than did the participating families.

The results of the New York study reveal a serious and basic flaw in modern medical practice. The internist, for all his concern for his patients, seldom attends them in their homes. He has facilities for diagnosis and treatment in his office that he could not possibly take with him on a house call. Yet the patient's complaint is frequently—perhaps usually—connected with his home and his family life; without firsthand knowledge of the patient's home situation, the modern physician's effectiveness is necessarily limited. Medical research has accomplished marvels, and today's internist is brilliantly equipped to diagnose and treat organic disorders. Yet all his knowledge and skill may fail him unless, like the family physician of old, he makes a special effort to understand his patients as people.

Tools of
the Trade

Like a mechanic or a carpenter, the physician must be skilled in the use of a variety of tools; among other things, they are indispensable in diagnosis. However, while some of these tools, such as the thermometer and the reflex hammer, have counterparts in the mechanic's gauges and the carpenter's T-square, the diagnostician's purpose is different from that of the craftsman. For the diagnosing physician uses his tools not to repair anything or to take anything apart, but to aid him in the search for hidden signs of trouble.

Each of the physician's diagnostic tools extends one of his senses or gives him a sense he lacks. The ophthalmoscope, for instance, enhances his sense of vision, enabling him to peer into the black recesses of the eye. A stethoscope sharpens his sense of hearing, a thermometer his sense of temperature. On the other hand, the electrocardiograph and X-ray machine put to use electrical signals and electromagnetic waves that no human organ can detect unaided. Today, diagnostic tools are becoming ever more sophisticated. Electronic machines are coming into use that can measure and record many of a patient's vital functions simultaneously, making possible the collection of needed information in a few seconds.

A DOCTOR'S TOOL KIT
Ready to be taken out on a house call, this physician's bag contains tools needed for a preliminary examination. A stethoscope lies coiled around an otoscope—a device used for inspecting the ear. A tuning fork, used to test for nerve damage, rests on a bunch of tongue depressors. Projecting from the bag at left is a rubber hammer, used to test muscular reflexes.

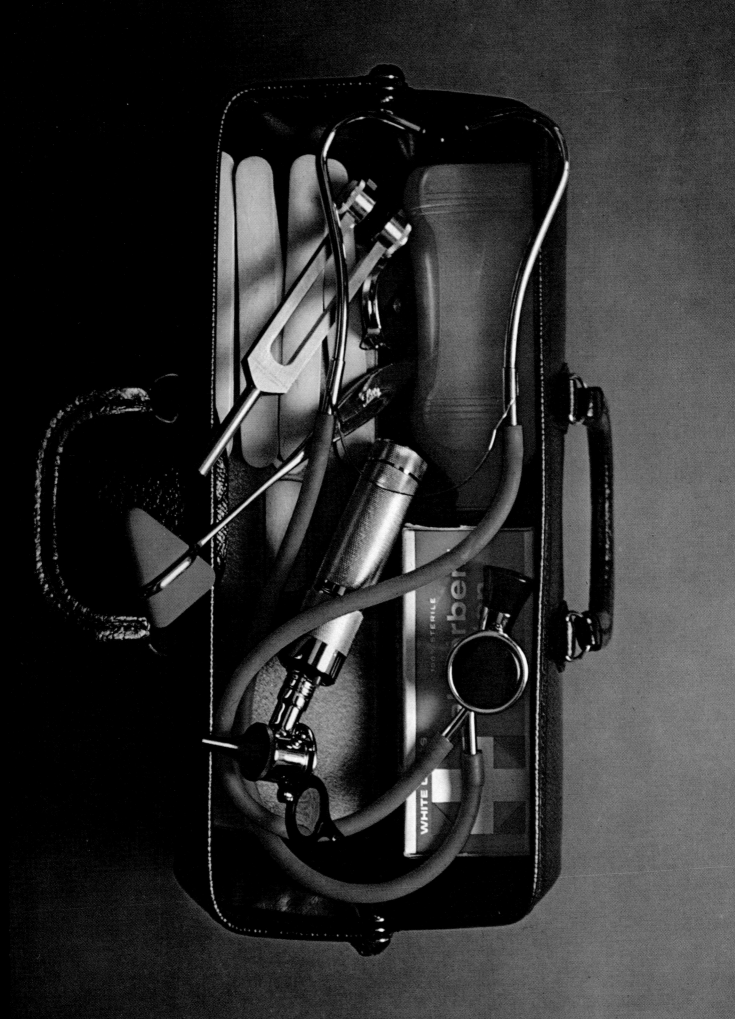

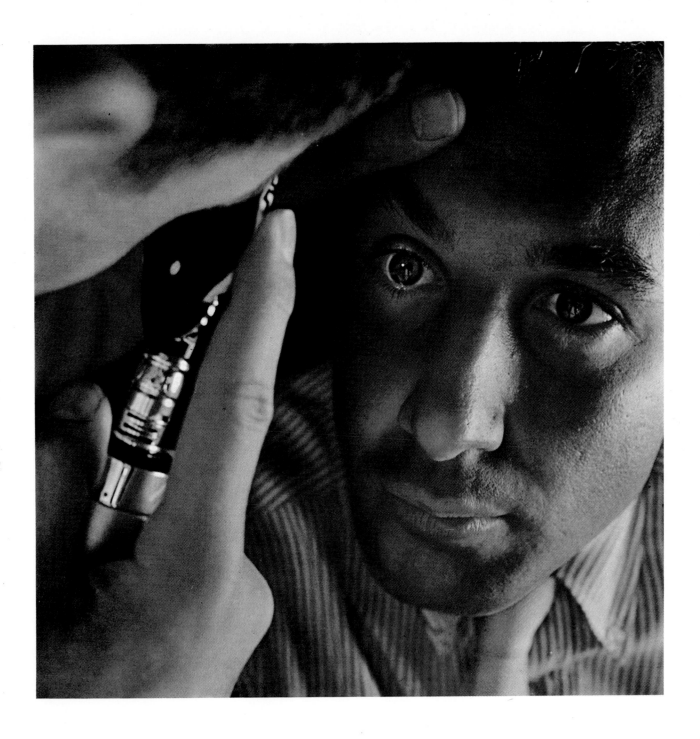

Lighting the Inside of the Eye

Although the eye is a small and fairly sturdy organ, rarely stricken by fatal diseases, it is one of the first parts of the body to be examined closely by the physician. He finds the eye especially useful in diagnosis because it offers the best interior view of the body in operation. Unlike the mouth or outer ear, which are simply openings lined with skinlike tissue, the eye is a completely enclosed, functioning organ. And it alone has a "window"—the pupil, sealed off by the transparent cornea—through which light enters and stimulates vision. Taking advantage of this window, the physician uses an instrument called the ophthalmoscope *(above)* to illuminate and observe nerves and blood vessels at work inside the body.

The general practitioner or internist usually examines the eye for injuries and infections, and for signs of disease in the lens, such as cataracts.

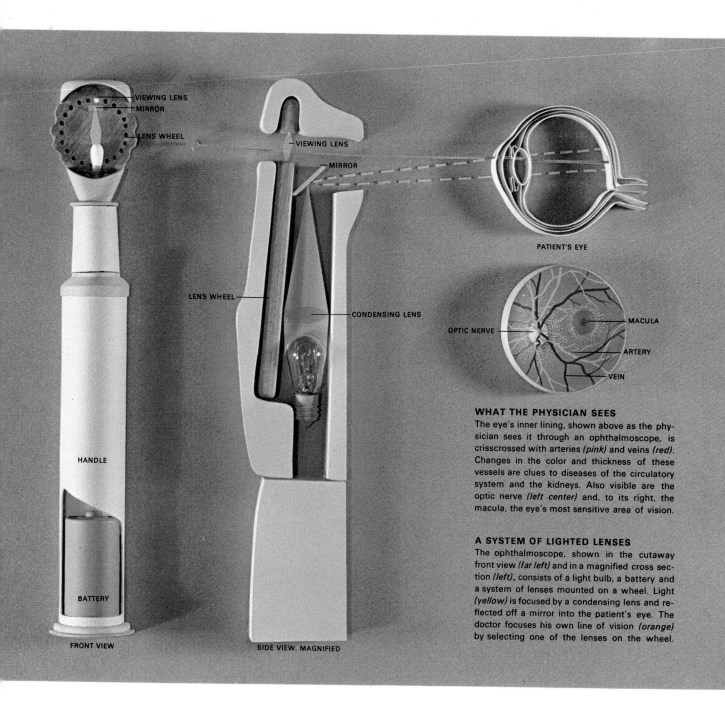

VIEWING LENS
MIRROR
LENS WHEEL

VIEWING LENS
MIRROR

LENS WHEEL
CONDENSING LENS

HANDLE

BATTERY

FRONT VIEW

SIDE VIEW, MAGNIFIED

PATIENT'S EYE

OPTIC NERVE
MACULA
ARTERY
VEIN

WHAT THE PHYSICIAN SEES

The eye's inner lining, shown above as the physician sees it through an ophthalmoscope, is crisscrossed with arteries *(pink)* and veins *(red)*. Changes in the color and thickness of these vessels are clues to diseases of the circulatory system and the kidneys. Also visible are the optic nerve *(left center)* and, to its right, the macula, the eye's most sensitive area of vision.

A SYSTEM OF LIGHTED LENSES

The ophthalmoscope, shown in the cutaway front view *(far left)* and in a magnified cross section *(left)*, consists of a light bulb, a battery and a system of lenses mounted on a wheel. Light *(yellow)* is focused by a condensing lens and reflected off a mirror into the patient's eye. The doctor focuses his own line of vision *(orange)* by selecting one of the lenses on the wheel.

But if he detects serious diseases of the eye itself, he usually refers the patient to a specialist. He himself is interested in something else: what the interior of the eye reveals about diseases of other organs and about the patient's general health.

By illuminating and observing the eye's inner lining with an ophthalmoscope the physician can, for example, study the end of the optic nerve, the only visible part of the nervous system. If this nerve is abnormally large and swollen, it may indicate a brain tumor. The eye is also the only part of the body where small blood vessels are readily visible, and changes in these vessels often give early signs of serious diseases. To cite one instance, clusters of swellings on the arteries are a typical sign of diabetes. Arteries that vary in thickness and veins that appear compressed where they join are often signs of hypertension.

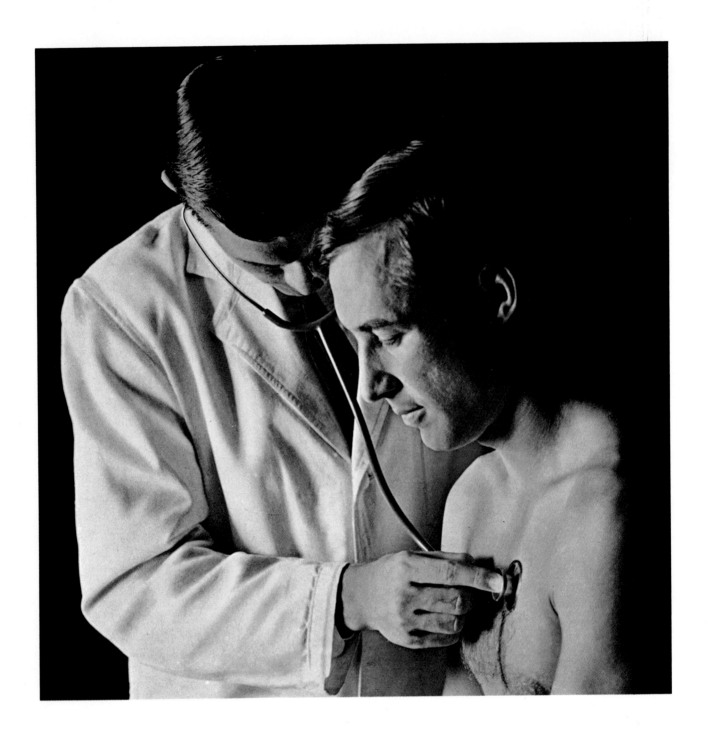

Listening to the Heart and Lungs

Just as the ophthalmoscope extends the physician's ability to see signs of disease, another tool, the stethoscope, improves his ability to hear such signs. He uses this aid most effectively in studying the heart and the lungs, because these organs make noises as they work, and thus reveal much about their condition. A physician could listen to these sounds if he simply pressed one ear directly against the chest—a method which occasionally still has to be employed in emergencies. But a stethoscope is generally used because it channels the sounds to both ears and blocks out extraneous noise.

To listen to the lungs, the physician applies the end of his stethoscope to different locations on the patient's chest and back, moving the instrument from point to point over a wide area covering both lungs. Normally, he hears a deep rushing sound, caused

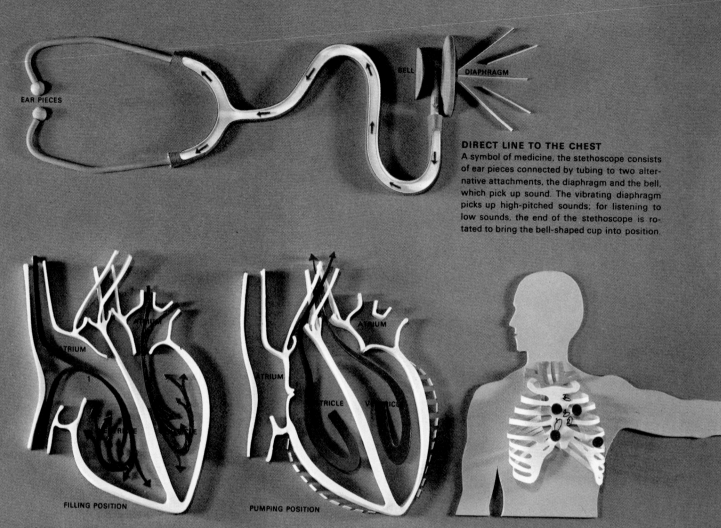

DIRECT LINE TO THE CHEST
A symbol of medicine, the stethoscope consists of ear pieces connected by tubing to two alternative attachments, the diaphragm and the bell, which pick up sound. The vibrating diaphragm picks up high-pitched sounds; for listening to low sounds, the end of the stethoscope is rotated to bring the bell-shaped cup into position.

EAR PIECES

BELL   DIAPHRAGM

ATRIUM

FILLING POSITION

ATRIUM

ATRIUM

VENTRICLE   VENTRICLE

PUMPING POSITION

A CYCLE OF HEART SOUNDS
In a single heartbeat, blood flowing in and out of the heart closes two pairs of valves to produce the distinctive "lub-dup" heart sound. In the filling position *(above)* blood from the body *(purple)* and the lungs *(red)* runs from the veins and each atrium, or receiving chamber, through the open valves 1 and 2, into the two pumping chambers, or ventricles. When the ventricles contract *(above)*, they push blood out, opening valves 3 and 4, and closing valves 1 and 2 to make the first heart sound, the "lub." Then, as the ventricles once more relax to the filling position *(dotted lines)*, valves 3 and 4 snap shut again to make the "dup," the second sound.

LISTENING POSTS ON THE CHEST
The locations of the heart valves *(black ovals)* do not correspond exactly to the points on the chest where the physician hears them best *(red dots)*, because the tissues of the heart and chest deflect the sounds away from the valves. In this illustration, each valve and its corresponding listening point bear identical numbers.

by moving air. If the lungs are diseased, however, the sounds are quite different. Asthma or bronchitis, for example, cause a high-pitched wheeze each time the patient exhales.

The stethoscope is even more valuable in studying the heart. In many cardiac ailments, the sounds the doctor hears offer the only clues to the nature and extent of heart damage. Using his stethoscope, he can distinguish the sound made by each of the four heart valves, which close in pairs as the blood rushes in and out of the heart's four chambers. The sounds that accompany each beat of a normal heart can best be described as a sort of "lub-dup," one pair of valves making the "lub," the other the "dup." But if a disease such as rheumatic fever has injured any valve so that it does not open and close properly, blood passing through it makes the soft rushing sound called a murmur.

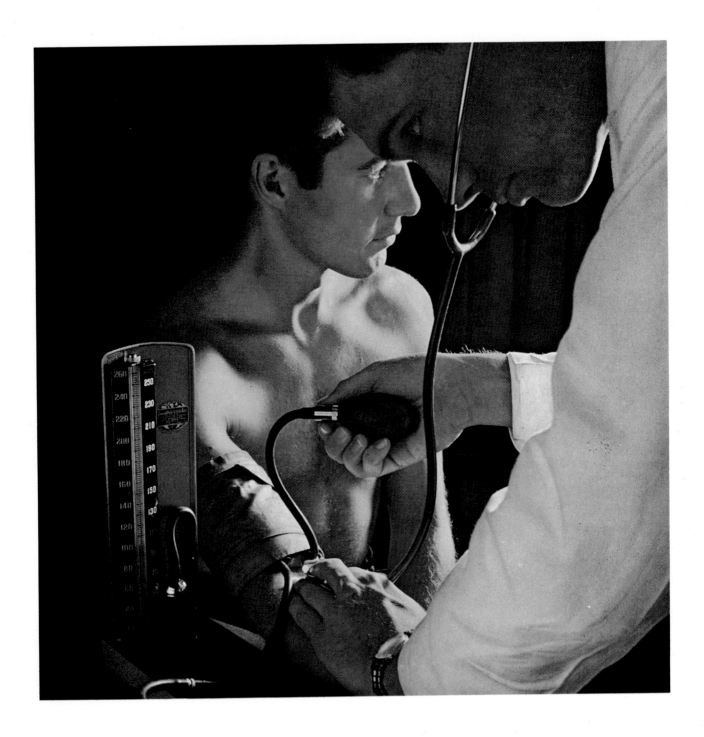

Measuring the Blood Pressure

One of the best clues to disease is the pressure that the blood exerts on the walls of the arteries. Blood loss can lower this pressure to nothing; some circulatory diseases can double it.

Blood pressure varies with every heart beat. It reaches a maximum when the heart contracts to force the blood into the arteries, a minimum when the heart relaxes. Both levels are important for diagnosis, and the physician records them both, using a stethoscope and a device called a sphygmomanometer.

The sphygmomanometer measures the blood pressure by comparing the pressure inside the brachial artery—the major artery of the arm—with air pressure generated in an inflatable cuff. The physician wraps the cuff around his patient's arm, covering the artery. He then pumps air into the cuff until its pressure exceeds the maximum blood pressure in the ar-

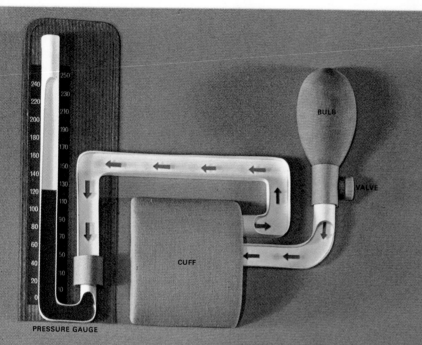

PRESSURE GAUGE

BULB

VALVE

CUFF

BULB, CUFF, VALVE AND GAUGE

Squeezing a sphygmomanometer's bulb forces air *(arrows)* through a tube into a cuff. The air then runs through a second tube, where its pressure raises a column of mercury. Air pressure is diminished with a valve until the physician determines, by the method below, that the cuff pressure matches the patient's blood pressure. He determines the pressure by noting the height, in millimeters, of the mercury column.

READING THE BLOOD PRESSURE

The illustration below shows how a physician relates the air pressure indicated by the mercury column to pressure of blood in an artery. Blood flows (1) until the artery is squeezed shut (2) by air that the physician pumps into the cuff. He then releases air. When blood flows intermittently (3), the mercury level indicates maximum blood pressure, and when blood flows freely (4), the mercury level shows the minimum pressure.

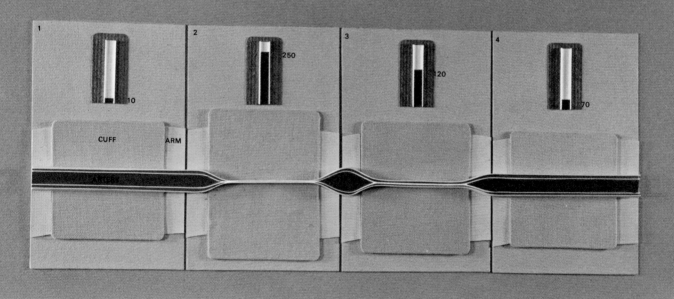

CUFF   ARM

ARTERY

tery and squeezes the artery shut, stopping the flow of blood. Next he puts a stethoscope over the artery and gradually lowers the cuff pressure by releasing air through a valve. When he hears a loud booming noise through the stethoscope, he knows that the blood is pulsating in spurts through the artery—and that the cuff pressure must be just below the maximum arterial pressure. At this point, the physician notes the cuff pressure, indicated by a mercury column, to determine maximum blood pressure. To measure minimum pressure, he continues to lower the cuff pressure until he no longer hears a noise. Blood is then flowing freely through the artery, and the registered cuff pressure indicates the minimum. An average blood pressure is 120/70, meaning 120 millimeters maximum and 70 minimum—equivalent to 2.3 and 1.3 pounds of pressure per square inch.

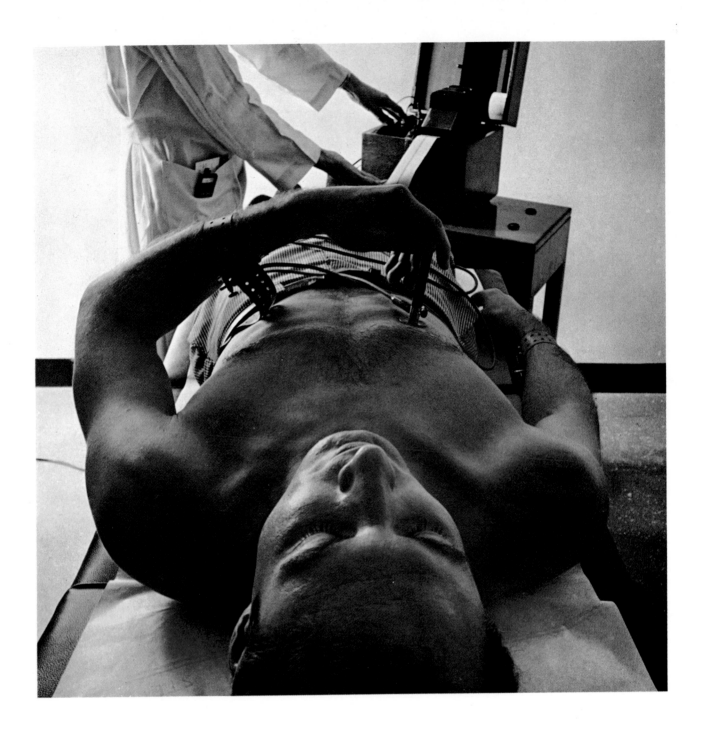

A Graph of
the Heart's Beat

For detailed examination of a patient's heart, the physician usually calls on a complex electronic tool, the electrocardiograph. Going far beyond the simple measurements of the blood-pressure cuff and stethoscope, the electrocardiograph can reveal not only damage to the heart but can even indicate the type of damage done.

It does this by recording the electrical pulses that originate in cells within the heart. These cells initiate an electric current at the beginning of each heartbeat, stimulating the heart muscle to contract. The current spreads through all the tissues of the body, and out to the surface of the skin. The voltages are about 3,000 times weaker than that in a flashlight —but they can be picked up by electrodes connected to the electrocardiograph and charted on a graph called an electrocardiogram (usually abbreviated to ECG or EKG).

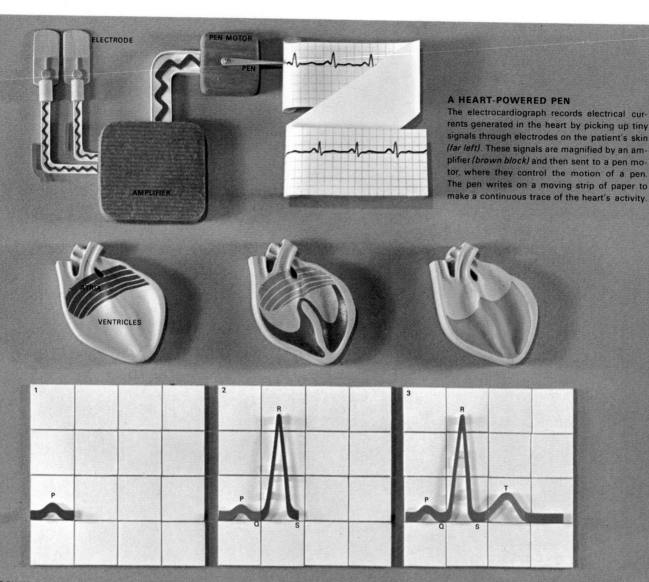

A HEART-POWERED PEN
The electrocardiograph records electrical currents generated in the heart by picking up tiny signals through electrodes on the patient's skin *(far left)*. These signals are magnified by an amplifier *(brown block)* and then sent to a pen motor, where they control the motion of a pen. The pen writes on a moving strip of paper to make a continuous trace of the heart's activity.

ELECTRODE

PEN MOTOR

PEN

AMPLIFIER

ATRIA

VENTRICLES

PROFILES OF A HEARTBEAT
The illustrations above show how the heart's electrical activity is reflected in electrocardiogram patterns. As a beat starts inside the heart (1), an electrical current *(red)* spreads through the cells of the collecting chambers, or atria, producing the small so-called "P-wave" shown on the graph beneath the heart. Next (2), this current passes through cells of the pumping chambers, or ventricles, making the big spike called QRS on the graph; at the same time the atria cells revert to their neutral state *(orange)* and prepare to trigger the next heartbeat. Finally the ventricles undergo the same electrical process (3) making the "T-wave." This wave often turns upside down after a heart attack.

Normally the EKG shows a three-peaked pattern which is characteristic of all healthy hearts. Diseased hearts, however, make distinct patterns of their own. Each of the three peaks is a reflection of the activity of a different part of the heart and the physician makes use of this fact to locate the area of the heart where damage has occurred. For example, the first peak reflects the activity of the heart's collecting chambers—disappearance of this peak indicates that these chambers are not working properly. If the third peak turns upside down, the physician knows that the pumping chambers have been damaged. To get even more specific information about the type of damage, the physician compares graphs made with electrodes at different parts of the body. From these he can often predict the patient's course of recovery and plan the best therapy.

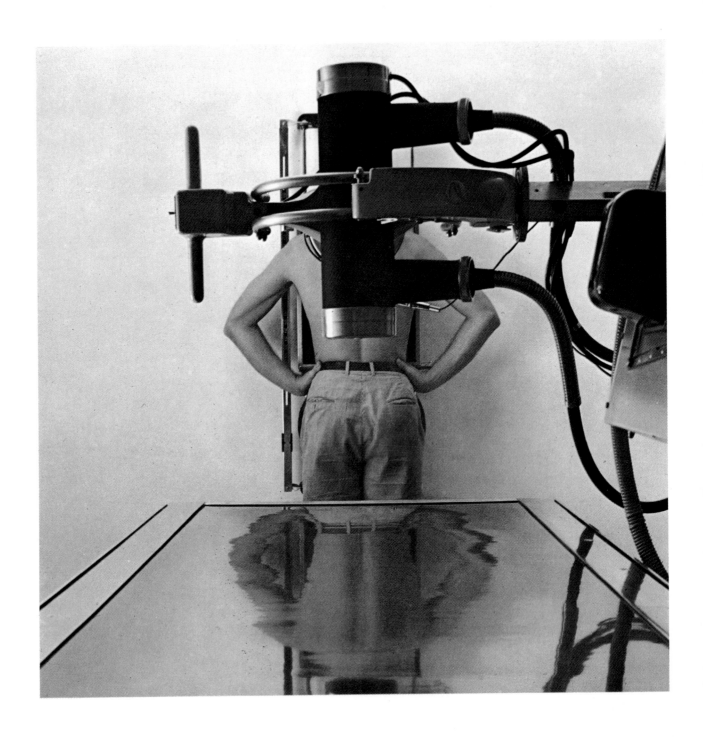

An Image of the Invisible

When Wilhelm Roentgen discovered the X-ray in 1895, he provided physicians with one of their most valuable diagnostic tools. With an X-ray machine, a physician can, in effect, see right through the skin into the body. A tumor in a lung, an oversized and straining heart, a broken bone—all are made visible. With an X-ray picture of internal organs the physician can often make a positive diagnosis even though every other method of investigation yields conflicting clues or none at all.

X-rays are high-frequency electromagnetic waves, very similar to light waves but generated in a powerful vacuum tube. Unlike light waves they pass through the human body; but like light waves they expose, or darken, ordinary photographic film. These two properties enable the physician to make a useful X-ray picture. He places the patient between an X-ray

96

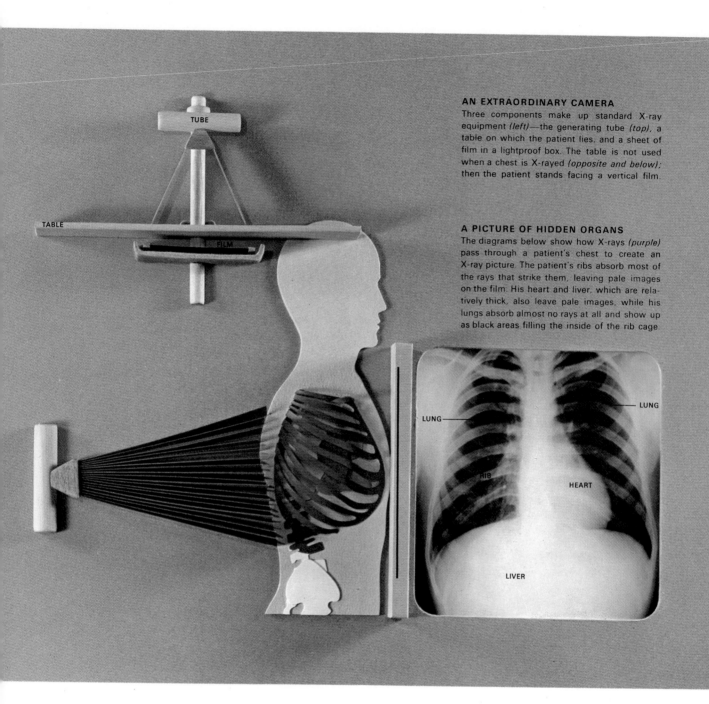

AN EXTRAORDINARY CAMERA

Three components make up standard X-ray equipment *(left)*—the generating tube *(top)*, a table on which the patient lies, and a sheet of film in a lightproof box. The table is not used when a chest is X-rayed *(opposite and below)*; then the patient stands facing a vertical film.

A PICTURE OF HIDDEN ORGANS

The diagrams below show how X-rays *(purple)* pass through a patient's chest to create an X-ray picture. The patient's ribs absorb most of the rays that strike them, leaving pale images on the film. His heart and liver, which are relatively thick, also leave pale images, while his lungs absorb almost no rays at all and show up as black areas filling the inside of the rib cage.

TUBE

TABLE

FILM

LUNG

LUNG

RIB

HEART

LIVER

generator and a sheet of film, and shoots rays through the patient's body onto the film for about one tenth of a second. Each of the patient's organs absorbs a certain quantity of the rays, allowing the rest to move through body tissue and expose the film. The quantity of rays any organ will absorb is determined primarily by its density and thickness. Dense tissues, like bone, and thick organs, like the liver, absorb almost all the rays; the few which get through make only pale images on the film. Light, air-filled lung tissue, on the other hand, lets almost all of the rays through to darken the film: thus, the lungs appear as a black image on the film.

Not all body organs are sufficiently distinctive in density and thickness to be distinguished in an X-ray. But the chest organs show up so well that a chest X-ray has become a routine part of every physical examination.

New Tools for Better Diagnosis

The huge machine at right, developed at the Texas Institute for Rehabilitation and Research, is one of the most elaborate tools of diagnosis. Actually, this device, called a physiograph, is not a single tool but a whole collection of instruments that simultaneously detect and record six different body functions. In less than a minute it gathers as much information as a physician might in an hour. Equally complex machines are being developed at several other medical centers. At New York's Mount Sinai Hospital, for example, physicians are experimenting with a computer that analyzes a patient's electrocardiogram and prints out a diagnosis for the physician to consider.

Both the Texas and New York machines are still experimental: other devices are already being used to perform routine examinations. In two California clinics, for example, machines perform 50 physical and chemical tests on 100 patients a day. A computer automatically prints out the results—and even singles out any abnormal readings to alert the patient's physician to a particular condition that might require attention.

A NEW COMBINATION OF TOOLS
Using a physiograph, a technician studies the continuous record of a patient's blood pressure, which has been picked up by a needle inserted into an artery in his arm. The machine also makes a standard electrocardiogram, measures respiration, registers the pulse at both neck and wrist, and records heart sounds through a microphone placed upon the patient's chest.

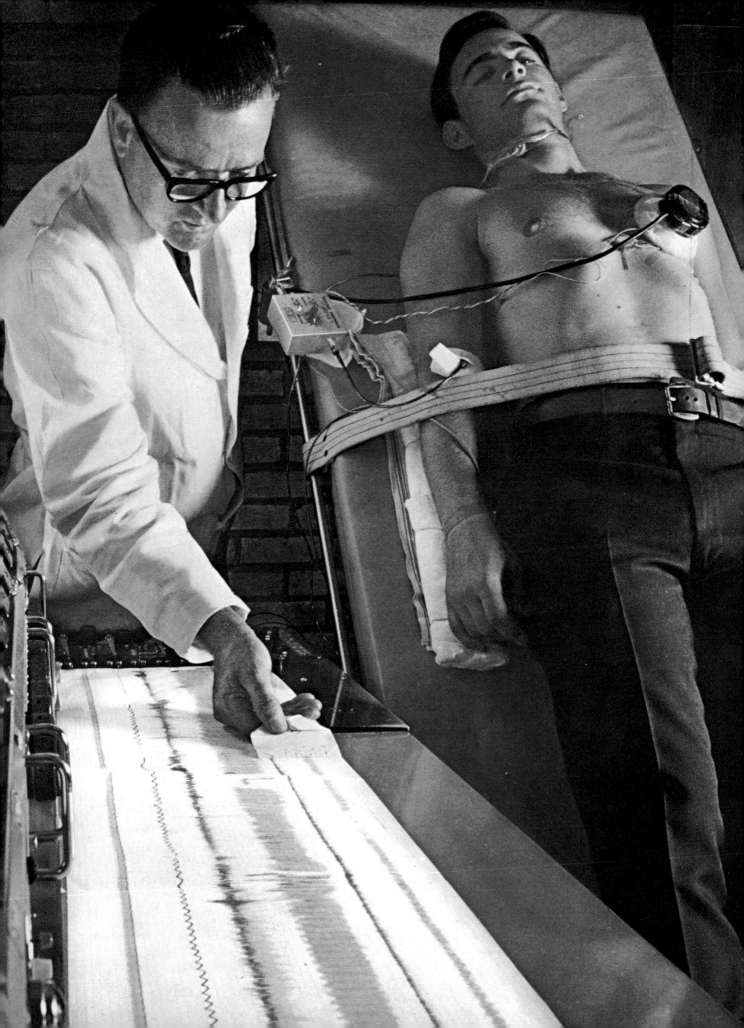

5

An Era
of Specialists

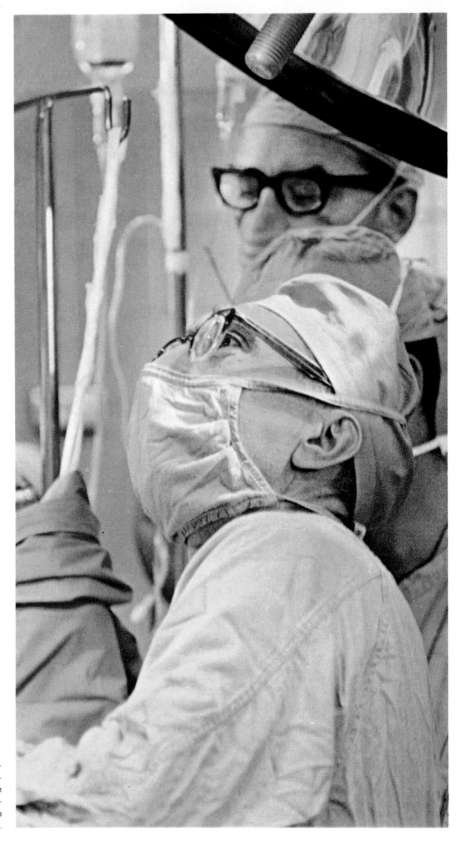

Dr. Michael DeBakey, a pioneer in open-heart surgery, watches a record of a patient's blood pressure as he conducts one of the first attempts to implant a man-made pump in a human chest. The pump relieves a failing heart until it can recover.

IN 1935 TWO THIRDS OF THE DOCTORS in the United States were general practitioners who treated all kinds of patients for all kinds of ailments. But since that time, American medicine has turned itself upside down. Today, more than 85 per cent of the young men who are just beginning their medical careers plan to be specialists—physicians who limit their practice to particular fields of medicine.

The specialist may be a surgeon, or an anesthesiologist, the expert whose delicate ministrations to the patient make modern surgery possible. He may be a dermatologist, diagnosing and treating disorders of the skin, or a radiologist, detecting tuberculosis and other ailments with X-rays and treating cancer with radioactive cobalt. He may be a psychiatrist, a pediatrician, an internist or a public health officer, guarding the health of an entire city. He may practice a specialty within a specialty, such as pediatric allergy, the treatment of children's sensitivity to dust or foods.

Whatever his specialty, it commands his full attention. He usually trains for two to five years after he has finished medical school and internship; he subscribes to journals that report the latest developments in his specialty and he belongs to medical societies that are devoted to his own specialty.

The modern specialist conducts his practice very differently from the general practitioner of other times. The old-fashioned G.P. made house calls, held his patient's hand, treated him by methods that seem simple today. The specialist practices in an office or a hospital clinic. He sees a patient for perhaps half an hour and does not have time to establish an easy friendship with him, as the G.P. did. Unless the specialist is a pediatrician or an internist, he rarely makes house calls—they take too much time, and he can give his patients better and more efficient treatment with the modern medical equipment and facilities available in his office or at the clinic. But the kind of medicine he practices is less personal and sometimes less appreciated than that of the old G.P.

The concept of specialization is not new. Surgeons are mentioned in medical literature at least as far back as 2500 B.C. *(page 32)*. Ancient Rome counted among its many physicians oculists, gynecologists and otologists. By the middle of the 18th Century in London, William Smellie was devoting himself entirely to the teaching and practice of obstetrics. And by the end of the 18th Century, physicians specializing in "nervous disorders" had anticipated the modern psychiatrist. But it was not until the 19th Century, with the acceleration of scientific discovery, that specialization really began to spread. And only within recent times have specialists come to dominate the practice of medicine, a revolutionary change that is a direct result of the explosion of knowledge.

Radiology came into existence only with the discovery of X-rays in 1895. Anesthesia was unknown before the 1840s; today three different gases are available for a difficult operation; the number of anesthetics that exist is at least 10 times that total. Diagnosis lacked even such a simple aid as the stethoscope until 1817; now the detection of disease depends on delicate electronic instruments and intricate chemical analyses—as many as six blood tests may be ordered to tell whether a patient with swollen lymph nodes and intermittent fever has mononucleosis or leukemia. In every field related to health and disease, so much useful information has accumulated in recent years that no man can hope to learn it all. Specialization is now essential for the physician who wishes to offer his patients the most advanced care.

Yet the expansion of knowledge is not the only force behind the rise of the specialist. Almost as important is the ever-increasing urbanization of modern society. As populations congregated in cities, the concentration of people provided physicians with so many prospective patients that a doctor could keep himself fully occupied even if he limited his practice to one field of medicine.

Along with the growth of urbanized, scientifically based medicine has come a larger role for the hospital. It offers the physician the facilities and technical help he needs if he is to dispense modern medical care; in return for this assistance, the hospital expects that its physicians will practice technically advanced medicine. Many big hospitals now insist that every patient be treated only by a recognized specialist, and this requirement has become one of the most powerful forces impelling physicians to achieve formal accreditation as specialists.

Qualifying the medical elite

The first such accrediting group in the U.S. was The American Board for Ophthalmic Examinations. Incorporated in 1917 by a group of outstanding eye doctors, its goal was the identification—for both the public and the medical profession—of those eye specialists who met high standards of training and competence. Today, to be certified by the American Board of Ophthalmology, as it is now called, a licensed physician must have served as a resident ophthalmologist in an approved hospital for three years and must have practiced for a year—after which he must take a seven-hour examination so stiff that one fifth of the candidates usually fail. Those who succeed are given diplomalike certificates—tickets of admission, in effect, to the upper strata of medicine.

The pattern established by the ophthalmologists has gradually been followed by other specialty groups. The American Board of Otolaryngology (for ear, nose and throat doctors) was founded in 1924, and the experts in gynecology and obstetrics established their board in 1930. By the 1960s, a total of 19 specialty boards and seven subspecialty boards had been organized. As purely private organizations, the boards have no legal authority. They cannot require that a physician pass one of their examinations before setting himself up as a specialist, and today there still are many competent specialists who are not board-certified. But the word of the boards carries great weight in the medical profession generally and in the hospitals particularly.

Specialists today offer medical services from the cradle (pediatrics) to the grave (geriatrics), and from the resculpturing of ladies' noses (plastic

SPECIALTY	DATE OF INCORPORATION OF SPECIALTY BOARD	NUMBER OF SPECIALISTS CERTIFIED IN 1965	TOTAL NUMBER OF SPECIALISTS CERTIFIED
OPHTHALMOLOGY	1917	268	6,268
OTOLARYNGOLOGY	1924	81	6,042
OBSTETRICS AND GYNECOLOGY	1930	416	8,284
DERMATOLOGY	1932	110	2,581
PEDIATRICS	1933	637	10,599
PSYCHIATRY AND NEUROLOGY	1934	311	8,682
RADIOLOGY	1934	398	8,569
ORTHOPEDIC SURGERY	1934	312	4,459
COLON AND RECTAL SURGERY	1934	12	362
UROLOGY	1935	138	3,279
PATHOLOGY	1936	413	6,039
INTERNAL MEDICINE	1936	775	17,107
ANESTHESIOLOGY	1937	290	3,716
PLASTIC SURGERY	1937	63	728
SURGERY	1937	735	13,690
NEUROLOGICAL SURGERY	1940	69	1,129
PHYSICAL AND MEDICAL REHABILITATION	1947	45	558
THORACIC SURGERY	1948	133	1,495
PREVENTIVE MEDICINE	1948	62	2,412

SPECIALIST CATEGORIES, into which most of today's physicians fall, now include the 19 listed above. They are largely determined and regulated by organizations, called boards, set up by outstanding specialists. Each board issues highly prized certificates to physicians who can pass stiff qualifying examinations. The certification figures indicate the rapid growth of some of the newer specialties such as thoracic (chest) surgery, in comparison to older specialties like otolaryngology, which deals with ailments of the ear, nose and throat.

surgery) to the training of amputees (physical medicine and rehabilitation). In this varied group of healers, two specialists stand out because they mark the ends of the medical spectrum. At one extreme is the surgeon, who takes drastic action to remedy the ailments or injuries that often threaten the survival of individual patients. At the other end is the public health physician. He is less concerned with individual patients than with entire populations. And his goal is not cure but prevention; he attempts to stop disease before it requires the ministrations of the surgeon or other physicians. Because their functions are so different, these two specialists merit closer examination.

Medicine's most romantic figure

The modern surgeon is the most glamorous and intriguing of all practitioners. Dramatically garbed in mask and gown, making life-or-death decisions under pressure, he embodies all that is romantic about the medical profession. He may be a general surgeon; in that case he usually concentrates on abdominal surgery—for ulcers, cancer of the stomach or intestines, hernias, appendicitis, gallstones—but may also operate for such conditions as varicose veins, breast cancers or goiters. Or he may be more highly specialized: he may limit his practice to very specific areas of the body, engaging solely in colonic and rectal surgery, or neurological (brain and nerves) surgery, or thoracic (chest) surgery. His specialty may be still more rarefied: some thoracic surgeons, for example, operate only on the esophagus or the lungs.

Today's surgeons work on the frontiers of medicine. They have developed new techniques for transplanting human organs from one body to another and for implanting artificial body parts in place of diseased or injured ones. Such procedures require a knowledge, skill and daring undreamed of a generation ago. Kidney transplants, first successfully attempted in 1954, are performed in many hospitals today. Eye banks supply new corneas for sightless eyes. And attempts are being made to transplant the human liver from one body to another.

The new techniques involve a broad variety of synthetic body parts as well as human organs. Dacron arteries, ceramic hip joints, plastic esophagi, and artificial heart valves have been developed. A synthetic shoulder—made of Vitallium, an alloy of cobalt, chromium and molybdenum—can be surgically attached to the top of the humerus, or upper-arm bone. And in the most daring surgical adventure of all, Dr. Michael DeBakey of Baylor University and surgeons in other medical centers have been developing artificial hearts that may some day replace the body's most vital organ.

To perform such exotic operations, and even to cope with the day-to-day problems of his exacting profession, the surgeon must possess special qualities that set him apart from other physicians. Basic, of course, is detailed knowledge of human anatomy. Equally important is a capacity for quick decision. Any operation is, in part at least, an exploration of the unknown, and the surgeon must respond instantaneously

—and correctly—to emergencies. During the repair of a weakened brain artery, for example, another blood vessel may hemorrhage and squeeze the patient's brain outward through the skull opening. The bleeding is usually invisible—yet the neurosurgeon must locate the source and stop the bleeding before its pressure damages the brain.

In addition to clear-headed authority and knowledge, the surgeon must also possess one skill that is usually expected only of craftsmen and artists: great manual dexterity. Many surgeons lavish as much attention on their hands as a concert pianist does, and for the same reason. They work with their fingers, precisely guiding a scalpel, feeling for one slippery body organ among many similar ones, sensing disease or injury from vague tactile clues, suturing with stitches that may be almost too small to be seen.

Stitching a paper edge

As an example of the delicacy of the surgeon's work and the dedication with which he approaches it, consider the case of Dr. Alexis Carrel, a Nobel Prize-winning surgeon. After he had developed the technique of joining together the smallest veins and arteries, in the early years of this century, he wrote: "We have availed ourselves of Kirby number 13 or number 14 needles and of linen threads, used in the manufacture of Valenciennes lace. . . . These solid, round, very sharp needles, finer than any used up to the present time, allow penetration of the venous or arterial walls without fear of oozing. . . . The only drawback is the smallness of the eye which makes it difficult to thread." To learn to manipulate such slim needles and gossamer thread, Carrel practiced sewing on paper, day after day—until finally he could sew the edge of a single sheet with stitches that did not show on either side of the paper.

Such finely honed techniques are only occasionally necessary, but the combination of skill, knowledge and judgment is demanded of every surgeon. How these elements fit together in his work can be seen by following, through one typical day, the activities of a general surgeon, the specialist who performs the bulk of the operations in a modern hospital —the gallbladder removals, hernia repairs and appendectomies.

The general surgeon's day begins early, since operations are usually scheduled for the morning, when the surgical team is fresh and the patient is rested. Our surgeon arrives at the hospital at 7 a.m. to check on recuperating patients and on the two persons who are to undergo surgery this morning—an 11-year-old boy with appendicitis and a 45-year-old woman with gallstones.

The woman's illness is one of the most common ailments treated by surgery. Following months of indigestion, especially after eating fatty foods, she finally had an excruciatingly painful attack. The family internist immediately suspected the gallbladder and ordered her to the hospital, where X-rays confirmed his diagnosis, showing several stones the size of large peas inside her gallbladder. These stones, formed from liver bile, had blocked the flow of this essential digestive fluid, which

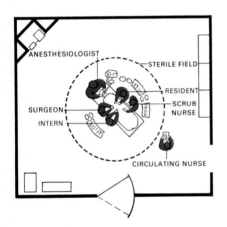

A TYPICAL OPERATION, diagramed from overhead, is performed by a team of five: the surgeon, assisted by an intern, a resident surgeon-in-training, a scrub nurse and an anesthesiologist who controls the flow of oxygen and anesthetic to the unconscious patient. All members of the operating team remain within a 10-foot circle (indicated by dashes), called the sterile field, inside which are permitted only those gowns, instruments and apparatus that have been sterilized. A circulating nurse, outside the sterile field, delivers supplies and handles emergencies.

passes from the gallbladder into the small intestine through the cystic duct and the common bile duct. Recurring attacks of increasing severity could be expected, as enlarging stones repeatedly tried to pass through the cystic duct. If her gallbladder was removed, the woman would have to follow a diet low in fatty foods for about a year, but gradually the bile ducts would take over the gallbladder's function, and she would be then able to lead a normal, healthy life. Weighing these factors, the surgeon and the internist together decided that an operation to remove the gallbladder was indicated.

This operation is the day's first case, scheduled for 8 o'clock. About 7:45, the surgeon, dressed in his white scrub suit, mask and cap, enters the operating room and stops briefly to chat with the patient, who has been given sedatives but is awake. Then he goes off to wash his hands, after which the scrub nurse fits him with a pair of thin-rubber surgical gloves and ties on his pale-green surgical gown. By now the anesthesiologist has injected the patient with thiopental sodium, a drug that quickly but gently brings sleep. Then, to induce the deeper level of unconsciousness and relaxation essential for the operation, he inserts into her windpipe a tube that supplies a mixture of ether and oxygen.

The sleeping patient is prepared for the incision by the nurse, who scrubs the abdomen and chest with soap and water and paints them with an antiseptic solution. Then she drapes the patient with towels and sheets so that only sterilized skin is exposed for the incision.

The moment of surgical truth

Now the surgeon is ready to do his part. Using a scalpel, an instrument with a blade an inch and a half long, the surgeon cuts open the patient's abdomen and inspects it to confirm that the gallbladder is at fault and to see if any other organs are diseased. The intern holds open the incision and gently pulls the liver out of the way with shoehorn-like instruments called retractors, and the resident presses aside the colon and the small intestine with his hand so that the surgeon can get at the gallbladder.

All through the operation, the surgeon works precisely and efficiently, extending his hand to the nurse for instruments that he needs—clamps, sponges, scissors, forceps or sutures. If he is competent, there is little danger that he will cut too far or in the wrong place. "It can happen, certainly," an experienced surgeon says. "If you are cutting the cystic duct, which leads from the gallbladder into the common bile duct, and you go half an inch too far, you've damaged the bile duct . . . jaundice will occur, and another operation to repair the damage must be performed. I suppose it could happen if the area is obscured with blood and you go blindly clamping away. But you should get the area cleaned up first, so you can see what you are doing, and then there is no reason to make that mistake."

The surgeon locates the cystic and common bile ducts and places two clamps side by side on the cystic duct. Next, after cutting and tying off

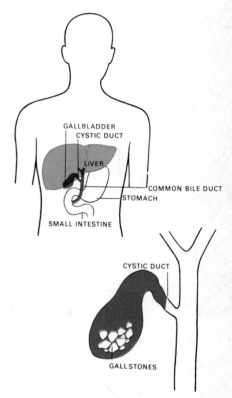

REMOVAL OF THE GALLBLADDER is often required to eliminate painful attacks caused by stones inside the organ. A nonessential part of the digestive system, the gallbladder *(color)* is located under the liver. Bile, a fat-digesting secretion from the liver, is transmitted to the gallbladder, which passes it through the cystic duct and common bile duct to the small intestine. Bile substances and fat chemicals often harden into stones *(detail drawing)*. If the stones irritate the gallbladder or block the cystic duct, the gallbladder and its stones are removed in one of the commonest of modern operations.

the gallbladder's artery, he cuts and ties the cystic duct close to the point where it joins with the common bile duct. Working with great care, he slices through the fibrous attachments between the gallbladder, the liver and the peritoneal sac, and removes the pear-shaped gallbladder. Then he runs his gloved fingers along the delicate quarter-inch-long common bile duct to make sure no gallstones have been forced into it, and finally, assured that all is well, he—or the resident—closes the incision, carefully suturing each layer: the peritoneum, the abdominal muscles and then finally the skin.

When the 45-minute operation is over, the surgeon goes downstairs for a cup of coffee. Then he visits postoperative patients. By 9:45 he is back in the operating room to remove the 11-year-old boy's appendix. The morning's operations completed, the surgeon visits each of his remaining hospitalized patients, listening to their complaints, checking their conditions, examining their dressings and discussing their cases with a resident as part of the teaching process.

Emergencies come on weekends

Hospital rounds usually take an hour and a half of the surgeon's time; then, if he can manage it, he breaks off for lunch. Often, however, he does not complete his rounds before 2 o'clock, leaving him time only for a snack before his afternoon office hours. He then sees patients who have been discharged from the hospital, and examines those who have been referred to him for surgery by other physicians. Usually he can go home at 6, after a working day of nearly 11 hours. But if he is taking his turn as the staff surgeon on call, he will probably be summoned to the hospital in the middle of the night, particularly on weekends, for that is when violence and automobile accidents fill the emergency clinic. The surgeon takes such calls as a part of his job. "I don't suppose there is anyone," a busy surgeon says, "who doesn't swear when the phone rings at 3 in the morning. But when you get there and you see how serious the situation is, your anger disappears, and you are glad you can help."

In contrast to the surgeon, whose task it is to repair existing damage, the public health officer has the job of preventing certain kinds of damage from occurring at all. In some respects he is like an army field officer whose enemy is disease. His function is to protect his community from disease attacks, and, if the attacks occur, to prevent them from achieving epidemic proportions. To achieve this he must often marshal experts from many fields, medical and nonmedical.

Dr. Charles Pigford, who became Public Health Officer of Houston, Texas, in 1961, supervises a staff of 500 that includes internists, pediatricians, obstetricians, venereologists and epidemiologists; as well as such nonphysicians as nurses, laboratory technicians and sanitary engineers. The department provides some medical treatment—mainly in city clinics—but its main job is the prevention of illness. Its experts inoculate 20,000 children every year against such diseases as diphtheria, smallpox, tetanus, whooping cough, poliomyelitis and measles. They watch over the preparation and distribution of the city's food, inspecting food-processing plants, restaurants and markets. They analyze drinking water, test swimming pools and check about 500 barbershops for hygienic procedures. The uneventful routine of such work is deceiving; it can uncover real danger.

Battling an epidemic

On the morning of August 13, 1964, Jean Pierce, a health department records clerk, walked into Pigford's office with a routine question. She had three death certificates in her hand, and she simply wanted to know how to classify the information on them. Each certificate listed the cause of death as encephalomyelitis, an inflammation of the brain and spinal cord that resembles mosquito-borne encephalitis. Pigford immediately became alerted. He had met encephalitis before, and he knew that if three adults had already died from it in Houston, there must be many more cases.

A quick call to the department's infectious disease office strengthened Pigford's suspicion: six similar cases had been reported in the previous eight weeks. He then telephoned Ben Taub Hospital, where the three deaths had occurred, and received even more alarming news. The hospital had among its patients 25 children and 35 adults with "encephalitis-like disease"; 12 death reports were being prepared at that time. Blood tests established that Houston was in the midst of an epidemic of so-called St. Louis encephalitis. No one had realized that it existed until Dr. Pigford noted the clues.

Armed with a positive identification of the disease, Dr. Pigford called on Mayor Louie Welch. "He asked what to do about the outbreak," Pigford later recalled. "I told him the only thing to do at this time was to kill mosquitoes." Entomologists spread through the city armed with machines like vacuum cleaners that sucked up mosquitoes—including the virus-carrying *Culex quinquefasciatus* variety. Ornithologists analyzed blood samples of wild and domestic birds—bluejays, mockingbirds, chickens, geese, pigeons—that often transmit the virus to mosquitoes. Fire engines, truck-mounted sprayers and a Coast Guard helicopter sprayed ditches, fields, school grounds and entire neighborhoods with insecticide. Newspapers, TV and radio stations urged residents to pour oil on accumulations of stagnant water.

Before the battle was over, 712 cases of encephalitis had been reported and 32 people died. But one of the most serious epidemics to attack a modern American city was on the wane within a month.

The source of that particular outbreak was readily identified as mosquitoes. Recognizing the origin of an epidemic is not always so easy, however, and the public health specialist must often follow elusive clues through unsuspected byways in tracking down the cause of a disease. Among the strangest—and most significant—medical detective stories is the mystery of Pascagoula's hepatitis.

Pascagoula, Mississippi, is a city of around 30,000 people on the Gulf of

Mexico; a shipyard at the mouth of the Pascagoula River builds nuclear submarines for the U.S. Navy. In February 1961, the Navy notified Dr. Alexander Langmuir, chief of the epidemiology branch of the federal Communicable Disease Center in Atlanta, of an outbreak of infectious hepatitis in Pascagoula, and asked for help.

A tough case for medical detectives

When the telephone call came through, Langmuir happened to be talking to one of his experts on infectious hepatitis, Dr. James Mason, who was immediately dispatched to investigate. Mason was well acquainted with the difficulties he faced. Infectious hepatitis is a serious liver disease that brings on jaundice and nausea; it often permanently impairs the digestive systems of its victims and sometimes is fatal. The disease is caused by a virus that is common in human waste and is easily spread when sewage contaminates food or drinking water. Locating the point of contamination is the puzzle. A sewer leak near a restaurant may infect a dozen people who have no apparent connection with one another and who quickly forget their chance connection with the restaurant. Or sloppy food handling at a picnic or club dinner can lead to scattered cases, seemingly unrelated. Finding the common thread linking victims to a potential source of the virus is the first task confronting the hepatitis detective, and Dr. Mason tackled this problem with the detective's standard technique. He collected as much information as he could, no matter how unrelated it seemed.

When he reached Pascagoula, he went first to the Jackson County health clinic, met the nurses on duty there and questioned them. Then he went to the Singing River Hospital, the only hospital in the area, parked himself in the doctors' lounge and interviewed local doctors as they happened to stop by. From them he learned that 13 cases of infectious hepatitis were currently in the hospital, and that there were also a number of other cases in the city.

Dr. Mason visited each of the 13 hospital patients, and almost immediately came upon his first significant clue. All 13 were adults. "Hepatitis usually is a disease of children," he later recalled. "It is spread by fecal-oral contact, and children wash their hands less often than adults. Adults can get it from children, but their cases come later."

As he mulled over this fact, Dr. Mason wondered what these people might have done together that could have given them hepatitis. Perhaps they had gone to a church supper where the water or food was contaminated, or perhaps they belonged to the same club, or had attended the same sporting event. His inquiries ruled out all of these possibilities, however, and Dr. Mason realized that something out of the ordinary must be the answer. "I began to try to think of something more esoteric," he said later. "I realized that this was a seacoast town. I began to wonder if some seafood that had been eaten raw could be the common source."

Although this possibility was so unlikely as to be outlandish, the next

A CORPSE IN THE STREET, victim of a 19th Century cholera epidemic, was drawn by French artist Honoré Daumier. Such scenes were common in Europe before public health experts learned how to eliminate polluted drinking water, the main source of cholera. The disease, which disrupts the digestive system, killed more than a million persons during one epidemic in Europe from 1847 to 1848, and it is still a hazard in India and other areas.

day Dr. Mason went back to the hospital and questioned the 13 patients again, asking them whether they had recently eaten raw seafood. Sure enough, he found that all of these patients had eaten raw oysters within the previous two months, a time that was consistent with the incubation period of hepatitis.

But no one had ever heard of a case in which U.S. shellfish had served as a source of hepatitis. Furthermore, Dr. Mason knew that oysters were a common dish in Pascagoula. If all of the population had eaten oysters during that period, the oyster theory meant nothing. He picked up the Pascagoula telephone book, selected 13 names at random and called them. None of the people whom he called had eaten oysters in the previous 60 days, and none of them had hepatitis.

Equipped with this information, Dr. Mason telephoned Dr. Langmuir at the Communicable Disease Center and related his suspicions. Dr. Langmuir's first reaction was: "Oysters! Are you crazy?" But when Mason told him of his telephone survey, Dr. Langmuir agreed that the lead should be followed up, and secured the help of Wilbert McLean, a sanitary engineer and shellfish expert, to assist Dr. Mason.

Finding the unsuspected culprit

McLean arrived the next day, and began visiting all the local oyster plants, stores, supermarkets and oyster stands. Meanwhile Dr. Mason was interviewing Pascagoula's hepatitis victims. From them he learned that, in all, two thirds of the hepatitis sufferers had recently eaten raw oysters. Some had gone oystering themselves or had been given oysters by friends, but most of the patients had purchased the oysters already shucked in cartons from one small group of stands and markets. Checking further, he and McLean learned that all these retail outlets had bought their oysters from the same oyster shucking company.

The end of the trail now seemed in sight. But the shucking plant, it turned out, was not the culprit. The source of the virus had to be traced still further back. Finally Mason and McLean learned that the oysters had been contaminated even before they were gathered. They came from a bed at the mouth of the Pascagoula River, in an area that had been ordered closed to oystering by the Mississippi State Board of Health as far back as 1931 because it was polluted by sewage.

The solution to the mystery of Pascagoula's hepatitis was a landmark in disease prevention. It furnished the first absolute proof that shellfish in the United States could be important carriers of hepatitis, explained the cause of similar epidemics in other cities, and led to closer regulation of both shellfishing and water pollution. But it is also noteworthy because the solution of the mystery required the assistance of about 20 specialists of six different kinds—epidemiologists, virologists, bacteriologists, internists, pediatricians and local public health officers—who applied their talents to the varied problems that were raised by the hepatitis outbreak. It was a remarkable demonstration of the role played by specialists in modern medicine.

MASKED AGAINST INFLUENZA, these policemen in Seattle, Washington, were using the only means of protection available against the epidemic that raged during the winter of 1918-1919. Today public health specialists can identify influenza viruses and develop vaccines to avert disasters like the flu outbreak of 1918, which swept the world, killing an estimated 20 million persons, including about 550,000 in the United States.

The Pediatrician and His Healthy Patients

Few of the great medical advances of this century have been as dramatic as those in pediatrics—the specialty concerned with the health of children. In 1900, one out of five American children died before the first birthday. Today the figure is one out of 40. No longer does the pediatrician concentrate on such childhood diseases as scarlet fever, diphtheria and rickets, for those afflictions are on their way to becoming mere footnotes in books on medical therapy. Now, the pediatrician's chief concern is the growth and development of healthy children, and his main objective is to keep them in good physical, mental and social health as they mature.

Pursuing this goal, Dr. Ralph Shugart (*right*), one of 15,000 pediatric specialists in the United States, practices in Littleton, a suburb of Denver, Colorado. During most of his working hours he administers the vaccines that prevent disease, works out nutrition tables and diets, and keeps a watchful eye on his patients' physical and psychological development. He is also a family counselor and—in his own words—"a bit of a professional wailing wall" for some 800 children and their parents. And, of course, he is a healer, for he is called on to treat a wide variety of children's injuries and illnesses.

EYEBALL TO EYEBALL
As part of a routine physical examination, Dr. Shugart peers through an ophthalmoscope into the eye of one-year-old Sheri Su Carrier. Sheri Su smiles at what she sees; but the doctor is deadly serious. He is hunting for cataracts or abnormal reflexes which would alert him to afflictions, such as tumors and metabolic disorders, that may be nipped in the bud.

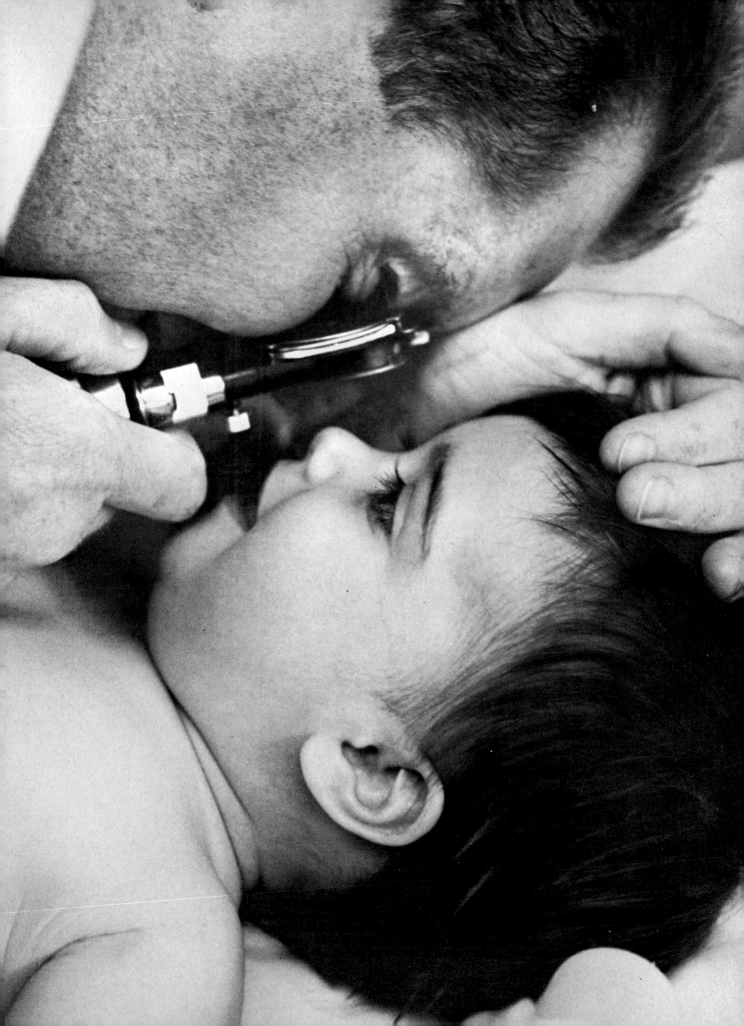

Treatment
in a Toy Shop

On a typical afternoon Dr. Shugart's reception room looks more like a permissive nursery school than a doctor's office. Bright pictures of clowns hang on the walls, toy trucks and trains litter the floor; the children scurry back and forth, puzzle over board games or seek the comfort of their mothers' arms. There is little in this room to suggest sickness—but few of the children waiting to see Dr. Shugart are sick. Most of them have come for the periodic examinations and preventive measures that keep them in good health. The babies—up to about six months old—see Dr. Shugart every month. Those of school age see him at least once a year.

This routine practice of preventive medicine makes Dr. Shugart a very busy man. During the eight hours he spends in his office every day, he sees as many as 50 children.

Predictably, this often creates a human traffic jam in his reception room. Dr. Shugart regrets the delays, and says: "Nothing bothers me more than a room full of mothers who have to wait, wait, wait. You can work out a perfect timetable and a kid ups and gets sick and you spend an unscheduled hour putting him in the hospital. So you're behind again." But he remembers the gracious remark of one mother to whom he had apologized: "I've never been to a good doctor but what I didn't have to wait."

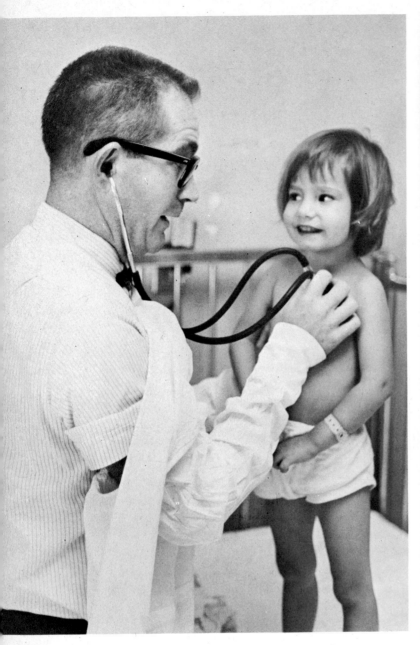

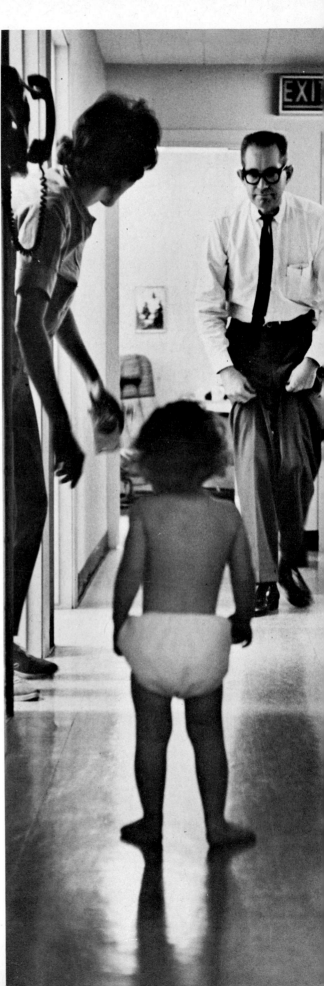

SMILE AT A CRIBSIDE

On his hospital rounds Dr. Shugart listens for signs of pneumonia in the chest of three-year-old Jo Ann Martinez, who "has been in the hospital so many times it's as familiar as her own home." She needs special attention because lung infections that might not prove too serious for other children present the hazard of heart failure to Jo Ann, who has a congenital heart defect.

STANDOFF AT KIDDIE CORRAL

Refusing to budge an inch, 18-month-old Melinda Rickard firmly stands her ground in the hallway of Dr. Shugart's office like a diapered cowboy waiting to draw on an advancing enemy. When she finally took a few hesitant steps, the doctor was able to observe her gait, balance and coordination to make sure that her bones, muscles and nervous system were developing as they should.

Demands and Joys of a Day's Work

In a single working day Dr. Shugart may go to six different hospitals in the Denver area, make three house visits and attend dozens of patients at his office. Countless telephone calls from frantic mothers punctuate his daily routine—he may be on the phone for as many as three hours a day. Throughout the night he is available for unpredictable emergencies.

Altogether, he often puts in from 60 to 90 hours of work per week. Though his patients are not often dangerously ill, the physical strain of his day-to-day practice and of the agonizing life-or-death decisions he must sometimes make have etched lines of concern on the face of the youthful doctor.

Yet there are compensations to match his responsibilites. For one thing, he genuinely enjoys his work —and his patients. "I often hug babies," he says, and he confesses to pleasure at the sight of a beautiful child. Best of all is the satisfaction of a decision well made, a responsibility met. Recalling a seven-year-old diabetic boy rescued at a critical stage of his disease by a perfect balance of diet and medication, Dr. Shugart muses: "I love him. I saved his life and it makes me feel near to him. I get a warm feeling when I see him, a good feeling inside that this child is alive because of something I did."

TWIST AND THRUST AT A TABLE
In a stance that might have come from a modern ballet, Dr. Shugart snatches a quick look at nine-month-old Peter Ismert's throat, while Peter's mother, sister and an interested young bystander *(left)* look on. "You have to be fast and agile," the doctor says. "At that age they don't give you very long to look." Once he had a stiff neck—and couldn't practice for several days.

Treatment at the Moment of Birth

In the past, the pediatrician's responsibilities for a baby did not begin until after the infant had been born. Today, many prospective mothers make their first visit to the pediatrician weeks before the baby is due, to discuss the problems of child rearing. In a sense, Dr. Shugart's care for the child begins at that point, for he will have provided a better home atmosphere for the infant by the reassurance he gives to a woman worried by her future duties as a mother. "Some people think books are the only way," he says. "They're afraid to rely on their instincts. Instinctive mothers really can be very good."

Like many modern pediatricians, Dr. Shugart makes a practice of attending births that present complications such as the surgical delivery of a baby by Caesarean section, shown below. The moment a Caesarean baby is removed from the womb, Dr. Shugart takes over from the obstetrician. He first uses suction on the infant's lungs and stomach, to remove the mucus and other matter that would

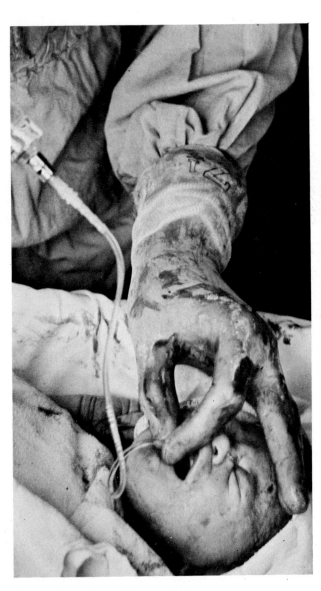

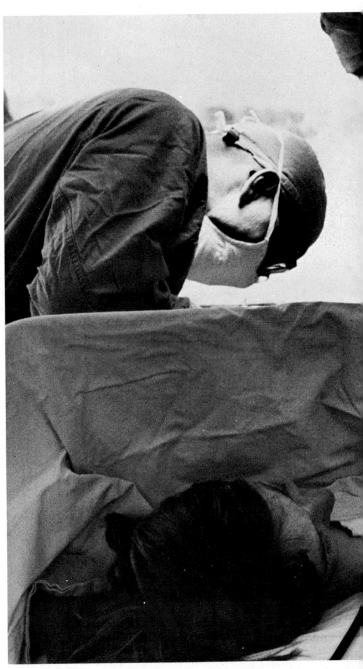

FIRST MOMENTS OF LIFE
Just seconds after its removal from its mother's womb, a baby delivered by Caesarean section has its stomach and lungs emptied of mucus *(above)*. A few moments later, after examining the newborn, Dr. Shugart shows it to its mother *(right)* who is beginning to recover from the anesthesia. "She naturally wants to see what she's done," he says. "You owe her that. And you're glad when you've got a good baby to show her."

normally be expelled by the pressure of natural birth. The technique is a relatively new one, in use since the early 1950s to prevent a Caesarean baby from choking on its own mucus.

Dr. Shugart also gives the newly delivered infant an on-the-spot physical examination. "You can tell a lot just by looking at a newborn," he says. "How its hands move, how it holds its mouth may indicate brain damage. Does it flex and tense or does it just lie there limply? It's a lot like picking a watermelon; it has to feel right."

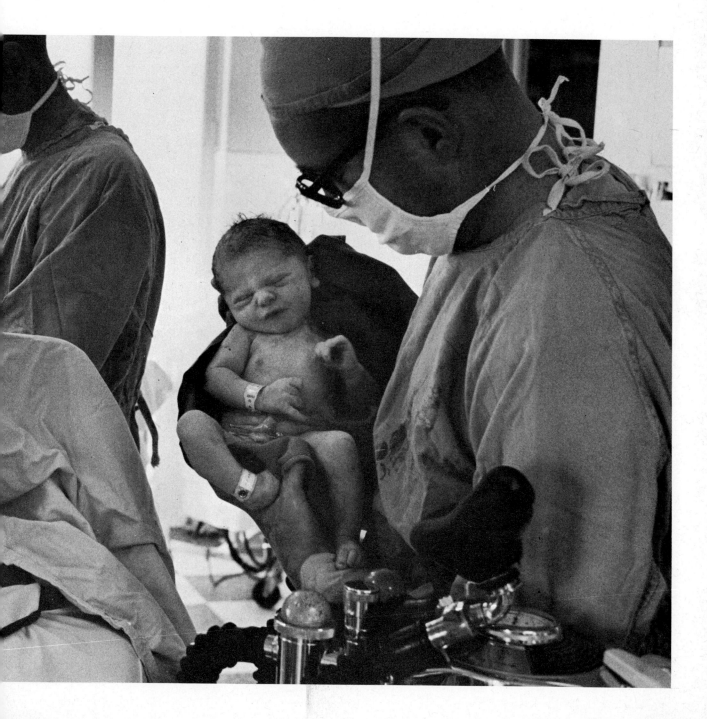

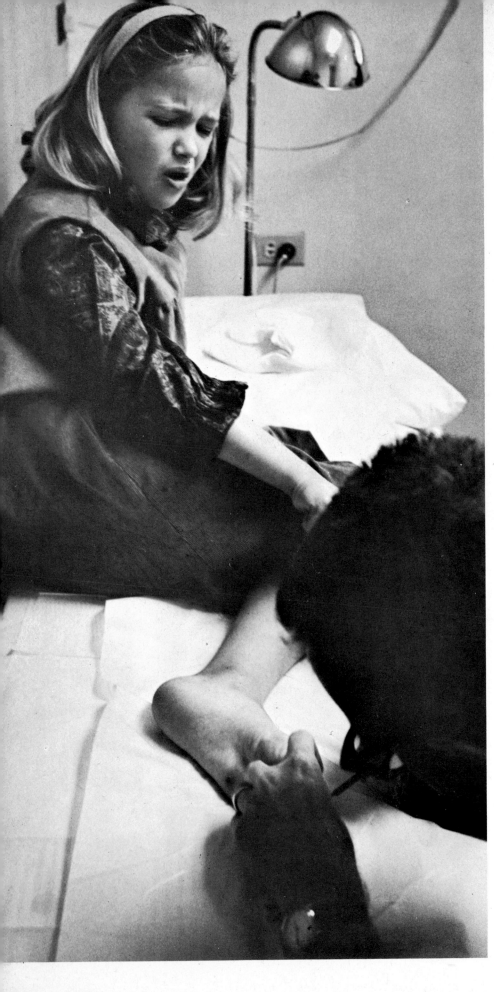

Causing Pain to Ease Pain

Occasional pain is a companion to medical care, even for healthy children. There is what Dr. Shugart calls the "brutality of the needle"—the hypodermic that injects a vaccine, the electric needle that removes skin blemishes. There is the pain of accidents, which are now the major cause of death or disability among children over one year old. That pain can be relieved, but what must follow is itself painful: swallowed poison must be pumped out, broken bones reset.

The infliction of necessary pain presents a major test of the pediatrician's skill at establishing an easy and trusting relationship with his patient. "The best way to establish it," says Dr. Shugart, "is to see him, get to know him, before you have to hurt him. That's not always possible." In a crisis, he says, "You sometimes have to establish rapport—with a loud voice. There is too much at stake."

A BURNING WIRE
The face of nine-year-old Sylvia Hutchison (left) twists in pain as Dr. Shugart burns a wart off her foot with an electric needle. The wart itself causes considerable discomfort and, unless it is removed, it might tend to spread; but the doctor admits that the treatment "stings like hell."

A PIERCING NEEDLE
Dr. Shugart comforts Johnny Connell, who fell and deeply gashed his forehead, and prepares the boy for the hypodermic needle that will inject a local anesthetic. "You must be light but truthful about the pain. Usually I tell them they're going to feel the bite of a big mosquito."

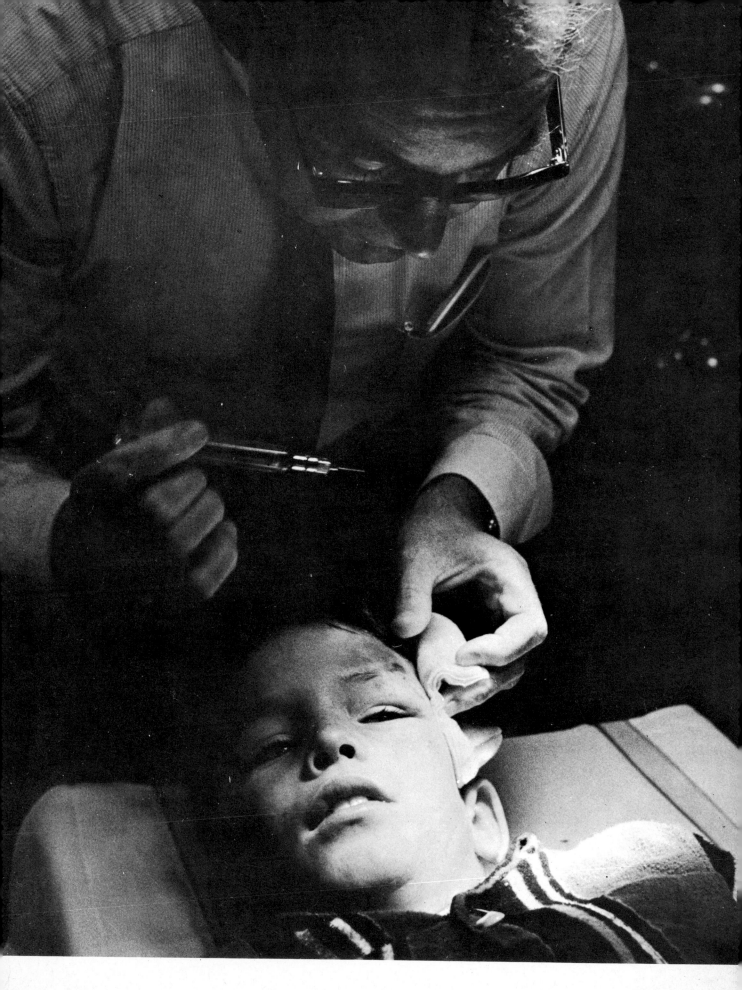

The Job of Friendly Counsel

As their patients grow older, many pediatricians find themselves called upon more and more to treat emotional problems. In these cases, the pediatrician must first decide whether he can resolve his patient's difficulty before it becomes serious.

Sometimes he may refer patients to practicing psychiatrists. In many cases, however, the pediatrician can handle such relatively minor problems as sleeping difficulties or misbehavior at school. Through informal sessions like the one shown at right, he acts as a buffer between parent and child, lending a willing ear to his patient and mitigating the tensions that often arise between generations.

In dealing with older children, Dr. Shugart faces special problems. "With teen-agers," he remarks, "it's imperative you don't lose contact. With boys I seek to be buddy-buddy or the all-knowing observer. To girls I'm a friend, sometimes a confidant." Dr. Shugart's experience with his own four children gives him an added insight into the problems of his patients. "Being a father," he says, "has made me a better pediatrician"—but he adds ruefully: "Being a pediatrician has not made me a better father."

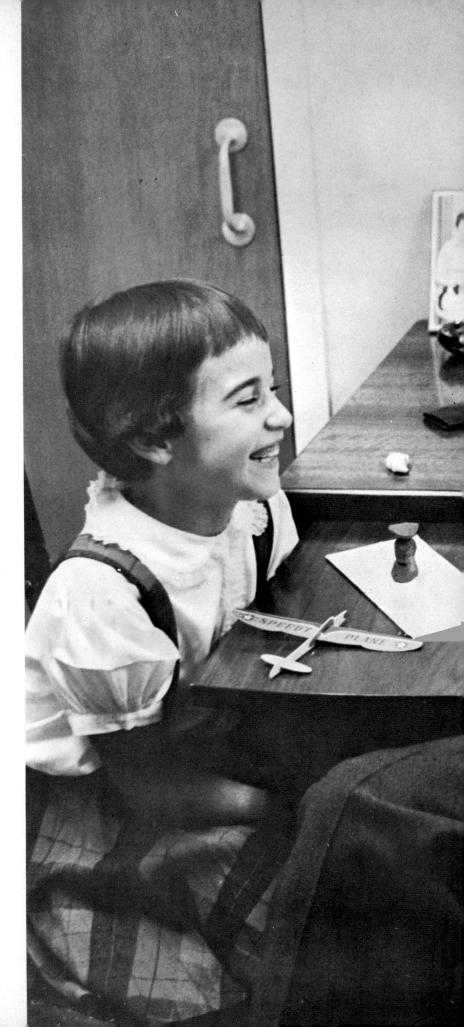

THE LIGHTER SIDE
Dr. Shugart and a pert little girl laugh as they share a joke during an otherwise serious conversation in which they have discussed the nightmares that had been bothering the child.

6
The Doctor Business

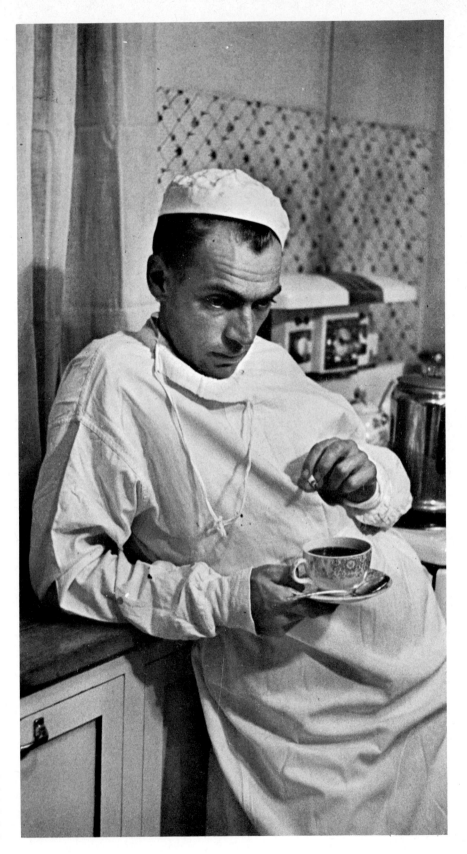

Exhausted after operating at midnight, Dr. Ernest Ceriani of Kremmling, Colorado, shows the strain that is the constant burden of individual practice. Unlike a physician who is in group practice, he has no one to share his work or responsibility.

"TIME WAS WHEN A PHYSICIAN setting up in practice merely hung out his shingle, got himself a set of surgical instruments, some simple medications and a good horse," says Dr. F.J.L. Blasingame, executive vice president of the American Medical Association.

In those horse and buggy days, the doctor business was nearly always a one-man enterprise. The young physician might begin by apprenticing himself for a time to an older physician, but in most cases he knew that he would ultimately open an office of his own and go into business for himself.

Today medicine is more complicated, and the doctor business is greatly changed. When a young physician completes his training, he faces a variety of choices. He may take a position as a full-time employee of a corporation, examining company workers and guarding their health. He may join the staff of a university, research laboratory or government agency, or he may work in a hospital as a radiologist, pathologist or anesthesiologist. In all these cases the physician is an employee, like an engineer or bookkeeper, and he enjoys all the advantages that go with a good job—a steady income, regular working hours and vacations, insurance and retirement benefits.

The amenities of a 9-to-5 job have now attracted 22 per cent of all physicians to salaried employment; nevertheless most young doctors still go into private practice. Unlike the old-fashioned family physician the young private practitioner has two alternative courses of action. He may follow the traditional path of going into practice for himself, becoming a "solo practitioner," in the jargon of the medical profession. As a solo practitioner, he must accept the full responsibility for his patients and the full burden of his practice. He must anticipate a difficult time in getting started, but he will enjoy complete independence and if he is successful he can earn substantial financial returns—the average net income of a private pediatrician in 1959, for example, was $20,700, and some outstanding doctors now enjoy incomes of $150,000 per year.

The fledgling physician may take still another course. He may decide to join the growing number of doctors who practice as members of groups, working under the same roof with other physicians and sharing patients and off-duty responsibilities with them. Such a position will mean a good income from the beginning—the American Association of Medical Clinics reports that group practitioners start at salaries ranging from $14,000 to $20,000 a year, and receive routine raises of $1,000 a year. Their financial rewards increase proportionately with experience— three fourths of the doctors in large group clinics earn between $20,000 and $49,000—and there are also other compensations, including regular working hours and regular vacations. But the group practitioner will not earn as much as the successful solo practitioner does in his peak years. He may have less opportunity to develop the close, friendly relations with his patients that the private doctor has, and if the group practitioner has a knack for business, he may miss the challenge and the excitement of running his own office.

If, after weighing all these factors, the young doctor decides to strike out on his own, he will be confronted with a host of problems at the start. The experience of an internist who set himself up in Mamaroneck, New York, a suburb of New York City, shows many of the difficulties and discouragements a physician must face on entering the profession. The internist was 33 years old when, having completed his residency and served two years in the Air Force Medical Service, he established his practice. Unlike many of his colleagues, he decided against apprenticeship to an older physician as a way of getting a start and abruptly launched his own career in an office of his own.

The young doctor had little trouble deciding where to practice. He had lived in Mamaroneck for 25 years; he knew people there; and the town was the kind of established community where he would meet the lung and heart diseases and other adult illnesses that occupy an internist.

No doctors in the house

Once the city was chosen, the next step was to find an office. At first the young internist thought he might use his home, but his wife was the daughter of a physician, and she was opposed to the idea. "Her father had used part of their home as an office," the doctor says, "and she had been shushed up all through her childhood. She remembered her mother saying, 'No noise, there are patients downstairs,' and she wasn't interested in repeating the experience."

The best location in Mamaroneck for a doctor's office was the large professional building downtown. Several physicians already occupied suites there, and the building's attractions included an established X-ray and clinical laboratory, as well as a parking lot outside. Happily the young internist found space there that provided an examining room, a consultation room, a small room for a nurse or secretary, a waiting room, a bathroom and an extra room.

The internist bought an electrocardiograph machine for checking hearts, a pulmonary testing machine for diagnosing lung diseases, and a small X-ray machine, together with an assortment of small instruments. He knew that he could manage without the X-ray machine, because there was a larger one down the hall, but he decided to buy his own anyway, so that he could take chest X-rays whenever he wanted to.

Next he bought a couch for his consultation room, so that patients could lie down while their electrocardiograms were taken, and he outfitted the other rooms with new furniture. Then he bought a second car because his wife needed the family car for shopping and other errands, and his practice required him to have one available every minute.

All told, the expenses of outfitting the office and buying the car came to about $10,000. The young doctor might have borrowed this capital investment from a bank or, if the bank turned down the loan, from the federal government (the Small Business Administration lends fledgling solo practitioners up to $15,000). He preferred, however, to scrape the money together himself. He had saved some money during his military

THE MAYO BROTHERS, pioneers in group medical practice, are immortalized by this bronze statue in Rochester, Minnesota, the small city they made world-famous as the site of their Mayo Clinic. William J. *(left)* (1861-1939) and Charles H. Mayo (1865-1939) were outstanding surgeons who pooled their talents with those of other physicians to establish the group practice. Today the clinic is a highly efficient diagnostic center that has been called "a medical mecca . . . amid the cornfields of Minnesota."

service, his wife had put aside some savings and his father helped out.

At last, in August of the year after his residency, the internist opened his office for business. Then he sat and waited. In the first five months only four patients appeared. Cash receipts from those patients came to exactly $28. Fourteen months passed before he took in enough from his practice to pay the office rent ($200 a month). "I had essentially no patients of my own," the doctor recalls. "A few friends came by, but sometimes you hate to charge them, or if you do, you underplay it a little bit."

Wrong man in an emergency

To help establish his practice, the internist called the Mamaroneck police and told them he was available, but the results were disappointing. When an emergency occurred, the police called the first doctor they could find, regardless of his specialty. "They would call a heart specialist if someone broke his neck in an automobile accident," the internist says.

The most effective stimulus to the young doctor's practice was the "covering" system, a common arrangement in which a physician substitutes for a colleague who is sick or out of town. "You see patients who are patients of another doctor," the internist says, "and if they come around to you later, you have to say, 'Please return to doctor so-and-so.' But at least you become known to the family, and then if their cousins decide to look for a doctor, very often they will mention you."

In his first full year in practice, the beginning internist spent $6,000 more to run his office than he took in from his patients. He made up the deficit and supported his family by dipping into savings and by working four afternoons a week, at $50 an afternoon, on the medical staff of a large corporation in New York City. The second full year his practice went into the red only $5,000, and the year after that he turned the corner, coming out $2,000 in the black. When he cleared $7,000, he took a two-week vacation, his first since going into practice.

After four years of practice, the internist was established. He was now seeing 30 to 40 patients a week, charging each seven dollars for a routine office call, $10 for a house call by day or $15 by night. His expenses came to almost $10,000 a year—including $200 a month office rent, $10 a day for a nurse who came in every weekday morning, $25 a month for the telephone, $30 a month for an answering service, and $40.80 a month for cleaning services.

The internist's wife is a registered nurse, and she still helps with his practice, answering the phone when neither he nor the regular nurse is in the office. "She's good on the telephone," he says of his wife, "and she has had enough experience to manage most things until they can be properly scheduled."

The practice is not large enough to warrant a secretary, and the young doctor keeps all of his own records. He sends bills himself, reminding delinquents three times before writing off unpaid sums as losses. (The system works well enough; 95 per cent of his bills are paid, which is better than average for a doctor.) Twice a year he takes his financial records to a local accountant who balances his books. "I just throw them in his lap and he laughs a little at my primitive bookkeeping," he says.

As a solo practitioner the young internist must pay all of the expenses of his practice out of his own pocket. He must protect himself against malpractice suits—legal actions charging him with negligent or improper care. Such suits are a major source of trouble for doctors today and can result in the award of very heavy damages to patients. About 9,000 suits are filed each year in the United States; settlements amount to $50 million a year, and the average jury award comes to almost $50,000. The young internist carries $100,000 malpractice insurance, which costs him $130 a year in premiums. He also carries accident insurance for the office ($25 a year) in case a patient slips on a rug or injures himself in some other way during his visit.

A day off—for work

To help meet all these expenses the internist still works for the corporation in New York one afternoon a week. "On Wednesdays you do not get many calls in Mamaroneck," he says. "People there assume that is every doctor's day off." He also spends one afternoon a week in a clinic in nearby Harrison, drawing $75 for four to five hours duty.

In addition to these financial responsibilities, the physician also faces very stringent professional responsibilities that go beyond his current treatment of his patients. He must devote a substantial amount of time to reading and attending lectures so that he can keep up with medical progress, and he is required to belong to several organizations.

Unless he is a member of the Westchester County Medical Society, he is not allowed to use the facilities of the voluntary hospitals in that county. The county society, in turn, requires him to join the New York State Medical Society. Along with these mandatory memberships, the internist voluntarily maintains enrollment in the American Thoracic Society, which concentrates on the chest diseases that are his particular field of interest.

Of all the medical organizations, the one that touches the internist's life most closely is the county medical society, which can exercise powerful authority over local physicians. In effect it possesses the right of veto over the practice of medicine in Westchester County. If it finds a physician guilty of unethical conduct or malpractice, it can bar him from practicing in Westchester voluntary hospitals, a drastic step that usually prevents him from continuing his career in the area.

Punitive action of this sort is rarely administered, of course, and the young internist, a respected and admired physician, has had no reason to worry about such a disaster. His relationship with the county society is a pleasant one. He regularly borrows books from the medical library it maintains in nearby Purchase, and once a month he attends lectures, sponsored by the society's educational arm, the Westchester Academy of Medicine, to hear noted clinicians and laboratory researchers describe their work. For reports on the most recent advances in medicine, he also goes to the conventions of national medical organizations, such as the American College of Physicians, the American Medical Association and the technical branch of the American Heart Association.

Another important source of medical information for the internist is the periodicals and pamphlets that flow into his office. He receives *The Journal of the American Medical Association* and subscribes to half a dozen other journals devoted to internal medicine and chest diseases, but he also gets an unasked-for deluge of free pamphlets and magazines, most of which are sponsored directly or indirectly by drug companies. Some of this free literature—such as the magazine *Medical Economics* —he finds useful, but for the most part he acquires his professional news from the journals he subscribes to.

Much of the news of developments in prescription drugs is brought directly to him in what might be called face-to-face commercials, presented by "detail men." They are representatives of drug companies who come, unannounced, to his office two or three times every week to promote the wares of their firms. The information they have to dispense is usually of little value, the Mamaroneck internist says, but the drug samples they leave behind are another matter. "I pass them out to patients who can't afford a $10 drugstore bill."

Things are going well for the young internist. He is making money and finding time to enjoy himself because other doctors now "cover" for him. "I love the covering system," he says, "because if I want to go to the beach in the summer, I can go, and I will not be called back. And I can go out to dinner and know I will not be called."

Within 10 years he expects to be seeing 60 patients a week and clearing $35,000 a year. To reach that goal, he will have to receive fees totaling at least $45,000 a year, that is, take in about $200 every working day of his life.

The attractions of the group

Although the Mamaroneck internist is happy with his decision to open an office of his own, solo practice is losing its favored position in American medicine. Today more and more doctors are pooling their talents in groups, sharing office space and equipment, and taking turns answering night calls so that they can provide round-the-clock patient care without disrupting their personal lives. Since 1946 about 1,000 doctors a year have gone into group practice. Estimates based on Public Health Service statistics indicate that soon more will practice in groups than alone.

Group practice may range from membership in such prestigious establishments as the Mayo Clinic in Rochester, Minnesota, the Lahey Clinic in Boston or the Cleveland Clinic, to a loose arrangement for cooperation among three or four doctors in a city or town.

The oldest and best known of all the major medical groups in the United States is the Mayo Clinic. Its origin goes back to the middle of the 19th Century, when a young country doctor named William Worrall

Mayo, who had originally come to the United States from Manchester, England, and had practiced medicine for a time at Le Sueur, Minnesota, moved to Rochester and set himself up in an office over Quale's Drugstore on Broadway. Dr. William Mayo had two sons, later to become famous as "Dr. Will" and "Dr. Charlie," who helped their father on his rounds, often serving as anesthetists. When the Mayo boys finished medical school, they came back to Rochester and went into practice with their father. Under the aggressive leadership of the physician-brothers, the Mayo practice flourished and expanded, and by the early 1900s, it had grown to the point where people were calling it a "clinic."

Behind the Mayo Clinic's reputation

Today, the Mayo Clinic is a thriving institution, respected around the world. Located in the heart of Rochester, a city of 48,000, the Clinic now includes five main buildings, one of them a 19-story skyscraper and another 10 stories high. Within these buildings 450 doctors and 675 residents—no longer including any Mayos in their number—are available to Mayo patients. Every year 200,000 people come from all parts of the world by car, bus, plane and train to visit the Clinic. One third of these patients are referred by their home-town physicians; the rest come on their own, attracted by the Clinic's reputation.

The Mayo Clinic is known primarily as a diagnostic center. A patient goes there to be examined by highly trained specialists when physicians elsewhere have not been able to determine his illness. It also provides treatment methods not available in most medical centers.

The patient may ask to see a particular doctor; if he does not, he will be seen by the first available internist. The internist takes a complete medical history, gives the patient a thorough examination and usually a few routine tests. More complete tests may follow, including X-ray examinations and one or more of 130-odd blood tests. After the internist reviews the test results and his own observations, he most often calls in another specialist, and together they decide on the treatment to be followed.

The Mayo Clinic is strictly an outpatient clinic, which means that it has no beds or hospital facilities of its own. Once the patient's ailment has been diagnosed and his treatment prescribed, he may go home to his own personal physician or he may enter Rochester Methodist Hospital or St. Mary's Hospital, also in Rochester, for treatment. Both of these hospitals are staffed by doctors from the Clinic.

The Mayo Clinic, its physicians and the hospitals they staff stand in the vanguard of progressively enlightened American medicine. St. Mary's was one of the first hospitals in the country to accept all patients without regard to race, creed or social or economic status. A team of physicians at the Clinic was among the first to use a heart-lung machine to take over a patient's blood flow during heart surgery. Dr. John Lundy of the Clinic developed the widely used anesthetic, sodium pentothal, and at Rochester Methodist Hospital he set up the first recovery room, where a surgi-

PHYSICIANS AND SURGEONS
$14,561

DENTISTS
$11,858

LAWYERS AND JUDGES
$10,587

ENGINEERS
$8,361

NATURAL SCIENTISTS
$7,658

TEACHERS
$5,610

PLUMBERS AND PIPEFITTERS
$5,593

CLERGYMEN
$4,020

FARMERS AND FARM MANAGERS
$2,169

PROSPEROUS PHYSICIANS, as this graph of average incomes shows, are the rule in the United States. Among professionals, physicians make more than dentists or lawyers, and their annual income is more than three times that of clergymen. According to U.S. Bureau of Census statistics, the average physician earns nearly $720,000 in his lifetime, and many specialists top the million-dollar mark. Although figures given here date from 1959 —the most recent year for which figures are available—later estimates indicate that the ranking has not changed appreciably since then.

cal patient can be given special attention immediately after an operation, an innovation since adopted by many hospitals.

The founders of the Mayo Clinic were men with strong social consciences. "Our father recognized certain definite social obligations," Dr. Will Mayo once recalled. "He believed that any man who had a better opportunity than others, greater strength of mind, body or character, owed something to those who had not been so provided." Acting on this philosophy the Mayos endowed a research and educational foundation at the nearby University of Minnesota. The Mayo brothers gave $1.5 million to establish the foundation, and today the Mayo organization sets aside more than three million dollars annually for research. With Clinic support Dr. Edward Kendall, a biochemist, and Dr. Philip Hench, an internist, developed cortisone, the remarkable drug used in the treatment of rheumatoid arthritis, leukemia and rheumatic fever.

Yet for all the varied activities of its doctors, the Mayo Clinic represents a special kind of group medical practice. In many cases, when a patient goes there he goes for a particular illness or a specific medical episode; after the treatment is completed he seldom returns. Many group medical practices are designed to provide complete, continuing care for their patients. The physicians who work in the group may, like solo practitioners, provide separate services for separate fees, or they may offer all-inclusive care paid for in advance by subscribers to a health plan, such as HIP (Health Insurance Plan), serving 730,000 people in New York, or the Kaiser Health Plan, serving 1.5 million people in California, Oregon and Hawaii.

Total care by 1,400 doctors

The Kaiser Plan is America's most ambitious scheme for pooling medical talent. It furnishes total medical care to people who pay a fixed monthly sum that covers all the treatments they may need; members of the plan pay the same amount whether or not they receive medical services. The medical staff of the Kaiser Plan includes some 1,400 doctors, 90 per cent of whom are specialists. Available to them are the 18 hospitals (3,200 beds) and 43 clinics of the Kaiser Foundation.

This network developed from extremely modest beginnings. In 1933, a young surgeon named Sidney Garfield persuaded seven colleagues to join with him in building a hospital in California's Mojave Desert, where construction workers were building an aqueduct. Garfield and his associates borrowed money, built a 15-bed hospital and planned to charge their patients on the traditional fee-for-service basis. But it soon became clear that this approach would not work. Although the fees were modest, they were still too high for many of the workers on the project.

So the doctors decided to try a new idea. They offered to care for the workers for a charge of only $1.50 each per month. This fee, well within the workers' means, brought in sufficient income to Garfield and his colleagues to keep the hospital operating. The medical results were impressive, for the existence of the hospital cut absenteeism among the workers.

The sick and injured, who previously had to be taken long distances to hospitals, could now be treated close to the job site and returned to duty much more quickly than before.

Garfield's achievement came to the attention of Henry J. Kaiser, the builder and industrialist. In 1938, when he was supervising the building of the Grand Coulee Dam in the state of Washington, he decided to provide prepaid medical care for the 5,000 workers on the project; he offered to build a 75-bed hospital near the construction site, and he persuaded Garfield and his group to run it. During World War II the Kaiser Plan was expanded to include the 180,000 workers employed in the seven Kaiser shipyards that dotted the West Coast, and today all residents of California, Oregon and Hawaii are eligible.

A 15-cent hospital stay

On the Kaiser Plan, most subscribers pay a monthly fee ranging from $10 for a single person to $25 for a man and his family. For this regular fee, and in some cases a small additional charge, a member gets all his medical care; office visits as well as hospital stays—as long as 111 days for a single illness—are included. One subscriber, recently discharged from the hospital, remarked, "I was in 10 days and all they charged me was 15 cents for a telephone call."

For the physician as well as the patient, this kind of group practice has many advantages. The doctor never has to worry about the cost of treatment. The patient is fully covered by the plan, and if he needs them he can use all the resources of the Kaiser hospitals, specialists and clinics. If the doctor wants a test, he orders it; if he wants to refer the patient to another specialist, that specialist is at hand.

The group operation enables the Kaiser doctor to lead a normal, well-ordered life. So many physicians are available that even a junior member of the staff may have to answer night calls only about once a month. The hours are regular (roughly a 44-hour week), and the doctor enjoys regular vacations—usually two weeks a year at first, and one month a year after 10 years. He may also take from two weeks to a month off every year for study or research in his particular field.

In his search for the kinds of personal conveniences offered by group practice the physician is not limited to all-inclusive prepayment schemes like that of the Kaiser Plan. Similar work- and equipment-sharing arrangements are provided by a much more common form of group. This is the community service group, or medical center, now operating in many American towns and cities.

The Wenatchee Valley Clinic in the heart of central Washington's apple-growing country is a good example of this kind of practice. Located in the town of Wenatchee (population 18,000), the Clinic includes 21 specialists. Among them are six internists, three surgeons, two pediatricians and three obstetrician-gynecologists.

The management of the Clinic relieves the doctor of nearly all paper work. The business office keeps medical records, sends out bills, and

THE MERCENARY PHYSICIAN, derided for the size of his fees, has been the target of barbs for centuries. In this 1830 lampoon by the famous British caricaturist Robert Cruikshank, a physician is shown using a knife called "The Lancet"—the name of the British medical journal—to carve a "Proper Day" slice of profit during a cholera epidemic. He is surrounded by expensive remedies—all ineffective, since the cause of cholera was then unknown.

takes care of Medicare forms, insurance claims and office correspondence. The doctor starts out as a salaried employee of the Clinic at a salary of around $14,000 a year, but gets a raise every year, and in his fifth year he becomes a partner of the Clinic. He then shares the profits equally with other senior staff members, bringing his income to $35,000 or $40,000 a year. In his first year at the Clinic the doctor may take two weeks' vacation, and after six years he may take six weeks. He also gets an extra week off every year, to enable him to study, to attend medical meetings and to keep up with the latest developments in his field.

When a patient visits the Wenatchee Valley Clinic, he may call and make an appointment in advance or walk in and tell the receptionist his troubles. The receptionist makes an appointment with an internist, who examines the patient and refers him to another specialist—a neurologist or a surgeon, for example—if necessary.

The patient pays six dollars to $10 for each visit and is cared for by the Clinic rather than by an individual doctor. When he enters the Clinic all its specialists and all its facilities—labs, X-ray rooms and tumor clinic— are at his disposal. If he must go to the hospital, the Clinic finds space for him at Central Washington Deaconess Hospital, two miles away, or at St. Anthony's Hospital, three miles from the Clinic.

Instant doctors

The Wenatchee Clinic provides round-the-clock care for its patients by maintaining a duty roster under which a pediatrician, an obstetrician, an internist and a surgeon are available at any hour. Each of the four specialists on duty carries a light-weight two-way radio in his pocket. If a patient calls after 6 p.m., when the Clinic closes, his call is taken by an answering service. The telephone operator then calls a specialist via two-way radio, and he contacts the patient or visits him immediately.

The radio call system can get a doctor to a patient in a matter of minutes. One Sunday morning, Dr. Frank Kells, an obstetrician from the Clinic, was attending a service at St. Luke's Episcopal Church in Wenatchee. Dr. Kells was on call at the time, and had his radio volume turned low in order to avoid disrupting the service. But during the sermon, church members sitting near Dr. Kells could hear a distant voice call out, "Doctor 28!"

"Doctor 28" was Dr. Kells's code. He went out into the vestibule of the church, turned up the volume, and was told that one of his patients who was expecting a baby had gone to St. Anthony's Hospital. The doctor made it to the hospital in less than five minutes, in time to deliver a fine baby girl.

This almost instant availability of a doctor endears group practice to patients. The freedom—personal and professional—that it offers increasingly attracts physicians. Its rapid growth into what may soon be the most common form of practice in America is another sign of the great changes that have overtaken medicine since the day when one doctor with a good horse could care for all the needs of all his patients.

A Corps That Guards
a Nation's Health

Guarding the health of every American stands a corps of specially trained doctors he seldom sees. These are the physicians of the U.S. Public Health Service, full-time, salaried employees of the federal government, charged with controlling epidemics, finding the causes of disease and treating extraordinary medical problems.

Founded in 1798 as the Marine Hospital Service to care for sick and disabled seamen, the Public Health Service still provides medical treatment for special groups of Americans. But today its physicians and other specialists look after the well-being of the entire nation, and their main purpose is prevention rather than cure. To block infections that might enter the country from abroad, the Service has established more than 400 quarantine stations. To contain disease attacks within the United States, it maintains a Communicable Disease Center, which dispatches task forces of specialists to help local authorities quell epidemics. But most of the Public Health Service's effort is aimed at finding the causes of disease. Its principal bureau, the National Institutes of Health, spends over $1 billion a year on research—10 times as much as France, West Germany, Italy and Great Britain combined.

THE FIRST SURGEON GENERAL
Dr. John M. Woodworth *(right),* appointed the first Surgeon General of the United States in 1870, transformed the Marine Hospital Service into the national organization that has become the Public Health Service. Among its 34,000 full-time employees are 5,800 officers of the Service's commissioned corps, including physicians, nurses and other specialists.

A Tradition of Special Hospital Care

Since the administration of President John Adams the Public Health Service has provided hospital care for merchant seamen. Today it maintains 10 hospitals where seamen, Coastguardsmen and some federal employees are treated.

The seamen pose special medical problems, for in their travels to faraway lands they sometimes contract diseases that are quite rare in the United States. Fifteen cases of leprosy were admitted to the Health Service's hospital on Staten Island, New York, in 1966; there and in other hospitals Health Service doctors handle such ailments as loa-loa (a tropical eye disease) and leishmaniasis (a nasal and oral infection endemic in Central and South America).

Out-of-the-ordinary medical problems faced by other Americans are also a responsibility of the Public Health Service. It operates the country's only leprosarium, at Carville, Louisiana, and it has met the special health needs of Indians and Eskimos with such success that, over the past 12 years, the infant mortality rate among Indians has been reduced 36 per cent, and tuberculosis-caused deaths among Eskimos and Indians in Alaska have dropped 84 per cent.

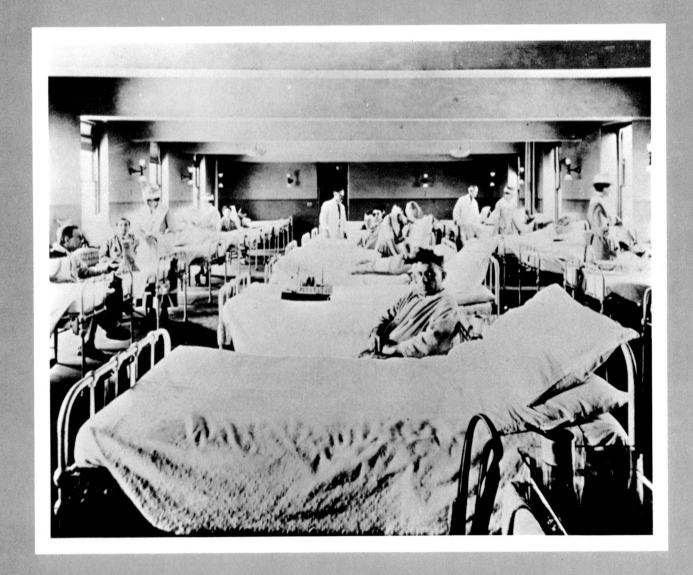

AN EARLY HOSPITAL WARD
During the 1920s, Public Health patients were still being treated *(above)* in the old Staten Island Hospital—built in 1831, when the care of seamen was the health agency's only mission.

THERAPY FOR AN INJURED SEAMAN
Seaman Kenneth Blair *(right)* of McMinnville, Tennessee, enjoys building ship models while recovering from an ankle injury at a new wing of the Staten Island Hospital, built in 1942.

Stopping Disease at the Gateway

In 1966 citizens and aliens made about 132 million entries into the United States from foreign countries (123.8 million of them from Mexico), yet not one case of a major communicable disease was traceable to this vast traffic. There was a time, however, when infected travelers coming into the United States from abroad posed a deadly threat to the health of Americans.

Through the 18th and 19th Centuries, deadly epidemics of yellow fever most often brought in from Havana frequently ravaged coastal cities of the South. Cholera outbreaks were not uncommon. In the summer of 1877, yellow fever struck New Orleans and then spread up the Mississippi River Valley beyond Vicksburg and Memphis, and along the Ohio as far as Cincinnati. More than 100 communities were stricken; 100,000 people were afflicted, and 13,000 died.

A SLOW CHECK AT ELLIS ISLAND
One of the millions of immigrants examined at Ellis Island before World War I pauses while a Public Health Service physician looks into her eye for signs of trachoma infection. In those days immigrants frequently had to wait for weeks before they could be cleared to enter the country.

Disasters like this one prompted Congress to pass the Federal Quarantine Act of 1878. Under it the Public Health Service was given the job of inspecting "passengers, crew, cargo and ballast" of incoming ships. By the late 1890s, fifty "ports of entry" had been established where incoming ships and their passengers could be examined and, if necessary, detained. But this plan proved cumbersome in practice; sick immigrants were held for long periods and many had to be sent back to their homelands as unfit.

Then in the 1920s the Public Health Service began to require that prospective immigrants be examined before embarking for the United States. Today new arrivals bring with them recent X-rays, blood-test reports and immunization records. Now an immigrant can be cleared in three or four minutes—and imported disease is no longer a major health hazard.

SWIFT APPROVAL IN THE JET AGE
A young Irish-immigrant family entering the United States shows its X-rays and health records to a Public Health officer at Kennedy International Airport in New York. Because these were completed in advance, the new arrivals will be cleared quickly by the health inspector.

Fighting for Safe Water and Air

Pollution has been a fighting word for the Public Health Service for more than half a century. In the early 1900s polluted water often caused widespread typhoid fever. That rarely happens now—but in the 1960s polluted air is killing an indeterminate number of the weak and aged. It is obvious that pollution is one of the worst health problems of our times.

Before World War I, devastating epidemics of typhoid fever raged in many parts of the country. Health Service agents traced the source of city-wide outbreaks of the disease to polluted drinking water and contaminated food coming from rural areas,

where sanitation methods were primitive. Public Health Service workers traveled through the backcountry, explaining to farmers the importance of better sanitation practices such as building flyproof outhouses at safe distances from wells; they also instituted new sanitation methods in the towns. This campaign proved effective; today typhoid fever is no longer a serious health threat. Now the most troublesome danger is in the polluted air.

In Los Angeles, automobiles add more than 10,000 tons of carbon monoxide to the air every day. And each year New York City is fouled by more

than three million tons of dirt, gases and chemicals, noxious products of industry and vehicles, that are spewed into the atmosphere. These poisons can be fatal: more than 400 deaths were attributed to intensely polluted air in New York City in 1963, as were 80 deaths in November 1966 when smog blanketed the city for four days.

To combat this new health hazard, the Public Health Service is guiding industry and state and local agencies in the development of filters and other control devices and in establishing regulations to guarantee that, just as our water is now safe to drink, our air will someday be safe to breathe.

CHECKING POLLUTION IN WATER
A Public Health Service worker of the 1920s stops at a rural home to explain the dangers of polluted water. Disease outbreaks that could develop into epidemics were almost inevitable when, as pictured here, the privy was located only a few yards from the family's well water.

TESTING POISONS IN AIR
The eyes of this Health Service volunteer are being exposed to components of automobile exhaust fumes to determine their irritating effect. Through such experiments the National Center for Air Pollution Control in Cincinnati studies pollutants and then proposes control measures.

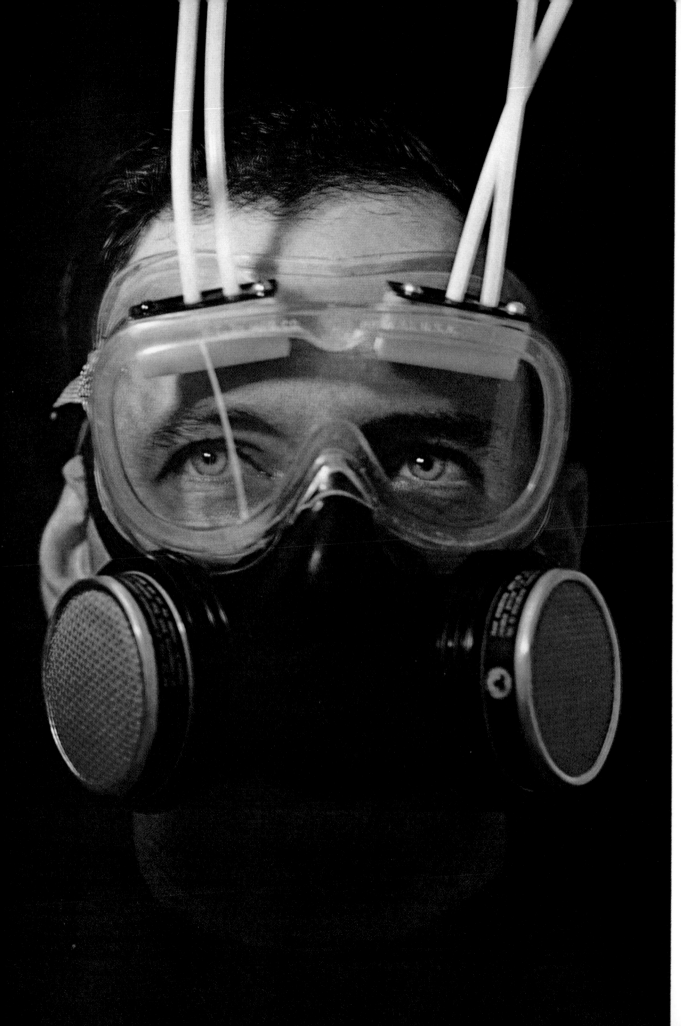

Progress toward a Healthy World

Following the Spanish-American War, United States troops occupying Cuba were threatened by yellow fever, the disease that had made many tropical and subtropical areas almost uninhabitable. Public Health officers were assigned to assist Major William Gorgas of the U.S. Army in an effort to end the scourge. Starting in Havana, where the disease was most prevalent, they worked to eliminate the mosquitoes that transmitted the germ. They fumigated houses and drained ponds and ditches, and even had a law passed to punish any householder whose property harbored mos-

GASSING DEADLY MOSQUITOES
During the campaign to quell the yellow fever epidemic of 1908 in the city of Santiago de Cuba, houses were wrapped in tarpaulins to seal them tight for fumigation. Lethal fumes, generated by burning sulfur inside, then killed any disease-carrying mosquitoes infesting the buildings.

quito larvae. In less than a decade, yellow fever was ended in Cuba.

Today, on the theory that disease anywhere can be a threat to people everywhere, the Health Service works closely with health organizations all over the world. Its Communicable Disease Center is studying viral dis-eases and tuberculosis in Yugoslavia, Brazil, Ceylon, Poland, Israel and India. In 17 tropical countries malaria is being eradicated, and in Africa, where smallpox kills up to 3,500 every year, Public Health Service specialists and local authorities plan to vaccinate 105 million people by 1971.

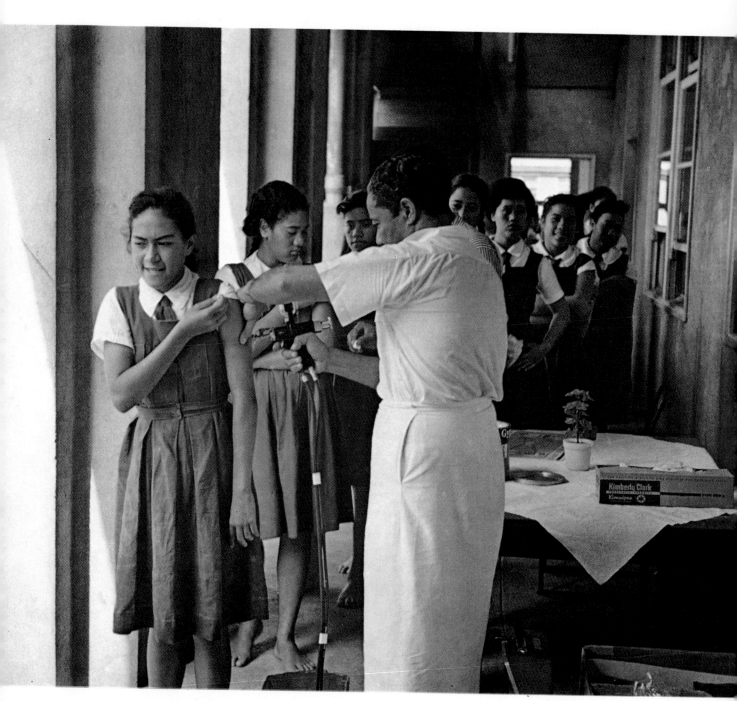

VACCINE FOR THE SOUTH PACIFIC
Wielding a pistol-handled hypodermic that will force vaccine into the skin, a Tonganese doctor inoculates a school girl against smallpox. The jet injector shown here works so fast that Public Health Service physicians and Tonganese doctors vaccinated 44,290 people in 37 days.

Fighting Disease in the Laboratory

Research now dominates the activities of the Public Health Service—and the Public Health Service very nearly dominates medical research. The Service, financing 40 per cent of all U.S. medical investigation, is the chief source of funds for this branch of science. Its own research center, the National Institutes of Health at Bethesda, Maryland, is the world's largest medical-research organization.

The record of Health Service scientists includes many noteworthy successes. They have found a vaccine for the often-fatal Rocky Mountain spotted fever; a promising vaccine for German measles, which can deform the unborn babies of expectant mothers, is being tested. And the Health Service also hopes to find an answer to the dreaded child-killer: leukemia.

EARLY LOCATIONS FOR RESEARCH
This modest laboratory, shown in an 1891 photograph was the first Washington, D.C., location for Public Health Service investigations in medical research. By 1937, the Service's Dr. Charles Armstrong, seen below dissecting a monkey, was helping to solve the riddle of polio.

ON THE TRACK OF LEUKEMIA
As part of the National Cancer Institute's leukemia research program, a baby monkey in a Kensington, Maryland, laboratory is injected *(right)* with human leukemia substances. Inducing the disease in the monkey may help to determine whether a virus causes the disease in humans.

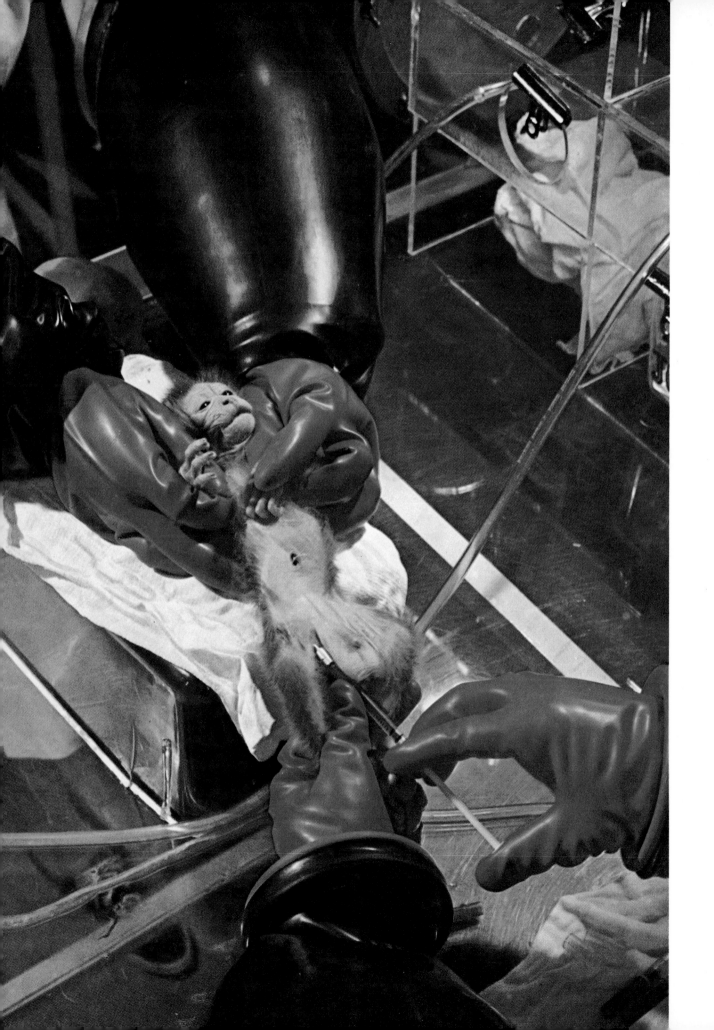

A Superplan
to End Leukemia

The experimental step pictured at right is part of the most massive attack ever launched against a single disease. Working with a grant from the Public Health Service's Cancer Institute, Dr. Marcel Baluda of the University of California is removing the yolk sac of a chicken embryo for use in the growing of chicken leukemia virus. From such experiments, scientists hope to find a method of tracing the development of human leukemia—a blood and bone-marrow cancer that kills more children than any other disease.

The crash program to solve the riddle of leukemia represents a bold new approach to cancer research. It applies to medicine the coordinated research and development techniques used so successfully on military and space projects, dividing the gigantic problem into dovetailing sections and then assigning each part to a separate group of investigators.

To identify the cause of human leukemia, and develop a vaccine against it, the research is directed into seven broad avenues. Already one avenue has led to the successful cultivation of different strains of leukemia cells in the laboratory—an achievement that could mark the turning point in the war against the lethal disease.

7
Headquarters: The Hospital

Operations like this, done without masks, gowns or gloves in a ward at New York's Bellevue Hospital, were common in the 1870s before scientific medicine changed hospitals from places of last resort to centers of hope for patients.

A GENERAL HOSPITAL may be a tall, gleaming building in the heart of a city, a dilapidated 19th Century relic surrounded by slums, a rambling one-floor structure located in the countryside on land where corn was recently grown. But regardless of how it looks or where it is located, the hospital plays a far larger role in the community today than ever before in history. For the average American, it is the place where he was born and the place where he will die. And in between his first breath and his last, he will receive much of his medical care—for many minor ailments as well as for major illnesses—within a hospital's rooms, emergency wards and outpatient clinics.

The hospitals that serve the vast majority of citizens are short-term hospitals, so called because the average stay of a patient in them is less than 30 days; they account for over 90 per cent of all admissions. The remaining 10 per cent are handled by psychiatric, tuberculosis and other long-term hospitals or by various kinds of institutions operated by the federal government.

To keep up with the ever-increasing demands for medical services, about 1,300 new short-term hospitals were established in the United States in the two decades starting with 1946—there are now nearly 6,000 of them—and many existing hospitals enormously expanded their facilities. This unprecedented growth added over a quarter million beds, bringing the total to nearly 750,000. It also accelerated the trend toward large hospitals, equipped with modern laboratories and staffed with specialists and their students. The expansion and improvement of hospitals were sorely needed; annual admissions almost doubled over the same period—from about 13.5 million to 26.5 million—a rate of increase that substantially exceeded the rate of increase in the country's population during that time.

The role of the hospital has not only grown; it has changed. The short-term general hospital, particularly if it is a large one, is now becoming the hub of medical practice in a community. Hospital clinics, for example, were once meant only for people who could not afford to pay for private medical care. Today many of the clinics are open to anyone who seeks treatment; those who can pay do so. For some physicians, the clinic has become a second office.

There are other ways in which the hospitals' role has changed. Many of them now provide services, unheard of a generation ago, such as classes for expectant mothers, clinics for the detection of cancer and poison-control centers. The last of these serves not only to treat victims but also to supply information about antidotes for the many kinds of toxic chemicals now found in the bathroom closets and kitchen cabinets of every home.

Education is yet another new and highly important function of many community hospitals. The 517 hospitals that are affiliated with medical colleges would, of course, be expected to have teaching programs. But today about 850 nonaffiliated hospitals in all parts of the country serve as educational institutions where interns and nurses are trained, and resident physicians are prepared for entrance into their specialties.

The new position of the hospital has brought about a radical change in medical practice. As recently as 50 years ago, the hospital was almost exclusively the place where surgery was performed and where patients suffering from serious illnesses were eased through their most painful days. To send someone there for any other reason was viewed as a family disgrace, a callous abandonment of responsibility. Most people were born at home, remained there when they were sick or injured, and eventually died there. A physician kept regular office hours, but most of his practice consisted of house calls to treat patients in their own beds.

This pattern of patient care is now all but obsolete, a casualty of the phenomenal advances of medical science that have turned the short-term general hospital into the center of medical practice. Two elements made the change inevitable.

Expensive equipment and skilled men

First, proper diagnosis and treatment often require the use of elaborate, expensive equipment and the services of numerous laboratories and technicians. This technical support is increasingly being located inside the hospital, where a wide variety of facilities can easily be made available to a large group of physicians.

Second, since no one man can keep up with the progress on all fronts of medicine, the doctor frequently needs to seek the advice or assistance of colleagues with skills in particular areas of medicine. The same logic that made the hospital the assembly point for machines, laboratories and technicians makes it a convenient meeting place for the specialists the doctor relies on.

As the functions of the hospital broaden and become more complex, the size of both medical and nonmedical staffs grows steadily. In 1946, there were approximately 150 full-time hospital employees for every 100 patients. Ten years later, the ratio had grown to slightly over 200 workers per 100 patients, and by 1965, about 250 staff members were needed to take care of every 100 patients.

Merely admitting a patient to a large general hospital may involve at least a dozen staff members directly and a number of others indirectly. And if the case is complicated, as many as 30 physicians, technicians, nurses, dietitians and others may play a part in the care of just one patient during his stay at the hospital. How this many persons work together to serve him can be seen by following the steps in the treatment received by a patient who has been hospitalized with a common but very serious affliction, lung cancer.

The internist who has been caring for the man, having completed a preliminary diagnosis, reserves a room for him at the hospital and orders him to report there for positive identification of the disease and possible treatment. On the appointed day, the patient appears in the hospital lobby and is first sent to the admissions clerk, who fills out a registration form on which is recorded the patient's age, his place of

HORSE-DRAWN AMBULANCES, the predecessors of today's swift emergency vehicles, were used to rush accident and sunstroke victims *(opposite page)* to 19th Century hospitals. This 1894 illustration shows such an ambulance entering a New York hospital through a special entrance that led to an emergency room—a novelty for hospitals of that period. However, most people of that era mistrusted hospitals and preferred to summon the obliging family physician to their homes.

employment, the tentative diagnosis, the names of his physician and of his next of kin. The clerk is also likely to ask a number of questions about the patient's financial position, his hospitalization insurance and other matters affecting his ability to pay hospital bills. She must also call a dozen different persons, including the ward clerk, telephone operator and information clerk, and tell them that the patient has been admitted and give them his room number. This assures proper disposition of the visitors, mail, flowers and telephone inquiries that will soon be coming for the patient.

A nurse's aide now takes the patient to the floor and section to which he has been assigned. There he gives his admission form to the station clerk, who copies and enters some of its relevant data on the patient's medical record sheet. Finally, a nurse's aide escorts the patient to his room. As soon as he unpacks his suitcase he is examined by his own physician or a hospital resident, who enters his findings on the medical record and orders laboratory tests such as X-rays and blood and urine analyses. The preliminary steps, which required a small army of trained personnel, are now completed. And another sizable group is about to start its collaborative care of the patient.

The next day, the patient's personal physician, the internist, comes in to examine the X-rays. He, however, wants another opinion, and so he consults with a radiologist who has already seen the films. Both men agree that cancer seems likely. But more evidence is needed. A chest surgeon is summoned. He inserts a bronchoscope—a long, slender viewing instrument with a light on the end—down the patient's throat and into the bronchial tubes and studies the affected part. "It looks like cancer," the surgeon reports to the internist, but this is still not the final word. A pathologist now joins the team. Using a snip of lung tissue that has been extracted with special forceps, the pathologist slices off a very thin section, colors it with a stain that makes cancer cells stand out and examines the section with a microscope. His findings, the conclusive evidence, substantiate the previous diagnosis of the internist, radiologist and surgeon.

Graphing heart action

All four physicians discuss their observations together and agree that the lung must be removed, but before undertaking this radical surgery they order an electrocardiogram to learn what heart problems may arise. Still another group is needed to perform the operation. This team will be headed by the surgeon who collaborated in the diagnosis; it will also include two surgeon assistants, an anesthesiologist and two surgical nurses.

When the surgeon operates, he finds that the cancer has spread to the lymph nodes, and that too many organs are probably involved to make additional surgery feasible. The pathologist again examines the tissue taken from the area, and he concludes that the cancerous cells are of a type that can be treated with radioactive cobalt, a material that emits

HOSPITAL TREATMENT was drastic and crude but often effective by the close of the 19th Century. The apparatus shown here, used on sunstroke victims at New York's House of Relief, consisted of a traveling electric crane that could lift an unconscious, overheated victim in a net and dunk him—sometimes fully clothed—in a tub of ice water. The frigid bath reduced body temperature quickly, and modern emergency rooms still use a similar technique, wrapping the victim in wet sheets.

atomic rays capable of destroying cancer cells even though they are deep inside the body.

As soon as the patient has recovered sufficiently from the operation, the radiologist returns to give the cobalt treatments. He determines from X-ray studies what parts of the body will be treated, and calculates how much exposure to the radioactive rays will be necessary. When the patient reports for cobalt therapy, he is taken into a windowless room with walls about three feet thick, which prevent the powerful rays from escaping to harm the radiologist or other persons outside. In the center of this cell-like room is a treatment table; above it hangs the cobalt machine.

Harnessing atomic rays

Although it looks like an infernal device in a television spy story, the cobalt machine is a comparatively simple piece of apparatus. The heart of the machine is a stack of cobalt disks, each slightly larger than a dime, that have been made radioactive by being bombarded in an atomic pile. The disks are enclosed in a lead "pig," a sphere about two and a half feet in diameter. A small opening at the bottom of the pig is closed by a shutter when the machine is not in use. The pig is held by a thick steel arm and a vertical column in such a manner that it can be moved up and down and from side to side.

When the patient is stretched out on the treatment table, the radiologist raises or lowers the pig until it is aimed so that the cobalt rays will be focused on the site of the cancer. Then, before starting the treatment, the radiologist leaves the room; he must avoid repeated exposure to cobalt rays for they can injure or even eventually kill him. At the outside control unit, from which he can observe both the patient and the cobalt machine through a small, heavily shielded porthole, the radiologist sets the machine for desired time of exposure. The shutter of the cobalt machine then opens, permitting the invisible cobalt rays to strike at the cancerous cells; when the preset time has elapsed—the average time is five to seven minutes—the machine's shutter automatically closes and the treatment is ended.

The cobalt therapy may continue over an extended period of time. But if the patient's condition takes a downward turn—for example, because of a blood clot in the lung—he may be rushed to another part of the hospital, the intensive-care unit. Here the hospital has marshaled modern technology and the latest knowledge of medical science for last-ditch efforts to snatch human beings back from death.

Every patient in an intensive-care unit is going through a life-or-death struggle, but he does have a chance for survival. No one is sent there who has a recognized terminal illness for which there is no known cure —such as someone in the last stage of leukemia. The average stay in the unit is from three to five days; as soon as a patient is out of immediate danger, and no longer requires constant care, he is transferred to a room or ward in another part of the hospital.

In a moderately large community hospital the intensive-care unit may contain six beds, separated by waist-high partitions, inside a single room of approximately 25 by 35 feet. Since every patient is gravely ill and requires minute-to-minute observation, three nurses are on hand round the clock, one for every two patients, and an intern is always available. The nurses are on the permanent staff of the hospital (private-duty nurses do not serve here), and they are especially trained for this duty. In an emergency, a coded call over the public-address system brings physicians and residents within seconds. In addition to this remarkable concentration of trained personnel, help is supplied by a variety of machines—probably the largest single collection of complex devices to be found anywhere in the hospital. Sometimes these machines literally keep the intensive-care patient alive, taking over functions that his body cannot perform. Because they are so vital a part of the unit, the machines are checked constantly to make certain they are working properly. The apparatus is always in full view of the nurses, even when they are seated at their desks.

Some of these devices are assigned to individual patients. For example, above each patient's head is a shelf on which stands a cardiac monitor, an instrument that looks like a large TV cabinet with a small, round screen in the center. Across the screen flickers an undulating green line that reports on the activity of the patient's heart; wires attached to the body carry electrical messages that are transformed into the image on the screen. More wires, attached to electrodes either under the skin or on the patient's chest, may lead to another piece of electrical apparatus called a pacemaker, which controls the rate of his heart beat. Nearby, for use in case of a heart emergency, is a defibrillator, used when the cardiac monitor shows that parts of the heart muscle are contracting without coordination, a dangerous phenomenon known as fibrillation. The defibrillator shocks the heart with an electric impulse, stopping the organ momentarily; when it resumes beating, the contractions of the muscle are again coordinated.

Tubes that sustain life

Next to the patient's bed is an apparatus that indicates the blood pressure in both the arteries and veins. Another machine may be forcing air into the patient's lungs, breathing for him. A tube in his right arm may be giving him blood; another in his left arm feeds glucose; a third tube may go through his nose down into his stomach to wash it out; and still other tubes remove waste. The patient can be covered with a special, thermostatically controlled blanket that will maintain his temperature at any desired level.

Scarcely dreamed of only a generation ago, the lifesaving equipment found in the intensive-care unit has extended the capacity of the hospital in several ways. The combination of complex apparatus and teams of specialists, specially trained in its use, provides extraordinary care not only for routinely admitted inpatients, such as the hypothetical lung-cancer victim, whose treatments can be planned and scheduled in advance, but also for the unpredictable flow of the injured and sick who come to the hospital without warning. Nearly every community hospital operates an emergency clinic and most also have clinics for outpatients, people who take treatment at the hospital but return home between visits. The facilities and responsibilities of both these sections of the hospital have grown tremendously and sometimes overlap.

Midnight emergencies

When a patient calls his doctor late at night and reports symptoms that sound ominous, the physician is likely to order the patient to meet him at the emergency ward. "Both patient and doctor *have* to, indeed *want* to, meet in the emergency ward when acute illness strikes," writes Dr. John H. Knowles, general director of Massachusetts General Hospital. "The technology is readily available, as are the teams of specialists and experts. The chief reason for the ever-expanding use of the emergency ward is simply that it is today the best possible place in which to solve a medical problem quickly and accurately. The public knows it, and so does the doctor."

The emergency ward of one hospital in a Midwestern city is typical. The ward is located on the ground floor. It is reached from a side street by its own driveway, which enables ambulances and police cars to deliver stretcher-borne patients directly to the ward. In a busy 24-hour period, the staff of the ward may see as many as 75 persons.

There are usually a resident, an intern and a nursing staff of five on duty, and at least one surgeon in each specialty is on call in the hospital or at some location where he can be readily reached. The intern sees each patient who comes in and either treats him or turns him over to the resident, who may decide to call in a specialist—or even several specialists—for help.

There are five rooms in this hospital for examination and treatment. One of them is equipped with emergency facilities for cardiac cases, and another is used for cleaning and sewing up wounds and other minor surgery. There is a portable X-ray machine, and the diagnostic laboratories of the hospital are available. There are two general-treatment rooms and one for psychiatric cases. Patients in need of treatment that cannot be performed in the emergency ward, such as extensive surgery, are of course moved to other sections of the hospital.

The traditional role of the ward has been to provide swift care for victims of accidents and other emergency cases. It still performs this function, but now it makes use of more specialized medical knowledge and greatly improved technology.

On one winter night an ambulance driver delivers a man hurt in an automobile crash. He is unconscious and bleeding profusely. His left eye has been badly damaged, his chest crushed and his spleen ruptured. X-rays, quickly taken and developed, show a broken spine. A technician takes a sample of the man's blood to determine its type; transfusions will most certainly be needed. Meanwhile, the senior resident is on the telephone assembling a team for the operating room: an internist, a general surgeon, a chest surgeon, an eye surgeon, a neurosurgeon, perhaps several residents in those various specialties, an anesthesiologist and nurses. The internist or general surgeon will probably act as captain of the team and determine the order of surgery. If the patient is having trouble breathing, the chest surgeon may first perform a tracheotomy—cutting a hole in the windpipe—to bring air directly to the lungs. Then, as the general surgeon works on the ruptured spleen, the ophthalmologist may simultaneously operate on the damaged eye. Whether the chest surgeon or the neurosurgeon takes over next depends on which injuries pose the most immediate and greatest threat to life.

While this team works feverishly to save the life of the automobile-accident victim, other emergency cases stream into the ward. An elderly man, beaten by a gang of hoodlums, is helped into the emergency room by a passerby who saw him lying in an alley. A faded-blonde woman of indeterminate years is rolled in on a stretcher; "Sleeping pills, maybe 30 or 40," the ambulance driver says. A boy who fell from the third-story window of his family's apartment; a wife with three bullets in her chest, the result of a domestic quarrel; a fireman who stepped on a high-voltage wire while fighting a blaze in a warehouse; a terrified, almost uncontrollable alcoholic fighting off giant spiders that only he can see—these and others are brought to the emergency room. There is a steady flow of cases every night—but the numbers multiply on the weekends and on holidays when hard drinking inflames arguments and impairs driving skill.

The open-door clinic

Ambulance patients are not the only ones who come to the emergency clinic. Increasingly, this clinic and the outpatient clinics that often adjoin it and may share some of its facilities and staff, are becoming the havens for anyone needing medical care. Some people simply walk into a hospital clinic because they are newcomers to the community and have not yet found a local physician. Other patients are sent to the clinic by their own physicians, not as a middle-of-the-night expedient but as a routine procedure, particularly if the case is likely to require special equipment or assistance. Until recently, simple surgery—the suturing of a cut, the removal of a small skin tumor—was usually performed in the doctor's office. Even broken legs were often set there. Today such a straightforward treatment as the lancing of an infected ear is most likely to be carried out in a hospital clinic. The reason is simple: the clinic has the facilities—sterile instruments, X-ray machines, testing laboratories—as well as a variety of specialists who are less readily available in the office.

So heavily does the modern physician depend on the equipment and staff of the hospital that it often becomes his second base of operations. Some doctors go so far as to maintain their offices in the hospital itself, and many others practice from medical centers adjacent to it. In Columbus, Ohio, for example, an office building for physicians forms one complete wing of Riverview Methodist Hospital.

The vastly expanded functions of the hospital—the operation of clinics and laboratories, the collaboration with many specialists—have had a profound effect on its internal organization, which, in turn, influences the way the physician treats his patients. The rigid lines of authority within a hospital, similar to those in the army, have always been clearly defined and strictly enforced, but the recent multiplication of specialties has led to an even more compartmentalized organization of duties and responsibilities. One immediately apparent indication of the modern hospital's chain of command and division of duties is provided by the varied uniforms worn by hospital personnel. Even a casual visitor can often tell who does what just by looking at the clothing that the staff wears.

Dual chains of command

These distinctions in dress are only superficial marks of a fundamental division of duties that enables the large hospital to meet its responsibilities. At many modern hospitals, there are two separate but related chains of command. The hospital administrator no longer need be a physician; more often he is a university-trained layman with a master's degree in hospital administration. He is responsible for hiring nurses, purchasing equipment, providing beds and meals for patients, and supervising the nonmedical staff. A medical board, usually composed of senior staff physicians who head their specialty groups and a president elected by all the members of the medical staff, is in charge of all matters having to do with medical care. It assigns and supervises residents and interns, adjudicates disagreements and guards the quality of medical treatment.

The medical staff is subdivided into separate specialist groups, called "services," each headed by a chief of service who sits on the medical board. At a typical community hospital there may be seven services: medicine, surgery, obstetrics-gynecology, pediatrics, pathology, radiology and anesthesiology. Some of these may include more than one kind of specialist; dermatologists and cardiologists, for example, often belong to the medical service, while urologists and orthopedists are part of the surgical service.

This type of organization directly affects the treatments given patients, because each service may establish procedures to be followed by its member physicians. These standard procedures are often powerfully influenced by the chief of service. He is usually an experienced and respected specialist in his field, and he is also likely to be a strong-minded individual who imposes his concepts and methods on the entire service. A chief of internal medicine, for instance, may prefer that certain drugs be used for high blood pressure, or a chief of surgery may consider that a certain technique for making an incision is best for ulcer

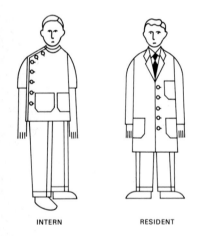

INTERN   RESIDENT

HOSPITAL UNIFORMS are a clue to duties in most such institutions. In one New England hospital, the white suit with a short high-collared jacket that buttons up the side *(left)* identifies an intern, newly graduated from medical college. More responsible tasks are assumed by the resident *(right)*, a specialist-in-training. He also wears a white suit, but the jacket is longer and, like a street coat, it buttons in front and has an open collar, permitting his shirt and tie to show.

operations. Whatever the chief's preferences, they usually become the standards of the hospital and are generally followed by the other physicians in his service.

Each service also acts as a kind of watchdog over its own area. For instance, the surgical service receives a laboratory report on all organs or tissue removed in an operation. If a surgeon removes a gallbladder that later is shown to have been perfectly sound, he will be called before his service to defend his decision to perform the operation. If he errs frequently or is suspected of performing needless surgery, he will probably lose his position on the staff and his right to operate in the hospital. Similarly, if an internist uses unorthodox therapy in a given case, he may be required to justify his choice of treatment before his colleagues in the service.

The division of treatment into services means that a patient in a hospital may be transferred from one physician to another, and then to still another—each of them, in succession, "his doctor," with authority over his care and responsibility for it.

In the past the family physician usually saw his patients completely through their illnesses and provided all the treatment they needed. If appendicitis struck, he not only made the diagnosis but also performed the appendectomy. Today he would call in a surgeon to do the operation. From the moment the surgeon takes such a case, he is legally and morally responsible for the patient; the surgeon's responsibility does not end until he releases the patient to the personal physician. This transfer of authority and responsibility is a common procedure in nonsurgical cases as well. For instance, if the hospital tests and diagnosis indicate that a patient's ailment is an allergy, the patient's internist will probably turn the case over to an allergist. The patient's doctor is usually consulted about treatment, but the allergist, like the surgeon, now assumes moral and legal responsibility for what is done during this phase of the treatment of the illness.

An "increasingly impersonal service"

This shuffling from doctor to doctor, service to service, laboratory to laboratory, often gives rise to bitter complaints by a hospital patient. He feels that everyone is treating him but no one cares what happens to him. "Both patient and doctor remain highly individualistic in their hospital needs," writes Dr. Knowles of the Massachusetts General Hospital in Boston, "but now, other people and other things are necessary for the best care of the patient. With the increasing subdivision of labor in all areas of the health profession, medicine has changed from an individual, intuitive, and intensely personal enterprise into a highly complex, interdependent, and increasingly impersonal service."

Impersonal the service in today's large hospital may be, and baffling and annoying as well—but it is effective as only specialized medical science can make it. No patient wants to go back to the good old days when he entered the hospital only as a last resort.

SENIOR VOLUNTEER   REGISTERED NURSE   JUNIOR VOLUNTEER

VOLUNTEERS AND NURSES can be identified by their attire. In one hospital the senior volunteer *(left)* dresses in an apricot-colored jumper and white blouse while helping in the gift shop or manning the information booth. The registered nurse *(center)* wears the traditional white uniform and cap. The type of cap denotes the nursing school she attended. A red-and-white striped jumper and white blouse distinguish the "candy striper" *(right)*, a teen-age volunteer.

The Man Whose
Heart Stopped

The time is 10:58 p.m. The place, the intensive-care unit of
St. Vincent's Hospital in New York City's Greenwich Village.
In the stillness of Room 463, a patient's heart suddenly sinks
into a random, ineffectual quivering called fibrillation. As the
heart stops pumping blood through veins and arteries, the
patient's pulse and breathing abruptly cease, his blood pressure plummets to zero and the pupils of his eyes dilate. Clin-
ically, he is already dead when a student nurse notices the
telltale signs. She cries to a nearby nurse, "*Code 99 . . . Code
99. . . .*"

This call will summon a specially trained team of doctors,
nurses and technicians from every floor of the hospital, for
there are still four minutes to bring the patient back to life,
four sweeps of a second hand before his brain breaks down
for lack of oxygen carried by the blood. In hospitals throughout the country, similar teams, called by such code names
as "Dr. Heart" and "Code Blue," are marshaling all the resources of modern medicine to bring human beings back from
the dead. St. Vincent's "Code 99" task force, summoned by
the young nurse, must undertake the most dramatic application of this new technique: restarting a heart that failed.

10:58:29

A switchboard operator takes the "Code 99" call relayed to her over a special

10:58:46

Doctors and nurses race through a corridor in response to the Code 99 call. Below, the first to arrive at Room 463 forces oxygen into the patient's lungs through a plastic tube. Within seconds, a specially trained nurse will take over this part of the job with an oxygen mask and a manual respirator.

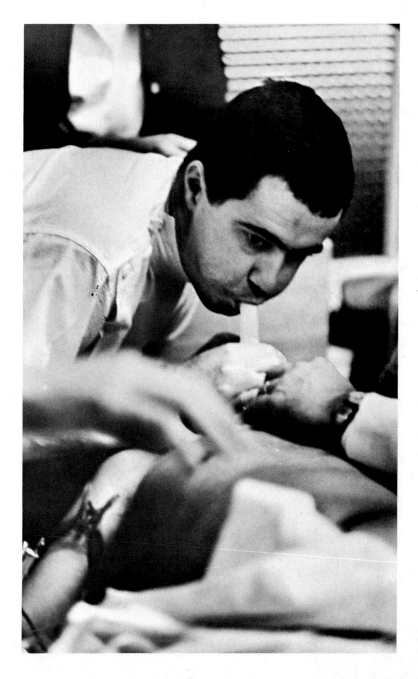

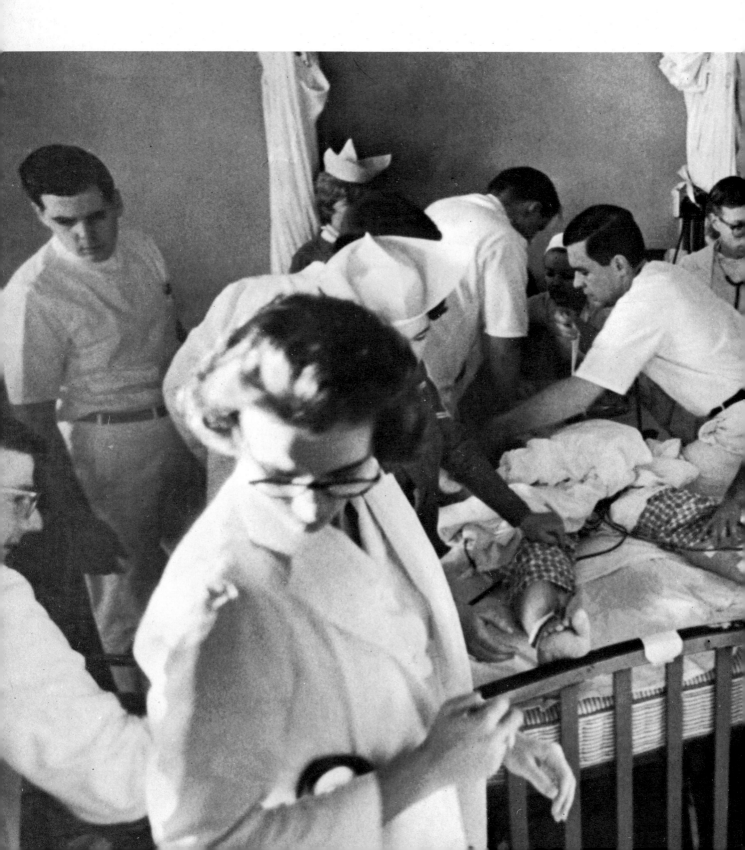

Some 25 doctors and nurses have now responded to the Code 99 call. Nurses and interns move other patients and all unnecessary equipment from the room, while the other team members work furiously to save the dying man. They must get air into the patient's lungs and blood into his brain; they must diagnose the cause of his heart failure; and they must get the heart working again. At the left of the bed, an intern presses his full weight repeatedly on the patient's chest to force blood from the heart through the arteries to the brain. Another intern attaches an electrode from an electrocardiograph (EKG) machine to the patient's wrist. The woman doctor in left foreground studies the EKG signals, seeking the sign that will tell them what step to take next.

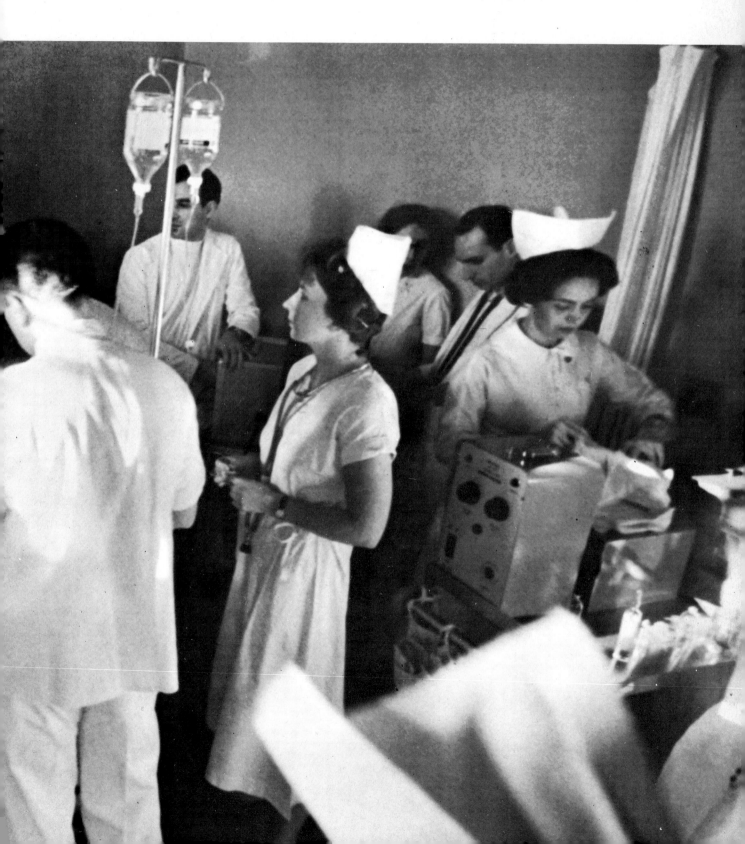

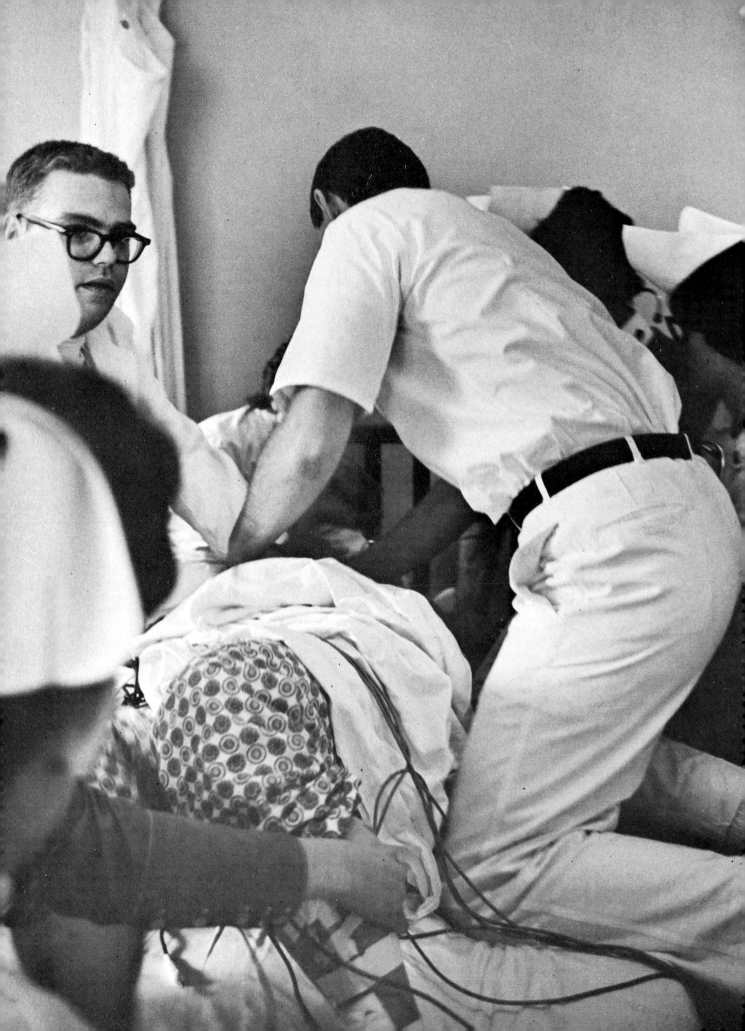

11:01:20

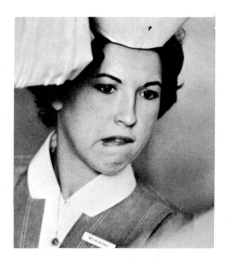

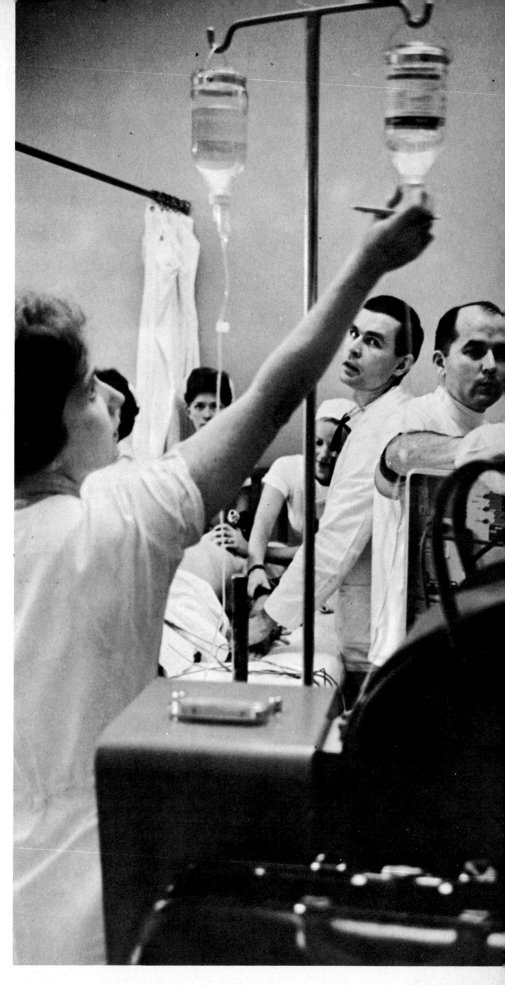

Biting her lip, the student nurse who sent the Code 99 watches the doctors. At right, glucose seeps into the patient's body. To this liquid, a doctor will add drugs to increase blood pressure. Meanwhile (left), an intern goes on squeezing the patient's heart between breastbone and spine with rib-cracking force. Said one patient later: "I feel like an elephant stepped on my chest."

11:02:26

Doctors and nurses confer anxiously (below), then decide upon a drastic course of action. To restore a normal heartbeat, a resident (right) positions a pair of electrodes and then, as nurses watch (above), sends 550 volts of electricity smashing through the patient for a tenth of a second. The patient's limbs twitch convulsively; at the height of the spasm his body arches up until only his head and heels touch the bed.

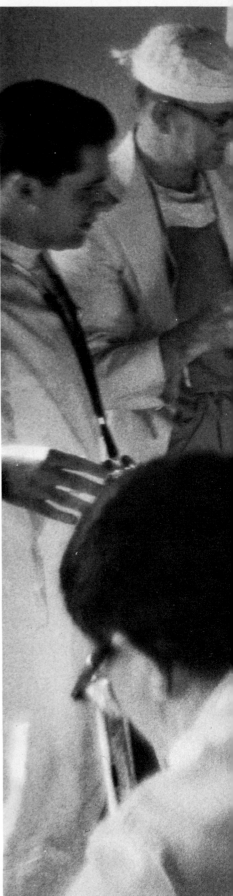

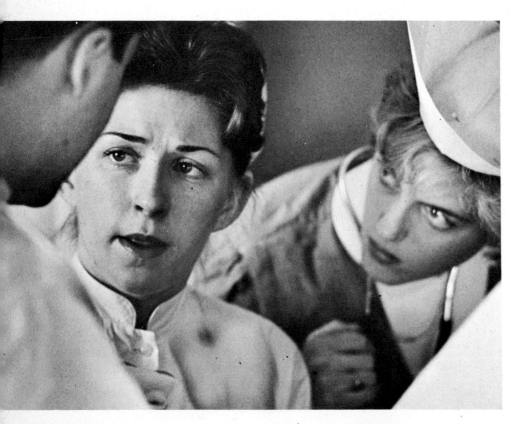

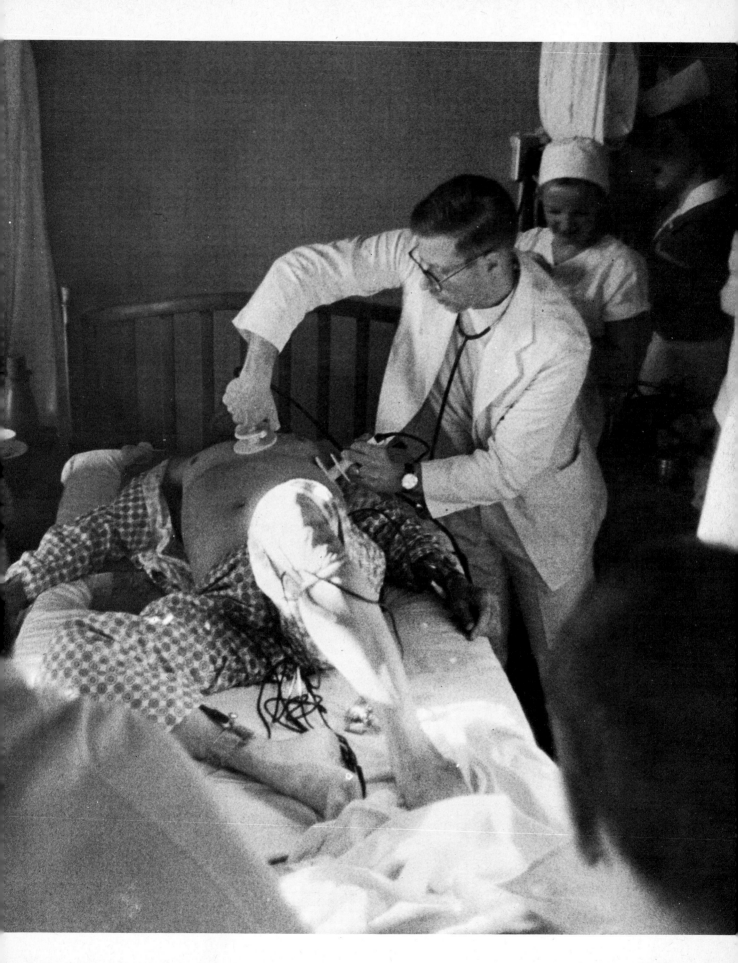

11:09:13

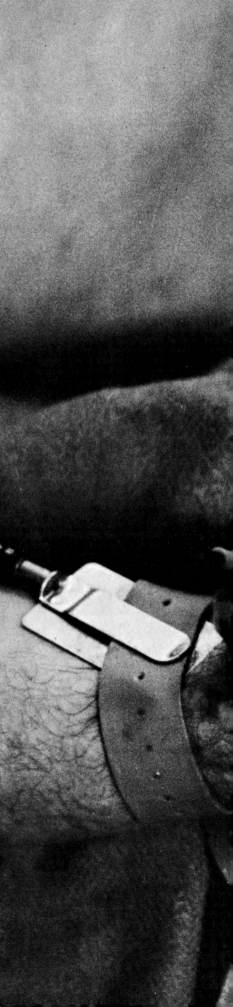

The shock technique works! Less than 15 minutes after the Code 99 alarm was sent, the revived man grasps the hand of his student nurse, a smiling symbol of life regained. Only the sophisticated combination of hospital equipment and teamwork can prevent the unnecessary deaths that often follow heart attack, respiratory failure, epileptic seizure and shock. One rescued patient, a vigorous 71-year-old now back at work as a printer, puts the case in a nutshell. "If I'd been sent home from work when the chest pains started, instead of the hospital, I'd be dead."

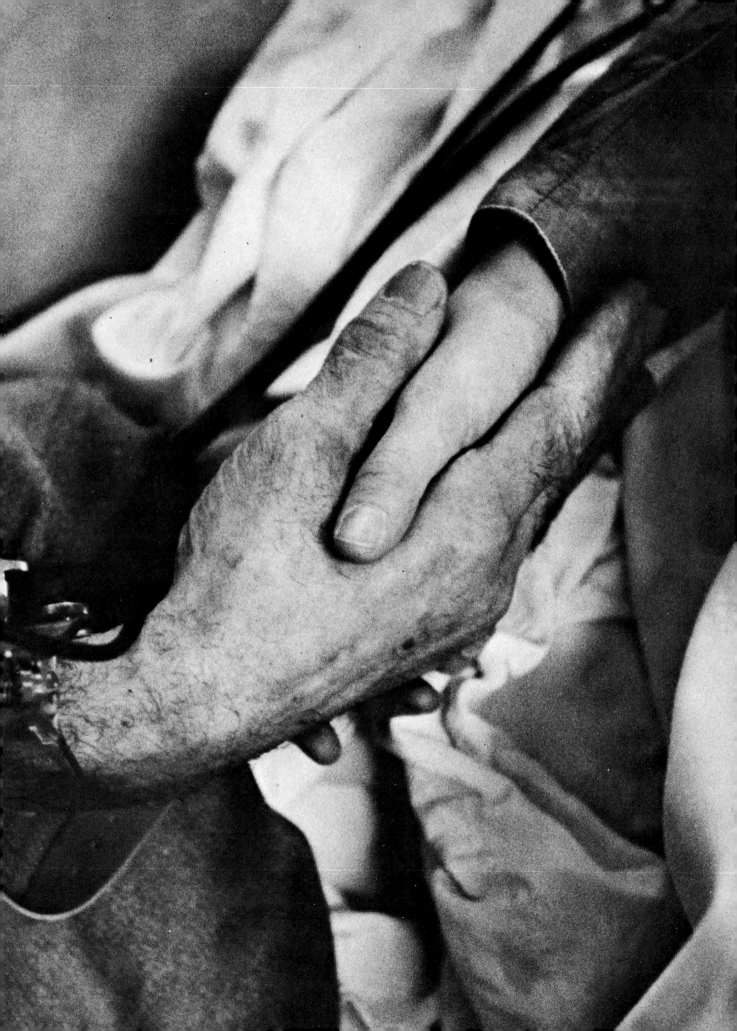

8

Who Shall Live, Who Shall Die?

This group of citizens, members of a Seattle, Washington, committee that selects the kidney-disease patients who will receive a special treatment, holds power of life and death. For without the treatment, the patients cannot live.

REGULARLY, two or three times a week, 70 men and women enter the Swedish Hospital in Seattle, Washington, for an overnight stay. During those 12 hours they lie in bed—reading, chatting, watching television or napping—while their blood is continually pumped out of their bodies into a complex filtering apparatus and back into their bodies again. This circuit is repeated over and over, perhaps 50 times during the night, until the blood is completely cleansed of impurities. In the morning the patients leave the hospital—the women to return to their homes and families, the men to their work as physicians, machinists, draftsmen, business executives and salesmen.

These brief visits cost close to $14,000 a year per patient and some of the patients have been coming to Swedish Hospital for as long as five years. They are resigned to the inconvenience and the expense. Without the regular blood-filtering treatments, every one of these men and women would be dead within two weeks. For all of them are victims of severe and irreversible kidney disease, and the filtering apparatus—a so-called dialysis machine—is actually an artificial kidney, which performs for them the vital purifying function their own kidneys are no longer capable of carrying out.

Serious kidney disease now strikes an estimated 5,000 to 10,000 Americans a year all of whose lives could probably, though not certainly, be prolonged by dialysis treatment. But only a limited number of patients can be accepted by Swedish Hospital, and those only from the Pacific Northwest. Another 125 or so American hospitals are equipped to serve a maximum of 1,100 people a year, and between 100 and 200 patients have home dialysis machines that they and their families have been trained to operate. While research continues on simpler and less expensive apparatus for both hospital and home use, the remaining kidney-disease victims are denied this lifesaving treatment; for all its usefulness it is so complex, and therefore so scarce and so expensive, that it cannot yet be provided to all who need it.

The plight of those who are left out illustrates one of the cruel dilemmas that perplex the physician today. His new knowledge and his steadily increasing technical skills have made him spectacularly successful in diagnosing and treating disease, in preserving health and averting death, in lengthening the life-span. But these very advances have brought with them equally spectacular problems—social, economic, scientific and ethical. There is, for example, the problem of cost. Many modern treatments, kidney dialysis, for example, are so expensive that improved methods of paying for them—insurance plans, prepayment schemes, government benefits and others still untried—must be devised to make certain that serious illness will not bankrupt the stricken person and his family. Inextricably linked with cost is the bewildering problem of the distribution of medical care, of providing the benefits of modern medicine to everyone—residents of slum and suburb, city and country. There is the awful problem of deciding how long and hard to struggle to offset the effects of usually fatal ailments, and of determining which lives are worth saving and which are past help. And as more and more people can be saved from death and as the world's birth rate rises, the population grows, raising concern not only over its size, but over its fitness and stamina as well.

Of all these problems, the one most people face most often is that of the cost of medical care. An operation as routine as the removal of the gallbladder cost approximately $1,200 in 1965: $510 for 10 days in the hospital, about $350 in surgeons' fees, about $125 for the internist, $85 for the anesthesiologist, and $120 for the various preoperative tests and examinations that are necessary.

Some of this cost is covered by the private medical insurance that now protects four out of five Americans. The typical policy pays the entire hospital bill, which accounts for almost half the total cost and provides $350 toward the physician's fees. But it allows nothing for the office visits, tests and examinations that preceded admission to the hospital. These uninsured charges—about $360 in this instance—have to be paid by the patient himself, subjecting him to an immediate and heavy expense.

A much greater sum may be needed for such involved medical treatment as an open-heart operation, which requires a long hospital stay, more expensive tests and higher doctors' bills. Most insurance policies cover the routine aspects of hospital care during that period, but the open-heart patient usually needs special treatment for which hospital insurance does not pay. Moreover, the physicians' fees in such a case are very high, perhaps $1,500 just for the surgeon. The total cost of an open-heart operation—which generally means three weeks in the hospital—can be as much as $5,000; the patient's direct out-of-pocket expenses may come to $1,000.

The cost of protracted illness

The most serious economic problem of all is that posed by extended illness. It quickly exhausts the financial benefits provided by the kind of medical insurance most people carry; only about 30 per cent of the population is covered either by all-inclusive prepayment plans or by the so-called "major medical" insurance that helps pay for lengthy and costly sickness. Yet such illness is common. The most common mental illness, schizophrenia, which afflicts about a half million Americans, often requires many years of expensive care in hospitals and outpatient clinics. Sufferers from deep-rooted neuroses must be wealthy to afford extensive psychoanalysis—a complete treatment for the average patient may take two to five years and cost from $8,000 to $20,000. A prolonged terminal illness such as cancer, with its lengthy hospital stays and repeated surgery, becomes a severe financial drain as well as a debilitating emotional crisis for the patient's family.

Hardest hit by the high cost of medical care are, of course, the poor. Although adequate treatment is, in theory, provided for them by clinic physicians and government-supported agencies, they actually enjoy fewer of the benefits of modern medicine than do other Americans. The poor receive less than the average amount of care (and, in the opinion of most observers, less expert care). A survey conducted by the U.S. Public Health Service shows that families with a yearly income of less than $4,000 send their children to doctors only slightly more than half as often as do families with higher incomes. The poor have shorter life-spans and they are subject to more illness than the middle class and the well-to-do. Perhaps the most depressing figures are those comparing the health of white citizens with that of Negroes, who are especially likely to live in poverty. The infant mortality rate among Negroes is nearly twice as high as among whites; the maternal mortality rate nearly four times as high. In 1964 the life expectancy for a Negro boy at birth was 61.1 years; for a white boy it was 67.7 years.

Where the doctors are

The difficulty of assuring adequate care for the poor is only part of the larger problem of the distribution of medical services. Even patients who are relatively well-off cannot always obtain the attention they need, for hospitals and doctors are not equally distributed throughout the country. In the Northeastern states the ratio of private physicians to population is almost half again as high as it is in the Southern ones: for every 100,000 people, the Northeast has about 112 doctors, whereas the South has about 80. Regardless of geography, urban areas have about three times as many doctors as rural sections: in the countryside there are 44 doctors in private practice for every 100,000 people as against 118 per 100,000 of population in the major cities. Specialists, particularly, are likely to open their offices in metropolitan centers. Of all the psychiatrists in the United States, 20 per cent are in the New York-New Jersey metropolitan area, which contains no more than 9 per cent of the nation's population.

The interrelated problems of the distribution and cost of medical services are, of course, far from new. Some solutions have already been provided by various governmental actions and through the efforts of doctors themselves. Since ancient times physicians have given their services without charge to those who cannot afford to pay; they are the only professionals who irrevocably and as a matter of course commit themselves to such a donation of skill. More recently they have developed the new patterns of practice described elsewhere in this book: by organizing in groups and clinics and centering their work in the hospital rather than the office, they have taken steps to make medical care more efficient and more readily available to those who need it. In pioneering prepayment schemes like the Kaiser Plan and the Health Insurance Plan of Greater New York, physicians have shown how costs can be more easily borne.

These voluntary efforts to make better care more widely available were supplemented by the federal government in 1965 with the passage of the Medicare Act, which set up a program of hospital and medical insurance for all Americans past the age of 65. Governmental responsibility for medical treatment on such a broad scale was an innovation in the United States, but it has long been firmly established in many other countries. In Europe nearly every nation has a governmental health program that directly or indirectly provides a broad range of medical services to everyone.

One of the most radical and inclusive of these national medical plans is Great Britain's, which has been in effect since 1948. Every Briton must support the program through his tax payments and nearly everyone uses it. Although physicians are not compelled to join, 98 per cent of the general practitioners and a great majority of specialists participate in it. Medicine in Great Britain is to a large extent the medicine practiced under the National Health Services Act.

Great Britain's health program

By the terms of that Act, the British government assumes responsibility for every individual's health care and pays for nearly all medical and dental treatment, largely out of tax funds. The government pays physicians for their services and underwrites the expense of all the care the patient receives with certain minor exceptions. Almost every health benefit—from hospitalization through laboratory tests to treatment in the physician's office—is completely free. This applies not only to British subjects, but to every resident of Britain and in some cases even to travelers passing through the country.

While the British program pays all the bills, it does not dictate the treatment the physician shall administer, or assign physicians to patients. The patient chooses his own doctor. Once he has made a choice, he enrolls in that physician's "list" by signing a card. Then he can make office visits as often as he wishes. If he becomes dissatisfied with his doctor, he can sign up with another.

But if the patient has full freedom to accept or reject a physician, the physician does not have a comparable right. Once he has joined the program, he cannot refuse any patient who applies for a vacancy on his list, nor can he discharge a patient he believes he ought not continue treating. He conducts his practice almost as if he were a government employee hired to serve the general public. Although he meets his patients in his own office, he is paid from government funds mainly on the basis of the number of patients he sees. He receives a flat annual stipend plus $2.80 a year for each patient on his list ($3.90 for a patient over 65)—whether he sees that patient once or 50 times. In addition, he may also see fee-paying private patients. But the limitations set up by the Health Plan on the physician's relationship with his "list" patients have aroused severe criticism among American physicians, most of whom believe that the British program seriously infringes on the doctor's freedom to practice medicine as he thinks best.

More conservative systems of medical benefits, closer to the U.S. Social Security program than to Britain's National Health Services, have

ROUTINE SERVICES (10-day stay)		SPECIAL SERVICES	
NURSING CARE	$99.50	OPERATING ROOM	$77.50
MEALS	44.00	CHEST X-RAY	10.00
CLEAN LINEN	12.10	BLOOD COUNT	7.25
CLEAN ROOM	19.90	URINALYSIS	2.50
UTILITIES	37.80	ANESTHESIA	10.00
ADMINISTRATION	72.10	BIOPSY	12.00
MEDICAL RECORD	7.00	VARIOUS TESTS	49.00
MISCELLANEOUS	7.60	MEDICATION	41.75
TOTAL	$300.00		$210.00

HIGH HOSPITAL COSTS, a financial headache only partly cured by medical insurance plans, bring the average charge for a routine gallbladder operation to about $510 —exclusive of physicians' and surgeons' bills. As shown in the list at right above, fees directly related to treatment—laboratory tests, operating room use, medication—make up only about 40 per cent of the sum. Approximately 60 per cent of the charges are for routine services *(left)*, such as food, room and ordinary nursing. These routine costs, which have nearly doubled since 1950, are mainly responsible for the recent steep increases in hospital bills.

been adopted in such European countries as West Germany, Denmark and Sweden. These governments assume responsibility for each citizen's health, but pay part rather than all of his medical expenses, and make that payment out of separate insurance funds rather than out of general tax receipts.

Medicine in Sweden

The scheme in force in Sweden is generally considered one of the most efficient and effective anywhere. Every Swede is covered by the country's National Health Insurance Program, which receives about half its support from annual premiums, averaging $14, which citizens pay along with their income taxes. The other half of the program's support comes from employers and from the government's tax revenues. This fund provides each policyholder and his family with a wide range of medical benefits: free hospital care; a small living allowance when illness incapacitates the policyholder; part payment for drugs; and part payment for all doctor bills. The Swedish program also gives the patient full freedom of choice of his physician, who may be either a government medical officer or a private practitioner.

The Swedish program stipulates a standard fee for every treatment and reimburses the patient for three fourths of that fee. If a patient goes to a government medical officer, the fee will be the standard one, and the patient pays one quarter of the sum while three quarters is paid by his insurance policy. If, on the other hand, he elects to go to a private practitioner, who can set fees as he chooses, the patient may have to pay more out-of-pocket, since he will be reimbursed only for three quarters of the standard fee.

The Swedish method of easing the financial burden of illness contains many features of medical practice that are traditional in the United States. It combines public and private responsibility for care, while giving latitude to the patient in his choice of a physician and to the physician in his conduct of his practice.

In the United States, patients have always taken for granted their right to select their own physicians, and physicians have rigorously defended their right to choose the pattern of practice they want to follow. Conversely, American patients have always assumed that they have an obligation to pay for the medical services they receive, if they have the means to do so.

While traditional rights and obligations have been altered by such relatively new developments as the advent of medical insurance and group-practice arrangements, the changes have been comparatively minor. Group practice, for example, involves some limitation on freedom of choice—for both physician and patient. A patient who seeks medical treatment from a group is most likely to be cared for only by the generalists and specialists who practice in that group. And physicians working in a group usually send their patients to specialists who are members of the same group. But this loss of freedom is more theoretical than real.

Even if a patient's personal physician is in private practice, his suggestions as to the specialists the patient should consult are almost always followed. And no responsible physician would join a group practice if he felt that the colleagues with whom he was working were incompetent. Similarly, the advent of doctor-bill insurance has altered payment methods. Before insurance became available, the patient paid his physician directly and in full for medical services: the transaction was not unlike the usual and traditional one between any customer and merchant. But the patient with doctor-bill insurance makes regular payments to the insurance company. Since these payments cover a significant part of his medical fees, the amount he pays the doctor directly is considerably decreased.

Side by side with the American tradition of individual freedom and responsibility exists the long-standing tradition that the government, acting for society as a whole, has a profound responsibility for the nation's health. The federal government has always made contributions toward this end, both in money and in services. Members of the armed forces have always been provided with medical care, and in 1798 hospitals for merchant seamen were established.

As the nation grew and medicine became more complex, so did the governmental role in the nation's health. Federal and state governments now undertake at least a part of the burden of training physicians by their support of medical schools, and most large cities have at least one municipal hospital, supported entirely by the city treasury and operated by the city health department.

Medicare: an American solution

With the passage of the Medicare Act, the federal government took its most radical step toward active and direct intervention in a national program of medical care. Medicare's broad outlines follow the tradition of American medicine. It is an insurance plan, under which individuals and government share responsibility for payments, and it guarantees patients the right to choose their physician and physicians the right to practice as they see fit.

But in one respect, Medicare represents a real break with the traditions of the past. For the first time Americans are compelled to participate in a national health program—a program of hospital insurance to which workers, government and employer all contribute. No one can be forced to take advantage of Medicare but everyone must contribute to its support.

The benefits, offered to everyone over 65, are extensive. For each spell of illness, they provide 90 days of hospitalization in a semiprivate room, at a direct cost to the patient of only $40 for the first 60 days, and at a cost of $10 a day for the next 30. In addition, they cover the total cost of routine nursing services, drugs and diagnostic services in the hospital. For hospital services beyond these—such as special nurses or conveniences like telephone and television—the patient must pay the hospital's regular fees. Medicare also underwrites up to 100 days of care in a nursing home, and in a separate optional program, reimburses patients for part of their doctor bills.

The passage of the Medicare bill is a step toward solution of one of the most pressing social problems with which the physician is now faced. The elderly are usually the least able to afford extended, complex medical treatment, and yet they need more such care than other persons. The problem is made more acute, paradoxically, by the very success of the physician in treating disease. As the illnesses that once struck down the young have been conquered, more and more people have survived to old age, and the number of old persons who must be cared for has increased tremendously. More Americans past the age of 65 are alive today than ever lived to reach that age in the history of the United States; in 1900 the elderly comprised 5 per cent; in 1966 they made up 9 per cent of the nation's population.

Not only are people living longer, they are also being born in greater numbers. World population, if it continues its present explosive growth, will double by the year 2000 and quadruple by the year 2050. These numbers will so strain food resources that in the opinion of some authorities, major famines are in prospect. How much of this problem can be attributed directly to modern medicine is a matter of controversy. (The rate of population growth is, oddly enough, greatest in underdeveloped countries where medical care is primitive.) But it is indisputable that the lifesaving successes of medical science have played a sizable role in creating this pressing social crisis, and physicians are taking the lead in efforts to resolve it. They are intensifying research on simple and effective methods of birth control and pressing for social measures that will help limit population expansion.

Nor is the world's population problem a problem of quantity alone; it is a problem of quality, too. At the worst it raises the question of the fitness for survival of the future inhabitants of the earth; at the best, it is a question of how to solve the new medical problems that are likely to arise.

Survival of the unfit?

The conquest of the serious infections, for example, has meant survival for large numbers of babies who were born with weak constitutions or the kind of defects that would, in the past, have doomed them to early death. A white baby boy born in the United States in 1900 had a 76 per cent chance of surviving past the 20th year of life; a white boy born in 1965 had a 96 per cent chance. As more people survive the perils of infancy and grow into adulthood, there is a corresponding increase in the number of people who live long enough to marry and have children of their own. Instead of succumbing to their hereditary weaknesses, more and more people are enabled to perpetuate their defects. Juvenile diabetes, for example, was once a fatal disease. Until the isolation of insulin in 1922, a diabetic child was not likely to live long enough to

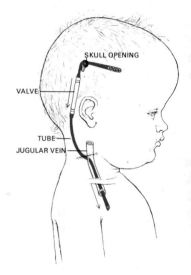

A DRAIN IN THE BRAIN is a new lifesaving device that raises unanswerable ethical questions about whether or not to use it. The tube was designed for children with hydrocephalus, in which an accumulation of fluid squeezes the brain and can lead to blindness, severe mental retardation and death. The excess fluid can be eliminated by implanting the device inside the child's body: the tube's valve opens under pressure and drains fluid, which flows through the tube and jugular vein to the heart, where it is carried away in the bloodstream. The tube saves a hydrocephalic child from almost certain death—but cannot always forestall mental retardation.

become a parent who might transmit his metabolic defect to future generations. Today juvenile diabetes has become no more than a handicap. Diabetics marry and raise families, and the number of people who carry within them the predisposition to this disease is therefore believed to be growing constantly. In much the same way, it is possible that other hereditary tendencies to illness are being bred into the population.

Contemplating the prospect of a human race steadily degraded by its own skill in sustaining its weaker members, some experts are dismayed. Dr. Herman J. Muller, the Nobel Prize-winning geneticist of Indiana University, foresees a distant but dismal future when so many people will require so much constant and complex care that this task will demand all the resources of society, and whatever civilization exists will be concerned exclusively with therapy.

This pessimistic view is not shared by most scientists. They believe that the laws of evolution and human skill may work together to maintain a human population well fitted for its environment. But they also recognize that this endeavor will inevitably meet with difficulties. As René Dubos of The Rockefeller University has said: "For the first time in the history of living things, we are allowing the survival of large numbers of biological misfits. . . . [Modern medical practices,] enlightened and successful as they are, may create new disease problems for generations to come."

Decisions of life and death

Similar problems—and the awful ethical questions they bring in their wake—already confront the physician today. Modern medicine can sometimes keep even the most desperately ill alive—can keep the body going long after it has become incapable of sustaining life by itself. Even when the heart has stopped, its beat can be restored and maintained by drugs and machines. People can survive—as vegetables—for months and even years.

How long should extraordinary effort be lavished on apparently hopeless cases? This is a question that the physician cannot answer but that he must face all too often. Every doctor knows the meaning of these words from a desperately ill patient: "You won't let me down when the time comes, will you, doctor?" And he knows what the patient's relatives mean when they ask: "How much longer can this go on?" Yet a little bit longer might be enough to save a human being who seems lost. Perhaps a cure or treatment will be found. Or perhaps the case is not as hopeless as it appears.

Repeatedly, men have been rescued from what seemed certain death by physicians' faith in their own skills, in medical science and in the great endurance of the human body. One of the most notable and unusual of such cases is that of Lev Davidovitch Landau, the noted Russian physicist.

One wintry day in 1962, Landau was riding in the back seat of an automobile a few miles outside of Moscow when the driver, swerving to avoid a little girl who had suddenly darted across the road, collided with an oncoming truck. Neither the truck driver nor the chauffeur was seriously hurt. But Landau, in the back seat, took the full force of the crash.

When he was brought to the hospital, he was unconscious and barely breathing, and his body was covered with blood. One description of his condition read like a "Dead on Arrival" report. Any one of five severe injuries he had endured should have been enough to have caused death all by itself.

Back from the grave

His physicians refused to accept defeat. According to some reports, Landau's heart stopped beating four times—and four times he was pulled back from the grave. For over a month he was in a coma, without even the basic reflexes. For seven weeks, an artificial breathing apparatus was required to supply his system with oxygen. He remained paralyzed for months.

Nine months after the accident, Landau sat up in bed and talked with the Swedish Ambassador to the U.S.S.R., who had come to the injured man's hospital room to inform him that he had been awarded the Nobel Prize in Physics for 1963. Three years later, according to official Russian reports, Landau was even further improved. He could not straighten the fingers of his left hand, and his right foot was useless. But he had been discharged from the hospital and was back at home with his wife and family. He could get himself out of bed, with the aid of a special railing, and could walk unaided. His vision, which had remained impaired until the spring of 1966, later improved so much that he could read. But he was unable to return to full-time work, and he never resigned himself to his handicaps. A month before his death in 1968, he told an interviewer: "I can walk. I can talk to friends, I can read. But I do not have the courage to resume other activities. Today, I am an ignoramus."

To treat Landau, outstanding physicians from many countries had been summoned. The medical team included Russian neuropathologist Nicolai Grachenkov; Gerard Guillot and Marie Garcin from France; Sdenek Kunz from Czechoslovakia; and Wilder Penfield of the Montreal Neurological Institute. Medication not available in the U.S.S.R. was flown to Landau from all over the world. His fellow scientists took turns at giving him nursing care.

In Landau's case the great effort was successful. But who can know—in advance—when similar expenditures of talent and resources are justified? Who can decide how far to go to fan the breath of life? That decision is not only the physician's to make. For the social, ethical and scientific problems that arise from modern medicine and its advances are never the concern of the physician alone. They are the concern of the entire society, and their solution is the responsibility of everyone.

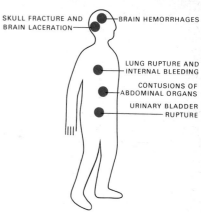

SKULL FRACTURE AND BRAIN LACERATION — BRAIN HEMORRHAGES

LUNG RUPTURE AND INTERNAL BLEEDING

CONTUSIONS OF ABDOMINAL ORGANS

URINARY BLADDER RUPTURE

IN A MEDICAL MIRACLE, Lev Landau *(top),* one of Russia's greatest physicists, was saved by doctors after a 1962 automobile accident left him deaf, dumb, blind and paralyzed. At least five of his many serious injuries, indicated in the drawing, could have been fatal. Revived from clinical death four times in the first 11 days, Landau later battled such deadly complications as pneumonia, uremia and body temperatures as high as 107° F.—and survived to resume some daily activity.

Assault
on the Killers

As today's ingenious medical researchers create revolutionary methods for prolonging life, ailments that once meant certain death may soon be considered routinely curable. Some of the new devices and techniques that are being perfected recall the fantasies of science fiction. Icy lances, colder than the dark side of the moon, freeze and kill deeply embedded brain tumors *(opposite)*. At the other extreme of temperature, rays hotter than the surface of the sun destroy more accessible malignant tissue. Plastic valves now operating in human hearts may herald completely synthetic hearts made of silicone rubber and driven by portable atomic-power plants. This innovation may one day drastically reduce the number of deaths caused by heart disease —now the nation's leading killer.

Looking beyond man-made spare parts, physicians are exploring the use of living substitutes for outworn organs. Animal livers are being tested as temporary replacements for diseased human counterparts. Eventually, surgeons may use entire organs from the dead as substitutes for the failing organs of the living, much as a mechanic replaces a worn-out automobile or airplane engine with a new one.

A FROSTBITTEN BRAIN

Ice crystals frost the tip of a needle chilled to −321° F. as it probes deeply into a patient's brain, freezing the tissue near its target—a malignant tumor. This new low-temperature technique, called cryosurgery, has also been employed to destroy the malfunctioning brain cells that cause such crippling nerve ailments as Parkinson's disease.

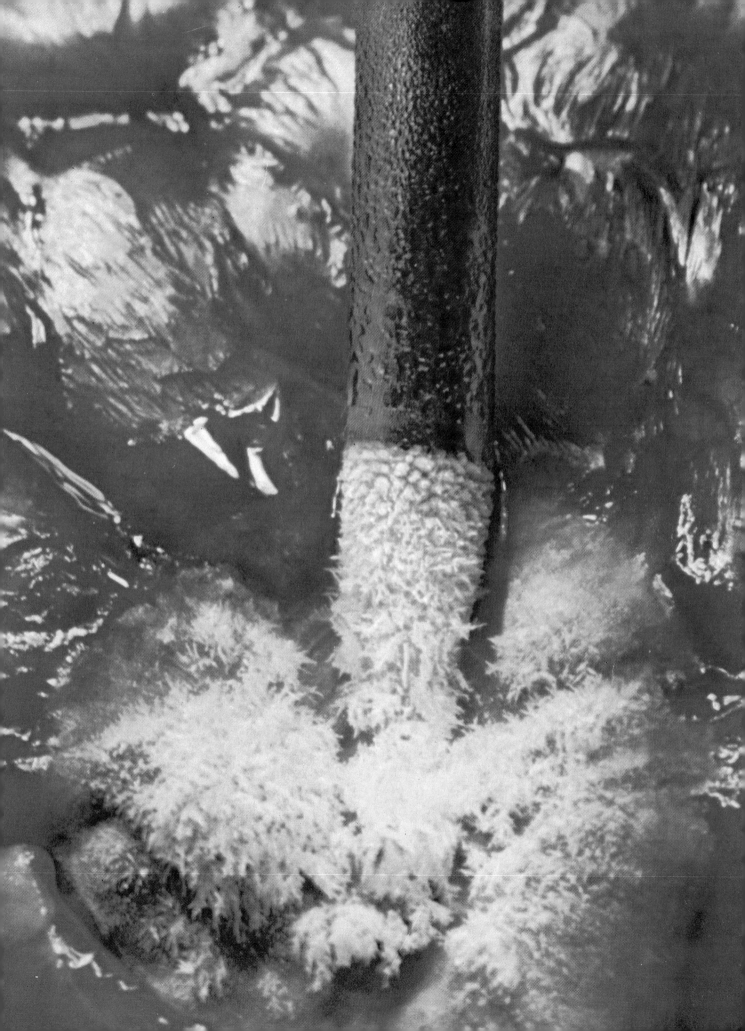

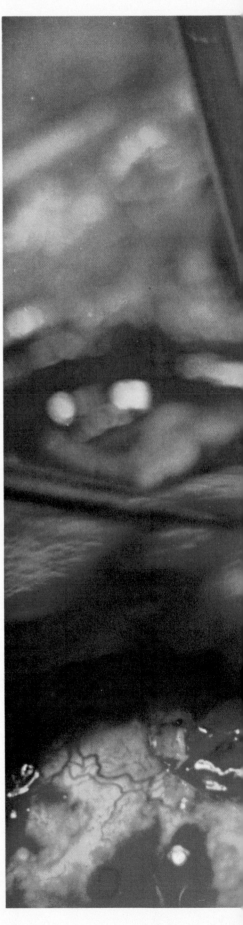

ZEROING IN ON THE TARGET
French neurosurgeon Jacques Le Beau lowers a nitrogen-filled needle through a guiding device centered over a brain tumor. The guide must help aim the needle through overlying tissue since the surgeon's hand is not steady or accurate enough to perform the operation unaided.

A WINDOW INTO THE BRAIN
Dr. Le Beau lifts away a piece of tissue to make a "window" into the recesses of the brain where the tumor is lodged. By freezing this unessential tissue before cutting it away and lifting it out, he can prevent hemorrhaging of surrounding tissue during the course of the operation.

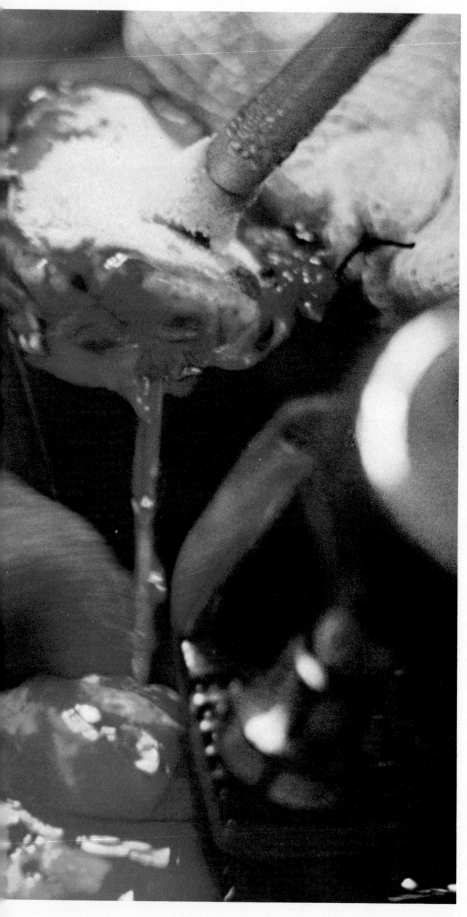

Operating with an Icy Needle

The difficulty and hazard that have long accompanied brain operations are now being removed by increased knowledge of the brain and by improvements in diagnosis and surgery. Several of these new techniques employ radical devices to lessen a risk that has always concerned the neurosurgeon. As he cut away diseased tissue, he often damaged surrounding healthy cells. To reduce this hazard, one new method, cryosurgery, freezes tissue temporarily instead of killing it immediately. The surgeon can stop in mid-course, test the patient's faculties and—if undesirable complications are developing—thaw out the frozen tissue.

In beginning a cryosurgical braintumor operation, the surgeon cuts open the skull. Then a hollow needle, filled with liquid nitrogen, is inserted into the brain until the tumor is reached. The nitrogen—its temperature –321° F.—cools the needle's tip, and the tip, in turn, freezes the brain cells on contact. But since the degree of chilling can be controlled, the tissue is first quick-frozen to a relatively mild 14°F.—cold enough to numb cells but not to kill them. At this crucial point the freezing is reversible.

The patient, awake under the local anesthetic, is told to repeat a tongue twister, make a fist or move his limbs. If he cannot do these things the surgeon knows he has struck vital tissue near the tumor. He lets the cells thaw, then refreezes the tumor from different angles, repeating the procedure until the patient's reactions are normal. Only then is the brain tumor destroyed by deep-freezing.

A Searing Beam of Light

The woman in the photograph below, dying of an incurable skin cancer, volunteered for a trial of an operation that may some day help other cancer victims. Above her in a Boston laboratory, Dr. Paul McGuff controls a laser, a new device that emits light so tightly concentrated that its energy generates extremely high temperatures. The searing pulse of laser light, lasting less than 1/1,000 of a second, burns away a tiny tumor on the patient's neck. The exposure to the beam is so brief that the patient feels no more pain than might be inflicted by a pinprick, yet the surface

tumor is destroyed by the radiation.

The future of the surgical laser is by no means assured. Physicians are intrigued by the speed, accuracy and painlessness of the device they call the optical knife, but not all of its effects on human tissue are yet known. Some doctors believe that the laser treatments may cause undesirable results; a few fear that lasers may actually induce cancer in human tissue rather than cure it. Even those who are more optimistic agree that years, perhaps decades, of intensive research will be needed before all the questions involved can be answered.

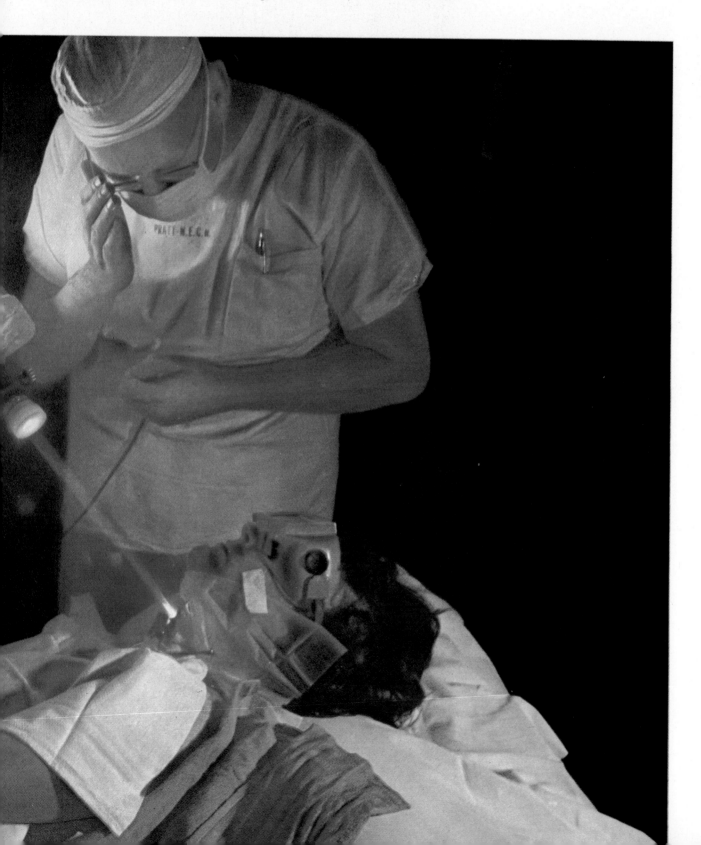

Prolonging Life with a Pig's Liver

A 34-year-old woman, her diseased liver unable to perform its thousands of life-supporting functions, falls into a coma; untreated, she will be dead in hours. But in a nearby room of the hospital, as part of an experimental operation called a perfusion, surgeons are removing a pig's liver in an attempt to prolong this woman's life. The pig's liver will, for a few hours, substitute for her own, permitting the human organ to rest and perhaps recover its ability to handle all its functions.

When this perfusion was ended, the woman's own liver had recuperated sufficiently to work by itself for a time. The next day she sat up in bed, chatted and watched television. Her improvement was only temporary, for her liver was too diseased to reap any permanent benefit from the time out. However, a series of five perfusions did prolong her life for 18 days.

Despite the very limited success in this case, doctors believe that a liver less ravaged by disease might have recovered completely. And what is possible for a liver should be possible for some other organs. Physicians foresee a time when several different kinds of animal organs—organs too complex in their functions to be duplicated by mechanical devices—will be temporarily mated to human bodies while their diseased, human counterparts are rested or repaired.

READYING A SUBSTITUTE LIVER

A team of Harvard Medical School researchers removes the liver of an anesthetized pig *(above)* at Boston City Hospital. The surgeon at the right cauterizes the pig's blood vessels with an electric needle to prevent hemorrhaging, which would render the liver useless. Moments after the excised liver has been placed in a tray, surgeons *(below)* insert tubes through which the human patient's blood will flow. The pig liver is now ready to be rushed to the bedside of the patient, where it will temporarily carry on the numerous functions of the human liver.

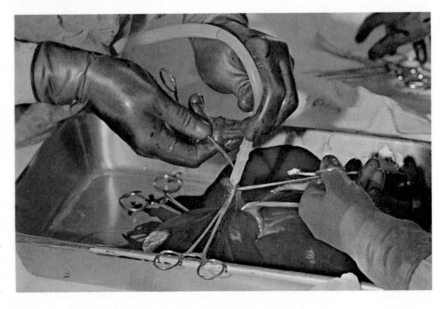

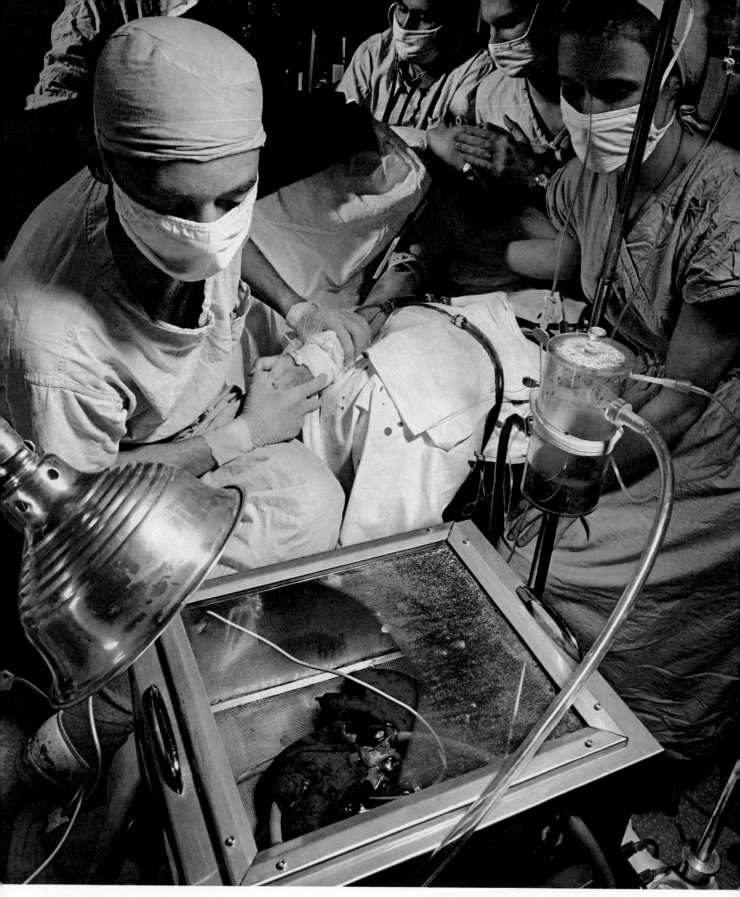

THE BORROWED LIVER AT WORK

During the period that the patient's own liver is allowed to rest, her blood is routed to the pig's liver for purification. The blood flows from an arm artery through the tube on the towel *(center)* and into a glass reservoir, where a chemical called heparin is added to prevent the blood from clotting. The purplish tube at lower right then takes the blood into the pig's liver. After leaving the pig's liver, the blood is cleansed of heparin, then returns to the patient through a vein in her arm. The lamp at left keeps the liver at the pig's own body temperature.

A PART AND ITS PLACEMENT

The action of a caged-ball valve, one of several types of synthetic heart valves, is shown at right. At first, the ball blocks the passage between the upper and lower portions of a glass tube. Liquid pumped from below forces the ball upward in the second picture. In the third and fourth pictures, the ball is moved to the top of its cage, allowing liquid to flow through. When pumping stops, the ball will return to its first position. In the picture below a surgeon is inserting this type of valve in a heart, guiding it with sutures which will hold the valve in place.

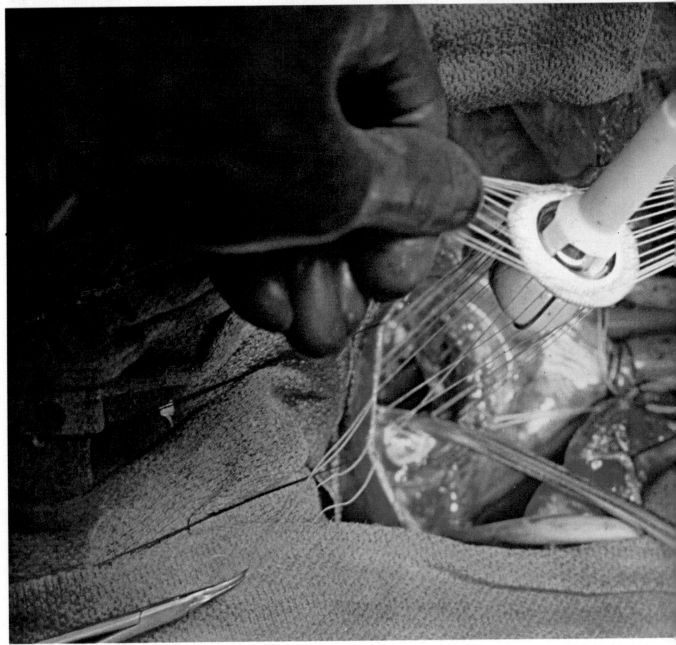

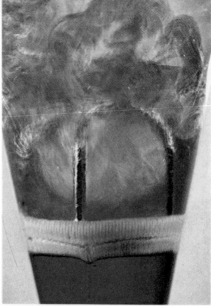

Valve Job
for a Heart

One of the physician's most dramatic victories over disease is his newly found and growing ability to repair the ravages of heart ailments, such as those caused by defective heart valves. If a valve does not close completely, the heart becomes an inefficient pump. It must then work so hard to keep up with its load that it may fail. Today, the victims of faulty valves can be saved by an operation, shown here, that replaces a diseased valve with a synthetic substitute.

Few surgical procedures require more complicated equipment, more precise timing, more accurate incisions. At the start, the patient is connected to instruments which keep track of such vital functions as pulse rate and blood pressure. Then, while one surgeon inserts a tube into an artery in the patient's hip, another opens the patient's chest and plugs a double tube into the two veins of the heart. The vein and artery tubes disconnect the patient's heart and lungs from his circulatory system; blood flows through the vein tube and into a "heart-lung machine," which performs both aeration and pumping functions, then back through the artery tube into his hip and the rest of his body. Only when the machine is operating and the heart bypassed do the surgeons open the heart itself. Now they remove the diseased valve and replace it with a synthetic one. This done, they retrace their steps, first taking the heart-lung machine out of the patient's circulatory system and permitting his own heart to resume its function.

The two- to three-hour operation calls for some 15 doctors, technicians and nurses working together with the coordination and teamwork of a ballet troupe. Yet the operation is relatively safe: about 25,000 Americans now pump blood through their bodies with the help of man-made valves.

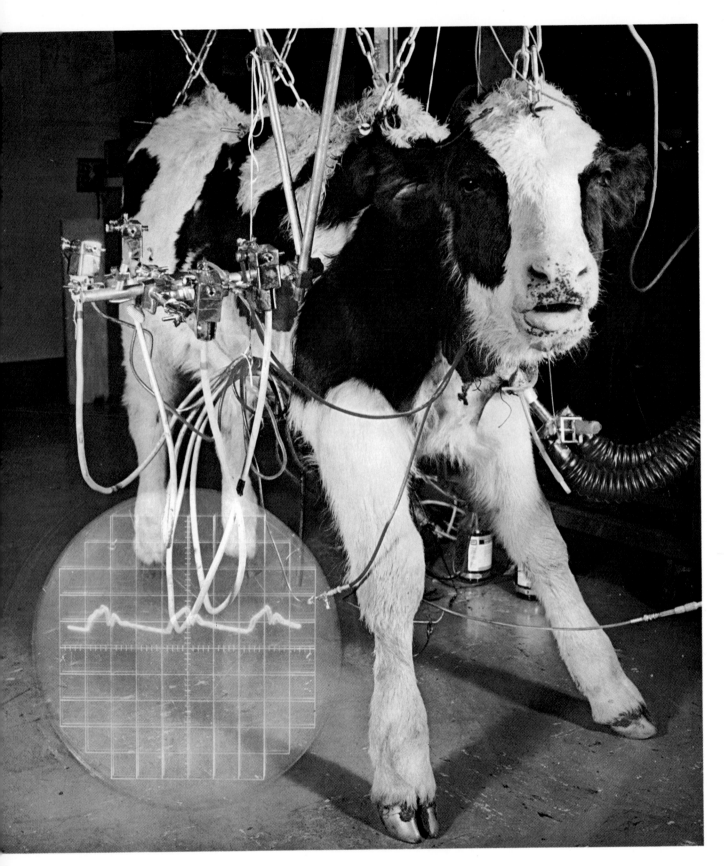

AIR PUMP FOR A CALF'S HEART

Hooked up to a maze of equipment, this calf lived for 31 hours with an implanted synthetic heart. Each of the heart's two pumping chambers consisted essentially of two sacks, one inside the other. The outer sack was rigid; the inner was flexible so that it alternately contracted and expanded as compressed air, fed through dangling tubes, was forced between the two sacks in bursts. This action squeezed blood from the inner sack and through the circulatory system, generating the blood pressure shown on the superimposed graph (lower left).

HEART POWER FROM A COIL
A lighted lamp demonstrates how a coil implanted in this dog could operate a synthetic heart. The coil picks up electromagnetic energy from wires entwined in slats of the dog's cage.

Toward a Synthetic Heart

Physicians, encouraged by their success in replacing parts of the human heart, are now advancing toward a far more difficult goal—replacement of the entire heart. Already hearts made of silicone rubber have kept alive animals like the calf at left—but only with the help of such cumbersome power sources as the electrically driven air compressor that operated the substitute. To keep a synthetic heart beating steadily year after year, medical scientists must now perfect a power system that will not only be small enough to be carried in or on the body but will also be durable and absolutely reliable.

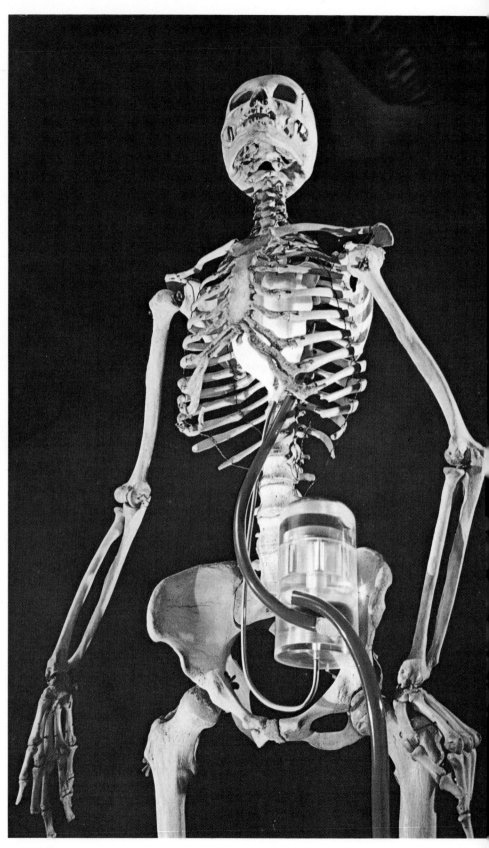

ATOMS FOR LIFE
The skeleton shown here is outfitted with both an artificial heart *(center)* and a mock-up of a portable atomic-power pack *(lower right)*. The pack is designed to hold radioactive materials that release heat to generate steam; the steam would drive the piston of a pump which in turn would create a regular beat in the synthetic heart, forcing blood to flow throughout the body.

Gifts of Life
from the Dead

Of all the physician's new lifesaving techniques, the most radical—and perhaps the most promising—is the transplantation of human organs. Already, kidneys removed from dead persons have taken over for the failing organs of desperately ill patients in last-ditch endeavors to prolong lives. The most important and baffling difficulty in the way of successful transplantation is immunological rejection—the individual body's destructive reaction to tissue other than its own. This reaction usually kills transplanted organs. Now, however, chemicals that slow down the rejection process have been found by researchers, and they are searching for newer drugs that will make transplantation even more practical.

Meanwhile, other researchers are working out procedures for keeping transplantable organs alive long after they have been removed from their original owners. The experimental equipment shown at right, developed at the University of Minnesota School of Medicine, has preserved the organs of dogs for relatively brief periods of time. If its methods can be improved and applied to human body parts, it could serve as the model for "organ banks" that someday may enable the dead to leave behind them the most precious of all gifts—the gift of life.

IN DEEP STORAGE
Their living processes slowed down by drugs and the chill of 39° F. temperature, a dog's heart *(chamber at left)*, kidney *(center)* and lungs *(right)* are kept in a state of suspended animation for experimental transplant operations. Floating in pots, the organs are supplied with oxygen by tubes connected to the gauge-equipped valves mounted above the three pots.

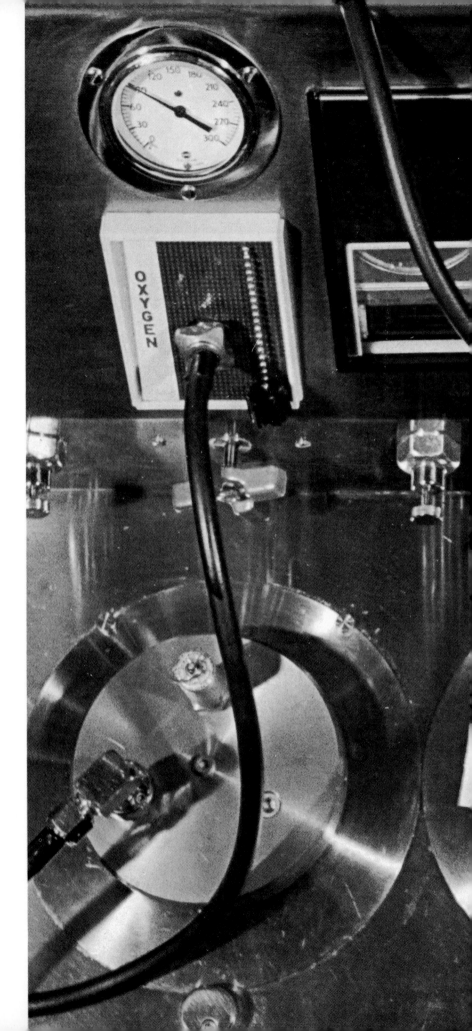

The Great Physicians

THE MODERN PHYSICIAN owes most of his skill in diagnosing and treating the ailments of mankind to his predecessors of recent times. Not until the latter part of the 18th Century did experimenters like the surgeon John Hunter and the anatomist Marie-François-Xavier Bichat begin to accelerate the slow pace of scientific medical progress; the most valuable lifesaving discoveries have been made in the two centuries since then by the great physicians whose contributions are sketched on these pages.

LEOPOLD AUENBRUGGER *(1722-1809)* was the Austrian physician who invented one of the simplest and most effective of diagnostic techniques: auscultation, tapping on a patient's chest and back for the sounds that tell the trained listener much about the health of internal organs.

JOHN HUNTER *(1728-1793)*, the father of modern surgery, was 18th Century England's most celebrated researcher, experimenter and teacher. By buttressing surgery with a thorough knowledge of physiology and pathology, he transformed it from a craft into a branch of scientific medicine.

WILLIAM CRUIKSHANK *(1745-1800)* was an epileptic who became an outstanding Scottish physician and an authority on human anatomy. His significant contribution was a treatise, published in 1786 after eight years of work, that gave the first detailed account of the lymphatic system.

EDWARD JENNER *(1749-1823)* achieved the first successful preventive inoculation in 1796. Using vaccine obtained from a milkmaid who had contracted cowpox, a mild disease, the English physician provided immunity to dreaded smallpox. His discovery began a new science: immunology.

JOHN WARREN *(1753-1815)*, member of a distinguished family of Boston physicians, was instrumental in founding Harvard Medical School in 1782 and was its first professor of anatomy and surgery. As a surgeon during the Revolution, he perfected several radical amputation techniques.

MARIE-FRANÇOIS-XAVIER BICHAT *(1771-1802)*, called the creator of descriptive anatomy, was a brilliant French physician. Working without a microscope, he was able to classify all body tissues into 21 groups, the essential first step in the accurate labeling of every portion of the body.

EPHRAIM MCDOWELL *(1771-1830)*, a frontier physician at Danville, Kentucky, made medical history in 1809 with the first successful removal of a diseased ovary. McDowell also perfected the modern surgical technique of lithotomy, for the removal of stones obstructing the urinary bladder.

THOMAS YOUNG *(1773-1829)*, a versatile English physician best known for his contributions to the science of physics, explained the structure and operation of the eye and developed the basic theory of color vision. He also worked out the exact physical laws that govern the flow of blood.

JOHN COLLINS WARREN *(1778-1856)*, son of John Warren, was a distinguished surgeon in his own right and a founder of the Massachusetts General Hospital in Boston, where in 1846 he opened the era of pain-free surgery with a dramatic demonstration of the use of ether in an operation.

RENÉ LAËNNEC *(1781-1826)* invented in 1819 the physician's familiar stethoscope, which helps identify lung and heart ailments. In 1826 this brilliant French pathologist increased the usefulness of his invention by describing the diseases that could be diagnosed with the new medical tool.

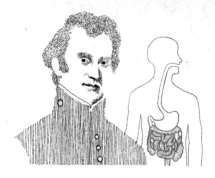

WILLIAM BEAUMONT *(1785-1853)*, used a living laboratory —a guide with a gunshot-caused hole in his stomach—in a remarkable series of experiments that began in 1825 at Fort Mackinac, Michigan. Using this "window," Beaumont became the first to study digestion by direct observation.

CLAUDE BERNARD *(1813-1878)*, French physiologist and master experimenter, laid down the principles of scientific research that have guided medical investigators ever since. Working with animals, he produced diseases in the various organs by using drugs and poisons and thus was able to supply clues to the functioning of the digestive system.

CARL WUNDERLICH *(1815-1877)*, a German physician, is best known for an 1868 study that proved fever was not a disease, but a symptom of disease. He showed the relationship between body temperature and various diseases, and made the clinical thermometer a key diagnostic tool.

IGNAZ SEMMELWEIS *(1818-1865)*, a Hungarian obstetrician, insisted, as early as 1847, that medical students prevent infection by washing their hands with a disinfectant before examining pregnant women. His aseptic technique, widely ridiculed, was accepted only after his death.

RUDOLF VIRCHOW *(1821-1902)* was a many-talented German physician who established the science of pathology. He proved that disease arises not from special body cells, but from the modification of normal cells, and showed how blood clots cause heart, lung and brain malfunctions.

JEAN CHARCOT *(1825-1893)* set up in Paris the first great clinic for treating nervous disorders. He pioneered in the scientific investigation of mental illness, including the use of hypnotic suggestion to study hysteria, which he correctly diagnosed as a mental, rather than a physical, condition.

JOSEPH LISTER *(1827-1912)* introduced the use of sterilized instruments, antiseptic dressings and disinfectant spray in the operating room in 1865 and helped to free surgery from its deadliest handicap—the postoperative infections that had formerly killed a large percentage of surgical patients.

THEODOR BILLROTH *(1829-1894)*, one of the foremost German surgeons of the 19th Century, perfected several types of new operations in the gastro-intestinal tract. In addition, he was the first to achieve success in the partial removal of the esophagus and complete removal of the larynx.

ROBERT KOCH *(1843-1910)*, a genius with a microscope, helped establish bacteriology as a science. Most famous for his identification of the tuberculosis germ, he also isolated the microorganisms that cause anthrax, wound infections, Asiatic cholera and conjunctivitis, a blinding eye infection.

WILLIAM OSLER *(1849-1919)* helped set the present pattern of U.S. medical education and medical practice. Under his influence, the scientific revolution of the 19th Century was incorporated into the training and work of the physician.

WALTER REED *(1851-1902)* was the U.S. Army surgeon whose dramatic experiments with human volunteers in Cuba after the Spanish-American War proved that yellow fever is carried by mosquitoes. Reed, an outstanding bacteriologist, also investigated other diseases, including typhoid fever.

PAUL EHRLICH *(1854-1915)* was a German bacteriologist who devoted his career to the search for chemical compounds that would cure specific diseases. After making hundreds of trial-and-error tests with aniline dyes, he came across his greatest discovery in 1910: Salvarsan 606, the "magic bullet" that kills the organisms causing syphilis.

EMIL VON BEHRING *(1854-1917)* showed how to protect humans against disease by inoculations with serums derived from the blood of immune animals. His greatest success came in 1890, when he extracted the serum that prevents diphtheria, a triumph for which he won the Nobel Prize.

WILLIAM GORGAS *(1854-1920)*, the U.S. Army's chief sanitary officer in Havana in 1900, directed a mosquito extermination campaign that in three months eliminated the insects—and the yellow fever they carried—from the city. By repeating this success in fever-infested Panama in 1904, he made possible the building of the Panama Canal.

SIGMUND FREUD *(1856-1939)*, an outstanding Austrian neurologist, is famed as the founder of psychoanalysis. His pioneering studies of psychoneuroses—nervous disorders caused by emotional conflicts—provided the first rational explanation for many peculiarities of human behavior.

WILLIAM MAYO *(1861-1939)*, son of a Minnesota country physician, was the elder of the famed Mayo brothers whose clinic in Rochester, Minnesota, became a model for cooperative group medical practice. His specialty was surgery, and he was noted for his cancer and gallstone operations.

CHARLES MAYO *(1865-1939)*, the brother of William *(above)*, was associated with him in the Mayo Clinic. He perfected new techniques for goiter and cataract surgery, served for 17 years as professor of surgery at the University of Minnesota, and was a leading advocate of preventive medicine.

KARL LANDSTEINER *(1868-1943)*, an Austrian who came to the United States in 1922, changed blood transfusion from a dangerous experiment to a lifesaving routine. He discovered the four blood types and showed that matching blood types from different persons could safely be mixed.

HARVEY CUSHING *(1869-1939)*, was the foremost American brain surgeon of his time. He established many modern techniques, including the use of local rather than general anesthesia for brain operations. Cushing also pioneered the use of X-rays and blood-pressure readings in diagnosis.

ALEXIS CARREL *(1873-1944)*, a French-American surgeon, opened a new era in medicine with his dramatic experiments in the transplantation and replacement of living organs. He perfected the technique of transplanting human blood vessels and built one of the first artificial hearts.

ALEXANDER FLEMING *(1881-1955)*, a Scottish bacteriologist, is famed for his 1928 discovery of penicillin, greatest of the drugs that kill disease-causing bacteria. Fleming searched for years for an ideal antibiotic before finding it in penicillium—the common blue mold of bread and cheese.

FREDERICK BANTING *(1891-1941)* saved diabetics from early death by his isolation in 1922 of insulin, a hormone ordinarily secreted by the pancreas. The Canadian physician showed how insulin injections could replace natural secretions and enable diabetics to lead near-normal lives.

FURTHER READING

History of Medicine

Bettman, Otto L., *A Pictorial History of Medicine*. Charles C. Thomas, 1956.

Castiglioni, Arturo, "Bologna," *Ciba Symposia*, August-September, 1945. *A History of Medicine*. Alfred A. Knopf, 1958.

Garrison, F. H., *History of Medicine*, 4th ed., W. B. Saunders, 1929.

MacKinney, Loren, *Medical Illustrations in Medieval Manuscripts*. University of California Press, 1965.

Sigerist, Henry E., *On the History of Medicine*. MD Publications, 1960.

†Singer, Charles, *A Short History of Anatomy and Physiology from the Greeks to Harvey*. Dover, 1957.

Biography

Cushing, Harvey, *The Life of Sir William Osler*. Oxford University Press, 1940.

*Clapesattle, Helen, *The Doctors Mayo*. The University of Minnesota Press, 1941.

Dubos, René, *Louis Pasteur: Freelance of Science*. Little, Brown and Co., 1950.

*Flexner, S., and J. T. Flexner, *William Henry Welch and the Heroic Age of American Medicine*. The Viking Press, 1941.

†Olmstead, J.M.D., and E. Harris Olmstead, *Claude Bernard and the Experimental Method in Medicine*. Collier Books, 1961.

†Sigerist, Henry E., *The Great Doctors*. Doubleday, 1958.

Medical Education

Becker, Howard S., and others, *Boys in White*. University of Chicago Press, 1961.

†Editors of Johns Hopkins Magazine, *The Education of a Physician*. Johns Hopkins University, 1964.

Knowles, John H., ed., *The Teaching Hospital*. Harvard University Press, 1966.

Merton, Robert King, ed., *The Student-Physician*. Harvard University Press, 1957.

Public Health

Rosen, G., *A History of Public Health*. MD Publications, 1958.

Smillie, Wilson G., *Public Health: Its Promise for the Future*. The Macmillan Company, 1955.

Williams, R. C., *The United States Public Health Service 1798-1950*. Whittet & Shepperson, 1951.

Special Topics

Greenburg, Selig, *The Troubled Calling*. The Macmillan Company, 1965.

Harris, Seymour E., *The Economics of American Medicine*. The Macmillan Company, 1964.

*Osler, William, *Selected Writings of Sir William Osler*. Oxford University Press, 1951.

Roueché, Berton, *Eleven Blue Men*. Little, Brown and Co., 1947.

*Also in paperback edition.

†Only in paperback edition.

ACKNOWLEDGMENTS

The editors of this book are indebted to Dr. Lawrence E. Hinkle Jr., Associate Professor of Medicine and Clinical Associate Professor of Medicine in Psychiatry, New York-Cornell Medical Center, and to the following persons and institutions: William F. Allyn, Welch Allyn Co., Skaneateles Falls, N.Y.; Wynn Baker, Wenatchee Clinic, Wenatchee, Wash.; Dr. Marcel Baluda, Prof. of Virology, UCLA School of Medicine, Los Angeles; Harry Becker, Executive Secretary of the Committee on Special Studies, New York Academy of Medicine, NYC; Dr. Frank B. Berry, Emeritus Professor of Clinical Surgery, and Dr. David Nachmanson, Prof. of Biochemistry, Columbia University College of Physicians and Surgeons, NYC; Richard E. Brenz, The Holter Co., Bridgeport, Pa.; Churchill Coe, Assistant Administrator, and Roberta J. Eisenhandler, Administrative Supervisor, Stamford Hospital, Stamford, Conn.; Sara Barr Cohen, American College of Surgeons, Chicago; James A. Coyle, NYC; Joseph Criscione and Robert Hughes, Kaiser Foundation Hospitals, Oakland; Dr. Michael DeBakey, Methodist Hospital, Houston; Dr. Ivan Dunaief, Bronx Eye Infirmary, NYC; Mary Elizabeth Feeney, Associate Librarian, New York Academy of Medicine, NYC; Dr. William Grace, Director of Medicine, Patricia Hurley, Public Relations Director, and Marilyn Michaels, St. Vincent's Hospital, NYC; Dr. Ralston R. Hannas, Secretary of the Commission on Education, American Academy of General Practice, Kansas City; Seymour E. Harris, Prof. of Economics, University of California at San Diego; Janet Koudelka, Curator of Books, Welsh Library, Johns Hopkins University, Baltimore; Michael Lesparre, Director, New York Office, American Hospital Assn.; Dr. Philip Lee, Assistant Secretary of Health, Education and Welfare, Washington, D.C.; Dr. Robert M. Lowman, Prof. of Radiology, Yale University School of Medicine, New Haven; Helen McCall, Balsam Grove, N.C.; Julian Mackewice, U.S. Hospital Supply Corp., NYC; Benjamin E. Marbury, New York Hospital, NYC; Robert N. Mazer, National Dialysis Committee, NYC; Dr. William Minogue, Westfield, N.J.; Dr. Eugene Pantuck, Columbia Presbyterian Hospital, NYC; Dr. Jerry P. Pendras, Medical Director, Seattle Artificial Kidney Center, Seattle; Dr. Charles Pigford, Department of Public Health, Houston; Lewis Reed, Chief, Office of Research Statistics, Social Security Administration, Washington, D.C.; Bruce Roberts, Charlotte, N.C.; Dr. Alan Spievack, Cambridge City Hospital, Cambridge, Mass.; Stanley D. Truelson Jr., Librarian, Yale Medical Library, New Haven; Dr. Carlos Vallbona, General Director, Research Center for Chronic Illness, Baylor University College of Medicine, Houston; Dr. Frank Vieth, Associate Prof. of Surgery, Albert Einstein Medical College, NYC; Frank von Richter, American Hospital Assn., Chicago; Ellen Wells, Asst. Picture Librarian, National Library of Medicine, Bethesda, Md.; the following persons from Cornell Medical College, NYC: Dr. George R. Holswade, Clinical Associate Prof. of Surgery, Dr. Jerome L. Meyer, Director, Electronics Laboratory, Dr. Russel H. Patterson Jr., Associate Prof. of Neurosurgery, and Dr. George G. Reader, Prof. of Medicine; the following persons from Western Reserve Medical School, Cleveland: Dr. Douglas D. Bond, Dr. Robert T. Breckenridge, Dr. John L. Caughey Jr., Mrs. R. J. Deitz, Dr. T. Hale Ham, Dr. Thomas W. Moir, Dr. Edra L. Spilman, James E. Vail, Director of Public Relations, and Dr. Israel Weisberg; the following persons from the U.S. Public Health Service: Dr. Ray Vanderhook, Chief Medical Officer of the Port of New York Quarantine Station; Marie Afferton, Associate Director of Education, and Thomas O'Rourke, Administrative Officer, Staten Island Hospital; Dr. James Mason, Deputy Chief, Laboratory Improvement Program, and Carolyn Robinson, Picture Librarian, Audio-Visual Library, National Communicable Disease Center; and the following information officers: Frank Acosta, Bureau of Disease Prevention and Environmental Control; Gordon Bourgin, National Center for Urban and Industrial Health; Margery Cunningham, Office of the Surgeon General; Julie Dickinson, Foreign Quarantine Program; Cecelia King and Dr. Charles Williams, Office of International Health; Leonard Levine, National Center for Air Pollution; Jean Nowak, Bureau of Indian Health; Daniel G. Rice, National Institutes of Health; Wallace Richter, National Communicable Disease Center; and Harry Weiner, Bureau of Medical Services.

INDEX

Numerals in italics indicate a photograph or painting of the subject mentioned.

PICTURE CREDITS

The sources for the illustrations that appear in this book are shown below. Credits for the pictures from left to right are separated by commas, from top to bottom by dashes.

Cover—John Murello and Charles Stewart.

CHAPTER 1: 8—Emmett Bright courtesy National Museum, Athens. 10 through 13—Culver Pictures. 15—The Bettmann Archive. 17—Walter Sanders courtesy Wuerttembergisches Landesmuseum, Stuttgart. 18, 19—Emmett Bright courtesy Palazzo D'Accursio—David Lees. 20, 21—Emmett Bright courtesy Biblioteca Universitaria, Bologna. 21—Bibliothèque Nationale. 22, 23—David Lees courtesy Donazione Putti, Istituto Rizzoli, Bologna. 24—Eric Schaal courtesy Musée de l'école de la Médecine, Paris. 25—Bibliothèque Nationale. 26, 27—David Lees courtesy Donazione Putti, Istituto Rizzoli, Bologna. 28—Left Vivarelli; right Emmett Bright courtesy Biblioteca Universitaria, Bologna. 29—David Lees courtesy Istituto Rizzoli, Bologna.

CHAPTER 2: 30—A. J. Wyatt courtesy University of Pennsylvania School of Medicine. 33 through 37—The Bettmann Archive. 39 through 51—Bruce Roberts from Rapho Guillumette.

CHAPTER 3: 52—Alfred Eisenstaedt. 54—The Bettmann Archive. 63 through 77—Cornell Capa from Magnum.

CHAPTER 4: 78—Alan Clifton courtesy The Curators of the Bodleian Library, Oxford. 80—Culver Pictures. 82—Drawing by John and Mary Condon. 87, 88, 90, 92, 94, 96, 98, 99—Arthur Seller. 89, 91, 93, 95, 97—Drawings by Nicholas Fasciano photographed by Neal Slavin. 87, 88, 92—Instruments courtesy U.S. Hospital Supply Corp.

CHAPTER 5: 100—Ralph Morse. 104—Drawing by Leslie Martin adapted from *Hospital Design and Function* by Todd Wheeler copyright McGraw-Hill. 105—Drawings by Leslie Martin. 108—New York Public Library. 109—Culver Pictures. 111 through 121—Leonard McCombe.

CHAPTER 6: 122—W. Eugene Smith. 124—Courtesy the Mayo Clinic, Rochester, Minnesota. 130—Culver Pictures. 133, 134—National Library of Medicine. 135—Robert Phillips. 136—National Archives. 137—Lee Lockwood from Black Star courtesy U.S. Public Health Service. 138—National Archives. 139—Robert Phillips courtesy U.S. Public Health Service. 140—National Library of Medicine. 141—U.S. Public Health Service-National Communicable Disease Center Audio-Visual Library. 142—Public Health Service World—National Archives. 143, 144, 145—Fritz Goro. 128—Chart by Raymond Ripper.

CHAPTER 7: 146—The Bettmann Archive. 148, 149—Culver Pictures. 154, 155—Drawings by Donald and Ann Crews courtesy Angelica Uniforms Company. 157 through 167—Charles Harbutt from Magnum.

CHAPTER 8: 168—Lawrence Schiller. 172—Article by Edwin L. Crosby, M.D. from *The Atlantic Monthly*, July 1966. 175—Drawing by Leslie Martin courtesy The Holter Co. 177—Sovfoto—drawing by Donald and Ann Crews. 179, 180, 181—J. L. Swiners-*Réalités*. 182, 183—Fritz Goro. 184 through 191—Ralph Morse. 193, 194, 195—Drawings by Nicholas Fasciano. Back cover—Drawing by Donald Crews.

A
STONEHENGE
BOOK

PRODUCTION STAFF FOR TIME INCORPORATED

John L. Hallenbeck (Vice President and Director of Production), Robert E. Foy and Caroline Ferri
Text photocomposed under the direction of Albert J. Dunn

xxx

200